❦ CHAUCERIAN BELIEF

John M. Hill

Chaucerian
B·e·l·i·e·f

The Poetics of Reverence and Delight

YALE UNIVERSITY PRESS   NEW HAVEN AND LONDON

Published with assistance from the foundation established in memory of
Amasa Stone Mather of the class of 1907, Yale College.

Designed by Nancy Ovedovitz. Set in Aldus type by G & S Typesetters,
Inc., Austin, Texas. Printed in the United States of America by Book
Crafters, Inc., Chelsea, Michigan.

LIBRARY OF CONGRESS CATALOGING-
IN-PUBLICATION DATA

Hill, John M.
  Chaucerian belief : the poetics of reverence and delight / John M. Hill.
  p.   cm.
  Includes bibliographical references and index.
  ISBN 0-300-04782-7 (alk. paper)
  1. Chaucer, Geoffrey, d. 1400.   Canterbury tales.   2. Chaucer,
Geoffrey, d. 1400—Philosophy.   3. Belief and doubt in literature.
I. Title.
PR1875.P5H55   1991
821'.1—dc20   90-45627
                                                                     CIP

The paper in this book meets the guidelines for permanence and durability
of the Committee on Production Guidelines for Book Longevity of the
Council on Library Resources.

10   9   8   7   6   5   4   3   2   1

TO BARBARA

❦ CONTENTS

❦ ACKNOWLEDGMENTS

*A*cknowledgment sections are clues to a kinship of indebtedness and therein to authorial identity. I write this in gratitude: first and deeply to my fellow adventurers in all realms possible to us—Leo Weinstein, R. Jackson Wilson, Sermon Woo—next to my teacher, Robert O. Payne, and to Betty; then to my enduring companions, Christine Hilary, Phil Jason, Al Lefcowitz, Bill Oram, and Thalia Pandiri; penultimately to wonderful Chaucerians, past and present, whose friendships have been sustaining beyond even their generous intentions—Mary Carruthers, Don Howard, Charles Muscatine, Glending Olson, and Lee Patterson.

I am grateful for the help of my editors at Yale University Press, Ellen Graham and Lorraine Alexson, and for the excellent advice of my readers. I would also like to thank the U.S. Naval Academy for its generous support, especially from Dean Karl Lamb, who provided a much-needed, entirely fruitful leave during which parts of this book were written.

But my most profound debt is to Barbara of the golden hair, for much more than which I love her and to whom I dedicate this book.

❦ CHAUCERIAN BELIEF

1 ❦ BELIEF AND TRUTH IN THE *CANTERBURY TALES*: TO KNOW FEELINGLY

eering through his pious writings—his translations of Boethius's *Consolation of Philosophy* and of Pope Innocent III's *De Contemptu Mundi*, along with moral lyrics, legends, and such treatises as the *Tale of Melibee* and the *Parson's Tale*—Chaucer finally condemns many of the tales of Canterbury. But generations of readers, finding that collection of tales a liberal entertainment, refuse to believe that Chaucer does not still inhabit those unspecified tales that he eventually retracts because they lead to sin. My study owes much to those readers, at least to those who see Chaucer as most capacious in the tales—as a lively, finally nonjudgmental author of the work, someone who brings tales and tellers into various relationships, such that he sometimes features the tale and sometimes, profoundly, deepens our sense of the teller. Whatever overall structure Chaucer hoped for, whatever thematic center he contemplated, undeniably he has achieved two things: a wide range of tales, probably drawn from every literary type he knew, and a hugely ambitious, often lively cast of characters, some members of which he makes particularly vivid, especially striking to our eyes and compelling to our ears.[1]

I think that few readers would quarrel with this. But we differ greatly whenever we wonder about questions of structure and theme, about Chaucer's purposes—if nonjudgmental, is he finally noncommittal concerning moral attitudes or points of view?—and about Chaucer's ordering devices (which may lead to what he would show or teach us). Chaucer's earliest editors understood the tales as a collection only, a *compilatio*, with no necessary or unifying order. Although framed and narratively connected, the tales could nevertheless stand alone for the sayings and bits of moralism each contained. Perhaps the tales even circulated singly or in pairs.[2] Whatever their use historically, however, we do have connected tales (as many as six in the longest fragment) and clearly Chaucer preoccupies himself with similar subjects from tale to tale (love, justice, order, marriage, "gentilesse," mercy, relations between authority and experience, intent and effect, mastery and accord, and so on). So modern readers have searched for organizing ideas or dualities (artificiality and realism, authority and art, stasis and flux); for moral categories; or for cognitive analogues of a formal, patterning kind (drawn from medieval images, Gothic architecture, or medieval divisions of the mind—with memory posited, for example, as the form of this work, which has a labyrinth as its structure).[3] There is no reason why fifteenth-century editors should understand Chaucer's creative intentions better than we do (especially if Chaucer is far from typical or merely conventional in what he does). Yet for all of our suggestions—despite George Kittredge's marriage group suggestion; despite attempts to organize the tales around themes of authority and experience, play and earnest, solace and "sentence"; and despite attempts to place them within moral frameworks such as the seven deadly sins or an earthly and a heavenly pilgrimage—still, I do not think we have searched successfully, no matter how much a particular proposal may illuminate aspects of the tales. Moreover, I have come to think that our difficulties do not reflect the collection's fragmentary state as much as a startling possibility: that Chaucer undertakes this work without a deep device, without any single way of transmuting the tales into an exemplary whole.

But clearly we have the idea of pilgrimage and everything that word connotes for medieval Christians. Surely, one might add, some sort of ordering principle arises from that if from nothing else. The characters meet in April, pilgrims all, bound for St. Thomas's tomb in Canterbury Cathedral—the resting place of that holy, blissful martyr who would help sick pilgrims. And the *Parson's Prologue* invokes that "parfit, glorious pilgrymage / That highte Jerusalem celestial." So there must be something to this idea of pilgrimage—given these and many other references to pilgrims and pilgrimage in the tales. Moreover, the entire event is remembered, each teller remembers a tale, and almost every pilgrim portrayed in the *General Prologue* has a satirizable vice.[4] Therefore perhaps memory is the form of the work, pilgrimage its controlling theme, and an estates' satire one of its aims. Yet I do not think so.

First, the pilgrims are neither pointedly presented as corruptions of their estates nor presented only as such. Second, the Parson refers to pilgrimage for his own, immediate purposes: He introduces us to the idea of a "meditacioun," and although Chaucer pairs that reference with his own to pilgrims and pilgrimage in the *General Prologue* (*GP*), the pilgrim gathering becomes a fictional device—a frame or plot—rather than an organizing theme. As a plot device it requires an exit from the game of tale telling, which the *Parson's Tale* provides.[5] Presumably, after hearing the Parson's treatise on penitence and the seven deadly sins, the pilgrims might then begin their individual penances at the shrine in Canterbury. For by agreeing to the Host's merriment—to the competitive game of tale telling, meant to shorten the way to Canterbury—the pilgrims become a social group set off from being pilgrims in the conventional sense. Their journey to the shrine becomes an excursion, a "wandering by the way" with occasions for quarrels and accords, rather than a penitential journey.[6]

Perhaps their agreement reveals the extent of their secularity or of their vulnerability to corruption. Chaucer leaves that judgment for us to make. He focuses instead on the world of tellers and tales created by Harry Bailey's game—a world recalled, to be sure, but only trivially a world of memory (memory devices do not organize the tales, and the tellers do not practice an art of memory). Still, the pilgrims and their wandering could suggest, if not an organizing theme, at least a labyrinthlike idea for the collection's possible structure—an idea that could make the tales a labyrinth similar to those arranged in cathedrals for pilgrims (as proposed by Howard). With these labyrinths set into or painted onto cathedral floors, an act of tracing or walking one of them may have been a pilgrimage in itself.[7]

However, when we enter the tales of Canterbury, instead of a pilgrimage on some road of penitence, and within the world as sacred sanctuary, we find a busy and partly profane world of tales and their tellers, with the tales understood as "out there," in the world. Everything is located in a fictional now within the frame of the collection, with tale after tale constructed dramatically and told by what I will call "imperfect appropriation." The full text of each "tale" is one in which a pilgrim teller tells a tale, often intrusively (breaking the fictional frame). The teller tries to appropriate his tale in some way, given his understanding of the tale and the relation he would have with his audience; but to some extent the tale or the tale material resists that appropriation. This functional world of dramatic tales is not new for the tales or for the drama in them. But when Chaucer invents appropriating tellers, tellers who misunderstand their material primarily because they would coerce a univocal meaning from it, then he leaves his own past behind,[8] and does something new for the middle ages generally.

This characterization of the relation between tellers and their tales seems unexceptionable: Chaucerians have long noted the insufficiences of tellers, seeing various tellers as deficient in understanding, in skill, in mental health, or in moral awareness. But these deficiencies are usually seen within terms controlled by readings of the *General Prologue* (*GP*) portraits, supplemented by attention to individual prologues, and ornately filled out by readings of the tales as dreamwork redounding upon the tellers. Such psychologized dramas have been rightly objected to by Benson, Lawton, Pearsall, and others. The tales are not pilgrim dreams. They are fictions that initially have only a tenuous relation to their tellers (in most cases); but which, in the course of being told, become extended occasions for attitudes and gestures on the part of the tellers, given the way a particular teller responds to his or her tale.[9] These performances are often surprising: They never merely fill out assessments posed in the *GP* portraits; rather, along with any prologue material for the tale, they become a largely independent way of recharacterizing most of the tellers, providing impressions that are different from but not inconsistent with the sense we have of the tellers given their *GP* portraits. And of course three tales belong to tellers for whom we have no initial, *GP* portraits (the Canon's Yeoman, Second Nun, and Nun's Priest). More than a mode of characterization, moreover, this business of intrusive tale telling provides Chaucer with a way of extensively highlighting aspects, parts, or moments of individual tales. Why does he do this?

Granted that Chaucer's tellers have subjective relations to their tale material, does Chaucer explore then the play of subjectivity for its own sake or for some extrinsic purpose? With a wide range of tale types, does he explore the reader's uses of different kinds of tales? Does he move toward the limits of human knowledge—however we might understand that in terms of a faculty psychology—given that different types of narratives organize and give meaning to experience in different ways? These have been attractive suggestions for what Chaucer may be doing in or through the tales, but despite some virtue in each suggestion—Chaucer does explore subjectivity, the human use and abuse of tales, the ways in which we know or claim to know, and the powers of different genres—we tend to think in these cases in ways too modern to catch Chaucer in his work. If by the play of subjectivities for its own sake we mean something like an integrating romanticism that would bring out the latent coherence of the world through a foregrounding of its own consciousness, then we have to excuse Chaucer. If by the limits of human knowledge we mean a radical skepticism that paradoxically presupposes a deep but unknowable structure, then Chaucer will elude us in his vaguely Boethian and confidently Aristotelian sympathies.[10] If by the use of tales we have in mind a democratic pathos like the elegant reflection of much Chaucer criticism in V. A. Kolve's *Chaucer and the Imagery of Narrative,* then we need to ask just how and why Chaucer gives us twenty-three voices bearing witness to their understanding of life through the tales they tell. How would Chaucer have these tales and tellers relate to knowledge of the world?

Certainly wisdom literature does not require so many voices and so much bearing of witness, although we can easily entertain a Chaucerian fascination for diverse folk diversely opining.[11] Does this crowd of viewpoints give Chaucer a way of arriving at moral nuances he could otherwise not approach?[12] Or does it provide him with a fiction maker's indulgence simply to explore characters, tales, and writing for their own sake?[13] Moral nuance is as available as thought itself. No late classical or medieval writer, from Augustine onward, needs an elaborate excursion for expressing nuances. But to explore the possibilities of understanding, to test moral claims—these are other matters indeed that could easily keep Chaucer from straying into a pure aestheticism (even for a time) or into an aesthetic of inconclusiveness, pluralism, or reflexivity, or some problematic for its own sake. Ideas such as these are more than useful; they become ways of coping with Chaucer's work—ways truly elicited by something in the tales themselves. But they are also, treacherously, our ideas, however they illumine Chaucer's concerns, and they slight the level of commitment involved in any Chaucerian exploration of how we understand anything, separate truth from falsehood, or would test moral claims.

Moreover, these ideas are shakily grounded on one or two of their deepest assumptions—sometimes held separately and sometimes together—assumptions that Chaucer, as I shall argue, simply does not share. The first is the ostensibly neutral nature of fictions in relation to truth claims about the world. Most of us have been educated to believe in the notion that fictions are fictions, utopian worlds unto themselves. Even Larry Sklute's perceptive readings founder on this notion when he writes that Chaucer "could translate or invent many kinds of stories in the *Canterbury Tales* that claimed to represent some truth about the nature of the world and about man's goals, yet that paradoxically remained mere opinions because their narrators were limited."[14]

When a critic like David Aers—committed to the individual consciousness against authority, to the human rather than the institutional, and to the personal against the oppressively ideological—can read Chaucer's tales as referentially concerning these issues in the real world, we at least are not gazing at aloof fictions. But here the second and more powerful assumption asserts itself everywhere: that our cognitions, our understandings, and our coming to knowledge are largely cerebral or rational affairs that enlist our emotions after the fact in persuasive gestures toward others.

Rather, for Chaucer, cognition is not mainly a function of reason, intellection, or some consistent pattern of anticipation, query, and problem solving. He holds instead to an emotive theory of perception and knowledge, to an affective theory that combines rationality, sense perception, and feeling into a mode of knowing that we might call cognitive credence. For Chaucer, the subjective act of extending belief is crucial to any nontrivial act of knowing nontrivial things. Our passions enter into the feelings with which we come to or confront complex and perplexing issues. What usually happens, if his tale tellers and the numerous events in his tales are any guide to his view of human nature, is that passions serve disruptive, even anarchic self-interests that distort views of whatever object is in sight. But passions can be transformed into perceptive feelings that in turn lead to an accord or community, to a prudential merriment. How then to approach fictions for our pleasure in truth, for our prudential gain when faced with vexing questions of order, justice, love, mastery, "gentilesse," or what have you? As this becomes the question, the *Canterbury Tales* becomes a cautionary collection about our use of fictions, along with an exploration of how we might come to understand facts about humans and other mysteries in a community-forming way, enabled by the power of our feelings and the openness of belief—a community (as I will argue in the chapters on Fragment 7) of fictions, audiences, and tale tellers accorded to one another in group-enhancing ways.

The "openness of belief" is another way of expressing what "cognitive credence" suggests: that an intellectual structure remains open to change and novelty as well as to a corroboration of the truths already believed in. Belief, not faith, is the crucial term here, if we understand it as Chaucer's way of entertaining seriously whatever comes his way through fictions, especially those truth claims found in old books. This does not commit him to a general relativism or to the emptiness of competing ideas juggled purely in a spirit of play. Rather Chaucer would gather all kinds of tales as his empirical ground for sorting through various claims about any number of subjects; the more claims on a given subject the better for finding either an increasingly clarified norm toward which those claims point or an equilibrium between them that in turn approximates that norm (tellers, not tales, oppose each other). Here the idea of "norm" is both transcendental and complex, as would be so with the "perfect" tale of any given type or with the "perfect" expression of any family of truths. Chaucer is vaguely Neoplatonic, although seemingly more Aristotelian than Platonic in placing truth within the materiality of tales.

One seeks in old books and in tales generally truths (however mixed with falsehood) that correspond (accord) with both worldly experience (experience in deeds) and with reason, with what is accordant with the mind. If experience and books correspond, then those books are certainly true; but if we lack experiential verification, then whatever accords with the mind commands more belief than do those claims that are discordant, perplexing, or painful. But in neither case is disbelief, given a lack of experiential verification, appropriate. As a structure, belief differs from faith in its provisional character. For Chaucer's bookish persona, belief involves such provisional attitudes as credence toward or delight in a number of notions or things, given an effort to relate those notions to each other. When he encounters something that confirms both a posited structure of relations between notions and the notions themselves, so much to the deepening good. But whatever does not fit, although tending to weaken any conviction that cherished truths or familiar authorities are indubitable, nevertheless is made room for, provisionally, and a search is undertaken for information that would organize this novel material into the belief structure or else force a change in the belief structure itself.[15] In the meantime, one is not paralyzed, because actions in accord with convictions that exceed but do not contradict the changeable grounds for various beliefs are still reasonable; indeed, they are likely to be ethical.

Thus Chaucer's notion of belief would be nondeductive and usually incomplete, involving attitudes that neither reach for closure—toward dogma or certainty—nor collapse into skepticism (even when faced with either contradictory authorities or truths). For those truths that we cannot confirm immediately, old books are our only witnesses; but as keys of remembrance, such books are only necessary, not sufficient witnesses. We must always bring our sense of what accords with reason and with general human experience when assessing claims in old books about the heavens or hell (including, of course, those more mundane but equally puzzling subjects of love, justice, order, and so on). But a delight in old books, and reverence for them, is also central to Chaucer's openness of belief. Humor, wryness, even friendly irony—these give Chaucer a way of confronting the anomalous or the discordant, of entertaining truths that would force gaps within his own beliefs. What seems to happen is that when Chaucer talks about reverence and delight in the credence we extend to old books (*Prologue to the Legend of Good Women* [*PLGW*], ll. 81–88), he approaches the issue of awe, which shades into wonder, which in turn brings us back to delight in a circle that keeps us open to a sense of beauty and the knowledge of harmony and proportion that accompany beauty. Without even a distant hint of beauty, the discordant and the painful—truths that would prove painful to believe if true (such as the lack of a heaven or hell)—could not be long entertained, and the search for truth would have to retreat to the enclosures of faith. Moreover, reverence and delight are feelings, not conclusions—feelings that deeply affect our ability to remain open and therefore to perceive.

How does Chaucer come to the way of confronting old books and tales sketched above? Such a question is impossible to answer in one sense; we have no autobiography of the poet's mind, given the inception of questioning consciousness. But we *can* trace some of the strands that materialize in Chaucer's affective sense of truth and in his view of fiction as a mixed bearer of truth and falsehood. Philosophically, we can begin with his own translations.

Chaucer would probably sympathize with the Boethian position that words, propositions, and even tales show or signify something outside themselves. They do not make the thing they signify, any more than the knowledge of something fully creates the thing known (see the *Consolation*, bk. 5, pr. 2). Thus Chaucer would not move toward a modern idea of subjectivity that would have the perceiver essentially create the truth perceived within a relativistic universe of perceptions. Chaucer is medieval, perhaps even vestigially Neoplatonic (if only through the accident of his sources), in considering the possible participation of fiction in truths. He believes in God's *Treuthe* and in truth, but he is acutely aware of our limitations in perceiving whatever truth we manage to understand, and thus of whatever truths we would tell in our tale telling. That awareness ramified is half of his project in the tales and supports critical attention to the multiplicity of tellers and their views. The other half concerns the tales themselves: if you will, their essential truth function in some syncretic sense. Chaucer thinks of stories, of tales, and of fictions as being compounds of artfully rendered truths and falsehoods, the truths in turn being mixtures of true and false report, experience, and the moral and the intellective (which he could understand as involving capacities for wonder, delight, and a sense of beauty). This would be true for all "tydings" and "gestes" despite their fame or obscurity.

As I shall demonstrate, Chaucer does not doubt that tales, "tydings," contain mixtures of truth and falsehood (perhaps sober truths and outrageous lies). In his day and in ours this is an easy claim that we can justify only with difficulty. In thinking about Truth, Chaucer could have thought and sometimes did think about God. In thinking about linguistic bearers of truth, Chaucer could have thought about propositional truth as developed within scholastic discussions of grammar, logic, and reference.[16] But considering fiction as having an affecting truth function should have committed him to the notion of fiction as exemplum, yet does not. Indeed, he has considerable trouble with that notion.[17] Moreover, he does not find much help, any more than we do, in the analytical thought of his day. Boethius provides oblique assistance in linking the heart to good understanding, with knowing well rather than simply knowing rationally (bk. 3, pr. 9, ll. 152–58). But because this is mainly a notion of inward light, of some spark that contains a knowledge we had when we were disembodied souls (Neoplatonic and Augustinian), it does not directly relate to feeling or the passions. In comparison, Aquinas seems more helpful when he relates knowledge to appetite insofar as each inevitably moves toward the true and the good, respectively, with the true and the good being convertible, the one supposed in the other (*Summa* 1, Q 16, art. 4).[18] Thus, when we think of the true as a kind of good and the good as a kind of truth, we can by some ratio close the gap between appetite and the order of desirable things, on the one hand, and the order of pure intellection on the other (where knowledge precedes the desire that then accompanies it and participates in it). Something like this tie between distinguishable orders may underlie those desires for knowledge—especially of love but also for what books convey—that animate the narrators of the early poems. Desiring truth as found in books and stories can be seen then as appetitive, albeit of an appetite refined of merely bodily hungers, and that desire may in fact become an essential part of the ground for understanding the object of desire.

As desire causes discernment in the reason, it may become more than a stimulus, achieving the status of an exclusive way of knowing familiar to us in late medieval mysticism.[19] But, Chaucer's emphasis (for example, through the *Troilus* narrator) always remains prosaic, participatory, and collaborative. What is this business of love? The knowledge question for the narrator of the *Troilus* concedes possible correction by those who have feeling in love, who have felt it and experienced it. Such people should correct the narrator's account, render it more true. Otherwise, the narrator must go by his own understanding and his own feelings as best he can—all the while crediting the depictions of love-experience found in his books. His feelings involve his powers of empathy and lead to a belief in phenomena he only partially understands. To feel, believe, and understand more fully is a conjoint problem for him and for any Chaucerian persona in the early poems. When we come to the tellers of Canterbury, however, we find tellers who are less reflective than willful and whose tales then become more problematic for us: To what truths do these "tydings" of Canterbury bear witness? What are the efforts and gestures of understanding produced by sometimes wayward pilgrims? These thoughts bring us to a motivating purpose for Chaucer's great undertaking in the tales of Canterbury.

Exploring the mixture of truth and falsehood in tales is Chaucer's extrinsic purpose for beginning the collection of tales. He chooses a wide range of tales in this Canterbury "experiment," because he undertakes a comprehensive exploration of truth in fiction—primarily "more-or-less" truths that therefore require appraisal. But in working with a host of "constructed," human "referents"—the pilgrims and their voices—he provides a way of apprehension for each tale and the truths each may bear.[20] That those apprehensions in many cases are either faulty or fall short hardly counts against the project. Instead the problem opens out to us, to our active engagement as we look with the pilgrim teller and consider the truths he or she finds along with our own. These truths would be matters of fit— a reductive fit, given the narrow feelings and preemptive beliefs of various tellers, and a more considered, perhaps circumlocutory fit given other tellers and our own considerations.[21] Thus how one's feelings and beliefs shape one's efforts toward an adequate symbolization of felt meaning for a tale is central to the truths the tale will bear for one, to whatever it is about the world that the tale illuminates as one manages to understand it.

Of course, fictions refer internally, given their own relationships. But also, and more importantly, fictions refer to the world, to life, to reality, to whatever it is outside themselves that we see they illuminate. This reference for us, however, is not the philosopher's "sense and reference"; it is not a propositional reference in that, for example, a depiction of the common room in Sympkin's house is a claim about some actual room in Chaucer's material world. But that room and the action in it reveal something that we want to know about human behavior, motivation, revenge, mischance, and comeuppance. Revelation is a referential function; it may not claim a fact about the world, but it informs.[22] I think Chaucer is closer to this view of fiction than he is to the notion of tales as illustrations of moral truth or as exempla. Indeed, his entire, inherently participatory theory of truth significantly anticipates the notion of premonitory inquiry through dynamic classification that Charles Peirce formalized in the nineteenth century as a triadic logic of reference—one in which our symbolizations both sport their own figurations and tell us what they represent while revealing the ground or quality they organize.[23]

Chaucer would have tales engage us in acts of exploration—sometimes open-ended acts and sometimes eventually closed at some level of understanding short of doctrine or easy morality. A sympathetic confrontation with tales leads us to the nontrivial truths tales may contain. Truths do not, for Chaucer, lead tales in any interesting way; we are led into the tales, in many cases, by the lines of sight of limited tellers. This sorting by an initial misreading becomes an original way of focusing on whatever truths tales contain, even if they contain only "storyal soth"—something true given the stories we know (perhaps puckishly applied to the legend of Cleopatra in the *Legend of Good Women*: "storyal soth, it is no fable," l. 702).

As one would expect, Chaucer concerns himself mainly with truths about human experience, conduct, and morality. For example, we can ask how we know what it is good to do, and how we should do it: What contexts do we consider? What consequences? Should we rely on unexamined tenets, perhaps on matters of faith or rule? Or should we look to experience and pose experiential likelihoods? We can catch Chaucer presupposing questions like these if we look to *Melibee* and notice that Dame Prudence invokes worldly likelihoods both to dissuade Melibeus from revenge and to counsel mercy toward the men who stabbed Sophie. If this is so, we need to reconsider those dualisms often invoked as thematic poles for the tales: authority and experience, "game" and "earnest," and "sentence" and "solas." They are often opposite sides of the same coin, with truth the coin and its manifestations appearing in either half of each pair. We are asked to entertain a great deal in each case—looking for truths that are "more-or-less" rather than self-evident or necessary and sufficient. Feeling and belief enter into our assessments; they participate in our perceptions and understanding of "sentence" and in the varying ways in which we can take "solas." As thematic pairs, these terms are enigmatic, reflecting an invitation to assess more than to judge, and suggesting in each case a dialectic of both the hierarchical and the subversive: "sentence" and earnest suggest whatever is serious and most valuable; but "solas" and play provoke questions and assert values of their own (if only those of recuperative entertainment). Of course the dialectic is really an interpenetration as we consider true "solas," false "sentence," fruitful play, and so on. The instability here is such that we can mistake play for earnest and see earnest only as further play, missing the earnest in play, just as we can mistake "sentence" and look for an inappropriate "solas." Chaucer's point, then, is that these terms are cautionary, not clarifying; they invite attention rather than direct it. As *themes* they are insubstantial nothings.

The pairing of authority and experience would seem to promise more substance. After all, the references seem fairly clear: "Authority" is all that is received as authoritative—judgments, claims, definitions, beliefs, and observations that we should credit because they come down to us in books or are vouched for by someone considered authoritative. Experience is what we know in our lives, through our senses and in our bodies (urges, feelings, memories, thoughts), and what we have direct acquaintance with. But to make sense of authorities and to understand our experiences require assessments that inevitably bring the two together in an interpenetrating way. We credit most those authorities and those experiences that lead to other authorities and other experiences in a way that confirms expectations raised by the original authorities or in the original experiences. And we try to understand our experiences (and the authoritative) by cognizing them— a task that involves acquired skills (from authorities and trial and error), as well as individual sensitivities (intelligence and feeling). Unlike the other two pairs, this one involves something directly in each case, some body of experience or of received witnessing and opinion. It does not involve attitudes or uses—orientations toward something or effects taken, although "sentence" connects its pair to authority more readily than to experience (however it is that we have opinions about and take from our experiences, often encouraged by the example of authorities). Thus the authority and experience pair feels primary. In fact it feels so for many readers, who then generate related thematic pairs (such as authority and art, stasis and flux) that directly play off Chaucer's voice for the Wife of Bath:

> "Experience, though noon auctoritee
> Were in this world, is right ynogh for me."
>   [ll. 1–2]

Experience is emphasized qualifiedly here, for the Wife is no champion of naked experience, although she feels satisfied enough that her five marriages qualify her to speak knowledgeably. Happily for us, she has authorities she can use and abuse as her primary means for saying what she has to say in defense of her sense of worth and her way of life. Here I think we seek, or should seek, not only some version of Chaucerian intention but also truth: Whatever Chaucer's Wife of Bath depiction illuminates about our humanness in terms of impulse, vitality, virtue, or vice (most commentators take the *Wife of Bath's Prologue and Tale* as more than a baroque gloss on a point of doctrine).[24] So it seems we are invited by these various pairs—"sentence" and "solas," game and earnest, authority and experience—to assess tellers and tales and to find truth where we can, in whatever spirit we can as Chaucer turns the gathering in the Tabard Inn into a world of chance, accident, and "aventure."

That fictions have compounds of truth and falsehood in them is something Chaucer "knows" from "experience"—the experience he projects in that highly playful dream vision, *House of Fame* (*HF*). There a Chaucerian persona finds himself in the House of Fame and the House of Rumor, where various medieval attitudes toward fictions and narratives coexist with some that are idiosyncratically Chaucerian. The narrator, upon approaching the House of Fame, first sees and hears all manner of minstrels and storytellers—entertainers who tell tales of weeping and of "game." This is pure entertainment, play without "sentence," unless we examine the tales themselves apart from their subservience to their tellers' performances. Within the House of Fame, the narrator sees various pillars holding up the fame of one "empire" or another—these are mainly in the world of histories, and so we have books and authors bearing witness to past events. Nowhere here does Chaucer raise the issue of fictional lies as matters of poetical or rhetorical surfaces, although he does address the issue of lies and poetry.

We might now ask how he escapes a general attitude of his time, given this question of truth in fiction, that literary language is only artful clothing, that fictions are lies by which one teaches moral truths but which do not in themselves refer to truths. Chaucer escapes that attitude—one either earnestly held or conveniently propounded by the likes of Petrarch, Boccaccio, and Dante—because he identifies fiction ("tydings," "gestes") with old stories or of a kind with old stories. And old stories he identifies in the *House of Fame* and the *Prologue to the Legend of Good Women* with history and marvelous experiences not granted to every man. Thus old stories tell, in the language and usage of their time, both marvelous and historical truths.[25] Indeed, for the truth about what happened in the past and for certain marvels or visions, old stories are our only way of knowing. This is what Chaucer means by thinking of books as the key to remembrance (unlocking remembrance in both the sense of memorial or testimony to something and of the soul's recollection of what it knew before embodiment in one's physical present). We should go to such books as we can, especially those that bring old things to mind, and extend credence in every reasonable way to the old, "approved stories" (*PLGW*, F l. 21). Without belief we dishonor truth; without countervailing proof, it is better to believe than to scorn. This is more than a provisional attitude. It is part of Chaucer's essential notion of truth in fiction and of the would-be knower's relation to stories. Extending credence is not just prudence or, something much less, a part of decorum. Rather, it is the necessary beginning for any truth seeking in books. It establishes the ground, even though one is largely ignorant, of delight and reverence—so that one allows neither one's faith nor one's skepticism to foreclose attention to "truths" that further reading and experience may or may not confirm.[26]

Of course the renown or fame of a story is no guarantee of truth, especially not if the famous can lie; still, anonymity is no sign of falsehood. A multitude of writers, whether agreeing or not, guarantees neither truth nor falsehood in their "gestes," just as the world of lesser stories, of gossip, talk, and report—of rumor, essentially—is a mixed world of truth, falsehood, compoundings, and distortion. In the rooks' nest world of "gestes," the heart of any story is some report, some tyding of war, peace, marriage, rest, labor, death, life, love, hate, accord, strife, and so on (the list occupies sixteen lines in *HF*). Today's news, today's rumor, is tomorrow's history. Of what has it been compounded? In some cases it is made up of a lie and a "sad soth sawe"; in others of a spark, perhaps, of truth that has been hugely exaggerated; and in others the tiding may not even have a verifiable spark—at least as far as anyone knows—being mere opinion much enlarged before it leaves the House of Rumor and enters the House of Fame. So tidings or stories are either enormously distorted and inflated or inextricably a mix of truth and falsehood in the House of Rumor (*HF*, ll. 2049–2109). Flying to the House of Fame, these tidings achieve fame or not through Fame's caprice.[27] It would seem that basically a story is news or is a history, even if peopled by fictional characters. The tiding may recall a happening that has some germ of truth in the recollection, some sober truth mixed with exaggerations, with lies. This, Chaucer goes on to say, is notoriously the case with the stories that shipmen and pilgrims tell, many of which are lies.

Apparently medieval pilgrims were notorious for their tales—a notoriety that lives well into the Renaissance. Harry Bailey, for one, supposes that the sundry pilgrims accidently gathered together in his tavern will tell tales and play. They do not strike him as the kind of company that will ride "by the way" as dumb as stones; they are a merry group, and there is no sport in mirthless travel. He so much expects tale telling that he offers, courteously, to organize this spontaneous entertainment into a game of tale telling concerning, appropriately enough, the worldly subject of "aventures that whilom han bifalle" (*GP*, l. 795). He then offers himself as the leader of this organized entertainment and as prize giver for the tale of "best sentence and moost solaas" (l. 798). The pilgrims had not troubled to oppose the Host in his desire to propose a "myrthe" that came to mind as he observed the merry company in his inn. They hear him out and grant his plan, swearing their oaths with glad heart and asking the Host to serve as their governor and as judge and reporter of their tales. By one assent, they all are accorded to this and to the Host. Thus a holiday social group is formed and structured, given a "grid" of personal competitions involving tale-telling play and judgment.[28] They will tell tales that concern the world in worldly play on the way to Canterbury. They anticipate mirthful experience, and they drink to that before going to rest, each to his own. Thus a realistic social game forms the group in a loosely competitive way and sets it off from other possible groups, especially from the antitype of mirthless, dumb, stonelike pilgrims. They will performatively experience something that later, back in the inn, will be a matter for true report, containing tales that in turn require assessment for the compoundings in them of truth and exaggeration, of "soth" and falsehood.

2 ❦ THE POETICS OF REVERENCE AND DELIGHT: COGNITIVE FEELING

esides having us read books in an openness of belief, Chaucer would have us assess the quality of belief, feeling, and perception given to various tellers. That the Canterbury tellers have partial and somewhat mistaken understandings of their tales is a truism in Chaucer criticism—true enough, but what follows from that? Usually readers move on either to a search for an organizing certainty in the tales—some underlying mechanism—or, resigned perhaps, keep to a surface of relativized, private assertions, finally leaving the play of tales and opinions behind in noting Chaucer's safe exit, the *Parson's Tale*. It is crucial that most of us fail to stay for long with Chaucer's exploration of private perceptions, of belief, and thus we miss the metaphysical context for Chaucer's great gathering of tales: a vaguely Neoplatonic, perhaps even decidedly Aristotelian search for the truths we can assay through the materiality of tales. What are those great issues we come across in tale after tale, such as justice, love, order, "maistrie," gentilesse," prudence, and accord?

We need to step back and observe the confidence with which Chaucer both creates and confronts different opinion in these matters, a confidence born of glimpses of truth rather than faith, of a clarity of orientation rather than the resolved certainties of dogma.[1] Having stepped back that far, we can then move again toward the collection of tales and toward Chaucer's works generally, first noting the centrality of mixed truth and falsehood in Chaucer's idea of tales, moving to a sense of the use and abuse of tales, and then settling down for a while with the issue of feeling, of how it is and just where that feeling both happily and unhappily guides our cognition and understanding. Confronting that issue is the main thrust of this chapter, but first we need to revisit the *House of Fame*, where Chaucer has arranged his most explicit remarks on the truth-bearing nature of fiction.

So the *House of Fame*, by raising the question of poets who are said to lie and by introducing us to the mixed character of tidings, essentially poses the question of truth—or of sparks of truth—in fiction, especially regarding those "gestes" for which no famous author will vouch. Because that world of "gestes" is a "ful confus" one, the narrator of the *House of Fame* passes it by. But in the tales of his comedy, these stories of "aventures that whilom han byfalle," Chaucer confronts that world directly, enters into it, and essentially descends into the midst of those "olde gestes" whose authors seem as amusingly numerous as rooks' nests in trees (*HF*, ll. 1515–16). Here, if you recall, Chaucer appropriately seeks truth in the hall of fame among those prestigious and poetical historians who uphold the fame of Jewery, Troy, Love, Rome, the matter of England, and the underworld; but he seeks it now not on their authority or in their masterful works but on the stock exchange floor, as it were, within the hurly-burly of the many.

However comically or mockingly Chaucer treats this question, assessing truth in a particular tiding has merit. The nature of tidings has been explained, given their origins in the House of Rumor and their resting or nesting places (rooks' nests) in the House of Fame. This amounts to a transcendental warrant for their status, a warrant that the rooks' nest simile underlines folklorically.[2]

At the least, and less sublimely, if we can stay for a moment with the metaphor of rooks' nests, tales are competing bearers of truth, of prophetic messages (whether ones of trouble or otherwise ["care"]). What they offer are ideas or claims to believe in, if only provisionally. A given teller may indeed point to a reality beyond the tale and even beyond the world as we customarily know it. But that teller's claims on behalf of his or her fiction, and the fiction itself, require independent scrutiny in the context of every other relevant tale, whether truths in other tales or the opinions of their tellers contradict the tale in question or not.

Moreover, this kind of procedure applies to Chaucer's gathering of various tellers, to his exploration of human nature, and to his recreative assessments of particular, characterized passions. In a belief structure of gathered and seriously entertained truths, contradictory claims do not cancel each other. What should happen instead is an overcoming of the narrow or the exclusivist focus of a given teller or of a particular claim, with all claims bearing on a particular subject spread out as variations tending toward a norm—an intimation that no particular claim will fully manifest and which not everyone will glimpse, if at all, to the same extent (however inclined a healthy mind and noble heart would be to acknowledge the truth upon being shown it). Thus we are left to our own assessments of the multitude of stories, of these jostling fictions always inspired by but not limited to the judgments and rhetoric of tellers who reveal themselves less in the kinds of tales they tell than in the ways in which they impose themselves rhetorically upon their tales or their tale material (which is different from textual voice in its seamless unfolding).

Here Kittredge's famous assertion that the tales are dramatic monologues makes only partial sense for two or perhaps three tellers (the Pardoner, the Wife of Bath, and the Canon's Yeoman). In those cases the tales involve resonant extensions of subject matter found in each pilgrim's prologue (a tale in itself). But when we consider the teller's strategy of telling—his or her obtrusively rhetorical moves, such as overt comments, intrusions, digressions, and other manipulations of the tale—then another mode of characterization comes into play.[3] For the way in which a teller imposes herself upon her material is what telling a tale comes to mean in many cases. The Canon's Yeoman, for instance, leaves his confessional rush behind, becoming an angry prosecutor when telling his tale of an alchemist-trickster. Like the Canon's Yeoman, many tellers simply do not reduce themselves to neutral, narrating voices; those who do should receive some credit for the economy and wit of their tales (such as the Miller and the Shipman). Although a few tellers fade away as rhetorical presences, their tales still come to us as tidings—as invitations for assessments of truth and falsehood.

However, this is not to say that a teller's mere intrusiveness inherently expresses, reveals, or betrays personality. Exactly what the teller says and in relation to what in the tale—these reveal attitudes that characterize and that, as attitudes, extend those revealed by the "voices" in the various prologues. Thus we need to separate, provisionally at least, various voices here, since many readers have rightly become disenchanted with dramatic, personality-revealing readings of teller and tale. A teller's voice appears in any teller's prologue; there we can track that voice for traces of attitude and tone. Then there is often a rhetorically responding voice in the tale telling, this voice being the teller's intrusions, comments, and often digressive responses. We could then move to the many voices of the story material itself, however, that would be beyond my scope here, into the culturally heterogeneous strands and textures that make up setting, plot, character, and speech in the tales.[4] Finally, having become sensitive to the different ways in which voice can apply, I will show in less textural terms that Chaucer's pilgrims do not simply understand or misunderstand the truth or falsehood of their tales. They understand what they do, for better and worse, because their posturings, responses, and feelings—their self-revealing, narrating voices—are crucially involved.

This is a modern idea for Chaucer to have had, which is why it has been largely overlooked in studies of Chaucer in favor of notions of cognition that are intellectual and problem solving in nature, to which the current vogue of phenomenological studies attests. The intersubjectivity of perception and creation is largely thought of in terms of intellection, intention, and will[5]—which brings us to the heart of the question and to consideration, in the pages that follow, of Chaucer's emphasis on feeling and understanding within a medieval context that connects wonder, beauty, and delight to desire and acts of knowing.

For Chaucer, our reaching into the world, especially for understanding, includes tales and virtually any human subject complex enough to have different aspects and various manifestations. We desire to know, to possess the truth of something—to understand individually. The understanding of others is useful, but it is not our own; it does not quite fit our own structures of perception and erotic experience.[6] This is why Chaucer's dream-vision narrators turn to books and read through them with great delight, even when little understanding seems to be their lot. They anticipate a consummatory fit between what they perceive, what they feelingly read about, and what they eventually hope to understand in some vivid way.[7] Problems arise, of course, when the narrator's feelings are confused, when he or she is astonished and perplexed (a state of wonder turned against possibilities of knowing); or a preliminary obstacle, a lack of feeling entirely, can prevent the narrator from delighting in anything. For example, some such state afflicts the melancholy narrator in the *Book of the Duchess*, who tells us he has great wonder that he is alive, for he cannot sleep or take pleasure in anything; he has "felynge in nothyng" (l. 11).

Unable to sleep, the *Book of the Duchess* narrator asks that his servant hand him a book, a "romaunce" (or collection of Ovidian fables, tales), so that he can read and thereby "drive the night away" (l. 49). This is not pleasure or desire but "play" that seems marginally preferable to chess or "tables." This is a fortunate choice, for he comes upon a tale that arouses wonder (the tale of Seys and Alcyone) and that leads him to "pleye" (half desperately) at a prayer for sleep, in which he mainly promises to give Morpheus, Juno, or someone a terrific featherbed and to redecorate their bedroom gorgeously, if only someone could make him sleep and get some rest (ll. 239–69). The story arouses a sensual, self-revealing humor that brings sleep, dream, a saved life, and eventually, thoughts of turning the dream into a poem. Without feeling in something, for something, no undertaking, no understanding, and no life is possible. However, amusingly and disconcertingly, the desperate narrator does not focus well on the tale he reads, if by "well" we ask only for some extended attention to the heart of the tale. Upon finishing the tale, his thoughts are aroused only by something that speaks directly to his own predicament. I will return to this characterizing and telling point later, because it is the earliest indication of Chaucer's sense that feelings have something to do with our perceptions and thus with our understanding of anything.

Along with largely ignoring this characterizing potential in the responses of tellers to their tales, Chaucer scholarship has not focused much on a fairly new insight that was available to Chaucer: that emotion, *feeling* in our sense—not compassion or pity in an abstract, moralistic, or traditionally medieval and ethical sense—profoundly affects one's perception and understanding of something, especially something as complex as human experience. In medieval love psychology, centered in part on *adfectus*, one has to be sensitive, one must have a tender heart, to perceive someone else's pain. Medieval theory here may extend to all acts of perception in human affairs; without feeling in the percipient, images would not impress themselves upon the mind.[8] A late medieval concern for love and pity is traced by J. D. Burnley back to Lactantius, then forward to Augustine and others: theirs "was an ethic based upon the holiness of the heart's affections, upon the scriptural injunction to 'love thy neighbour as thyself.' Its basis was not rational self-sufficiency like that of the philosophers but emotional inter-dependence: an ethic of relationships rather than individualism. The relationship involved was primarily that with God, but secondarily, and importantly, that existing between men" (both love and amity).[9] Chaucer clearly has similar concerns in his notions of pity, a "gentil" heart, and "gentil" behavior. But he seems also to have exploited a late development away from feeling as an ethical category—for example, penitential knowing; knowing as courtly sentiment; feeling as the "pite" or "gentilesse" appropriate to one's calling or to one's class—and toward feeling as an emotional category inherently linked to acts of knowing. Here feeling functions cognitively, perhaps in the way that a recognition of beauty deeply concerns knowledge in both the proportions and forms of things (Aquinas, *Summa* 1.4).[10] It is a love of books that leads two of Chaucer's dream narrators to want knowledge of them and an understanding of the experiences they depict, even though encounters with books and their delightful as well as perplexing contents are often frustrating. There is beauty in objects of love and reverence, just as there is in moments of renewal and natural awakening. Books, nature, and reverential delight are entertained together, sequentially in the opening of the *Legend of Good Women*, and with books dropped out, simultaneously in the grand, opening sentence of the *General Prologue* (which has struck many readers as reminiscent of the dream visions).[11] Apparently spring awakens more than nature; it awakens the longing to go on a pilgrimage, which in several turns generates a company of pilgrims and a collection of tales: a book of tales and tellers, finally, for our delight and reverence, for our engagement feelingly, and so for our knowing.

Because we have a natural affinity for proportion and therefore for the beautiful—our sense and our knowing faculties being in a kind of proportion says Aquinas—our sense of beauty and the feelings of delight and reverence involved are at the heart of knowing feelingly, which for Chaucer is the only way to know anything at all, especially in matters of love. But Chaucer extends this business to all topics of human importance, to questions of order, justice, accord, good fortune and bad, righteous and profane values, predestination and free will. Essentially, this brings the possibilities of knowing to everyone, removing knowing from the high ground of philosophers and theologians and transferring it to the products of Rumor's output—those expansively elaborated tidings we call fictions.[12]

We delight in what has a similitude to our own minds, and we extend belief readily in such cases, even with little or no worldly experience of the subjects depicted. This open crediting of old books is a disposition of mind, rather than the kind of judgment Lisa Kiser opts for in her careful review of the opening lines in the *Prologue to the Legend of Good Women*. There, at one point, Chaucer concludes that

> Wel ought us thanne honouren and beleve
> These bokes, there we han noon other preve.
> [F, 27–28]

Kiser thinks of Chaucer here as realizing that many things exist that people will never see for themselves, things that can be known only through "the 'doctrine of these olde wyse' (F, G, 19) as it is discovered in books."[13] But Chaucer does not "realize" or assert the existence of things here. Rather he speaks for an open mind, against those who would debunk those things in old books that they have neither experienced nor seen for themselves. The narrator speaks earlier of crediting accounts of joy in heaven and pain in hell; that it is so he readily grants because such matters accord with him ("And I acorde wel that it be so," G, l. 3). That such claims are true accords with him, which necessarily encourages belief, although we lack a univocal assertion that joy in heaven and pain in hell in fact exist. To believe otherwise, however, would be discordant and could have stunning consequences in one's life.

Beyond that we should, in every reasonable way, honor and credit what we read in books, both doctrine and story, even though we have no proof that certain doctrines or stories are true:

> And to the doctrine of these olde wyse,
> Yeve credence, in every skylful wise,
> That tellen of these olde appreved stories
> Of holynesse, of regnes, of victories,
> Of love, of hate, of other sondry thynges.
>
> [F, ll. 19–23]

In the G version of the lines immediately following this passage, Chaucer drops "honouren" as an injunction, retains believing, and modifies 'proof' by the notion of "non other assay" (G, l. 28). He tones down the notion of reverence (retaining the word in G, line 31, where it forms an end rhyme with credence in line 32) by cutting the narrator's references to faith and devotion in relation to books. Reasonable belief that accords with the mind is not faith. Moreover, the narrator's delight in books becomes more a desire than the gesture of honoring ("swich lust and swich credence" replace "feyth and ful credence"). Involved with feeling, then, and much neglected as a factor by modern readers, is this mental or cognitive and emotional or affective openness I call belief.

There are many things in books that we should believe are true, although we have no way of assaying them except as they accord with our minds, with our beliefs, and with the world as we understand it. Without such openness toward old stories and their doctrines, we will deprive ourselves of whatever truth or true remembrance is in them. It should be clear by now that "openness" is an affair of receptivity in mental and emotional connectedness. It becomes our only entry; given our relative ignorance, such openness is our only way of assaying the books we encounter. Thus belief and feeling enrich each other as a way of knowing, of assaying, old stories, the everyday offspring of which may be more delight in the reading of books, but the hope of which is truth.[14] Perhaps it is this stress on delight and feeling that separates Chaucer from Bernard's asceticism ("Bernard the monk ne saugh nat all, pardee!") while joining him in spirit to such successors of Bernard as Bonaventura and William of Auvergne.[15] At the least it marks an advance over ignorant faith in books and even the astonished, merely perplexed stages of wonder, wonder being a prerequisite for any undertaking that leads to knowledge.[16]

Chaucer's Canterbury pilgrims rarely show anything like the reverence, credence, and pleasure stressed here by Chaucer's narrator-dreamer. Most of them credit their tales in some way and find a "doctrine" in the stories they relate. But not only their feelings interfere with their understandings. Now we can think also about their reliance upon the senses and the ways their beliefs intermix with their feelings—beliefs that lead their understanding (unhappily in many cases, failing to achieve verification) to terminate in a reading of their tales. In the collection of tale tellings, then, Chaucer poses not only the truth content of tales and the vagaries of feeling but also the character of felt belief in each case of tale telling, or of believed feeling—that somehow a pilgrim's feelings in themselves can provide a suitable understanding of a tale. This dual focus may account for the prominence in the collection of impassioned tellers (whether or not confessional) and tales of pathos.[17] Indeed, experiences treated in a pathetic vein are ones Chaucer does not undercut. Because they involve innocent suffering, they express something pure in human nature, something true that victimization brings out unalloyed. How we understand the tales that encompass such suffering or the world in which such suffering occurs are of course other matters, susceptible to mistake and open to irony.

When complicated by notions of belief, feeling becomes the key issue in Chaucer's approach to truth in fiction. The essential, indeed, the novel way in which Chaucer seeks to know truth about the world or anything else in and through the tales we tell is by posing relations between feeling, belief, and perception in teller after teller: How it is that tellers' feelings and beliefs either hinder or aid them in perceiving something and in understanding what they see. This is to say that knowing anything complex at all about ourselves and our actions is not pure intellection. If so, another way in which to see many of the tellers and tales is as the result of this insight faced squarely. The understanding any pilgrim has of a tale is tied up in his or her emotional life. The pilgrim and we know or misknow feelingly: However else anyone claims to know anything is either a case of presumption or is indebted to divine revelation.[18]

By looking over a character's shoulder, we can hope to do better than that character in some respects. At least we can reasonably avoid the teller's mistakes and entertain intimations the teller does not see, although in seeing correctly from someone else's error (blindness rectifying sight,) we may not manage well for long without encountering problems of understanding. How, finally, are we to disentangle truth from falsehood and thereby suitably receive a tale? Chaucer, I think, would sober us up but still invite us to assay each teller who manifestly fails in different ways. Those tellers become an encouragement, particular guides over particular material about how not to proceed, as well as a cautionary multitude.

Chaucer studies have reflected much of this obliquely, but Chaucerians have not sufficiently faced these issues, which is justification enough for recapitulating those issues here before closing on a sense of Chaucer's democracy of knowing. Clearly, many readers have interpreted the tales idiosyncratically and *as* idiosyncratic, analyzing their themes, artifice, coherence, reflection of literary tradition, and rhetoricity. But few readers have seen the tales as compounds of truth and falsehood, which Chaucer invites us to assess as a project that poses the task of knowing and understanding in terms of perception intermingled with feeling and belief. Readers have long noted the limited understanding Chaucer gives his tellers, including his Pilgrim self, but they have not seen those limitations as stemming from perceptions both happily and unhappily driven, in particular cases, by mixtures of feeling and belief. And of course numerous readers have supposed that tales and tellers were matched in some revealing way. Robert Burlin (1977) has even suggested that the *way* a tale is told characterizes the teller. But typically readers assume that the tale (not the tale-telling intrusions, asides, digressions, and responses) is what reveals the teller to us. Even Burlin falls back upon an assumption of intimate connections between teller and tale, in the course of which he hardly analyzes the sense of the teller gained from closely following the teller's approaches and responses to his or her material.[19]

As I have said already, the so-called dramatic interpretation has recently been debunked by several readers, perhaps most powerfully by Robert Jordan (1987), who sees the tellers disappearing in their tale telling, tending to function mainly as presenters of material and offering, in their various appearances, no real sense of an inner life. Jordan's evocation of an essentially rhetorical rather than a realistic or a materialistically psychological poetics for Chaucer is adeptly managed and deserves the careful consideration in connection with particular tales given to it in later chapters. But initially it is not clear why such passages as the Manciple's comments on words and things or his quoting of Plato are the tale's rhetoric and not the teller's responses to a tale—however textual they are in a capacious, rhetorical sense. Rather than refer these extremes to the Manciple's character or personality—from which they would be seen to emanate—Jordan would simply have them express Chaucer's rhetorical methods of composition, an "expansive poetics" that allows Chaucer the "scope to orchestrate a spectrum of shadings from bombast to subtle irony."[20]

Of course one would be arguing circularly by positing a unitary persona and by then integrating his or her gestures into a suitably plastic conception of personality. But nothing prevents one from proceeding inferentially from the Manciple's comments to a sense of him, to an assessment of character (not some a priori character that is his—although the prologue to the tale gives us strong hints of personality, if not *a* personality). Chaucer's method of composition may preclude putting us inside a character's mind, but it hardly precludes the characterizing force of speech and gesture. When we attend to the Manciple, what appears is deviation, whether in a clerical or bombastic direction—deviation from an Aristotelian norm of a healthy, balanced mind. Positing organically integrated personalities for the Canterbury pilgrims is an unnecessary act, and probably un-Chaucerian. Organicism can provide, however, a useful model for highlighting those developments in which a latent "personality" emerges from discontinuous fragments, as when a teller's prologue voice emerges in the *General Prologue* and then carries into intrusive tale telling. This is especially so when the tale contains themes that resonate well with those developed in the teller's prologue account of self, witness the Wife of Bath and the Pardoner. Similarly, to posit a depth psychology for each of Chaucer's characters is otiose, although, again, depth psychology can provide a useful model for reflecting upon Chaucer's achievements in the creation of complexly voiced characters. Additionally, if we assume, for example, in the Manciple's case, that a relatable tale concerning Phebus, his wife, her lover, and a pet crow is essentially separate from, perhaps even alien to, the teller, then the tiding is one that the teller searches, assesses, and responds to in a self-revealing and characterizing way. Rather than a vague psychology of dream interpretation, following Kittredge, one could invoke the psychology of the Rorschach or thematic apperception test, thus moving from an important bête noir for such readers as Lawton, Benson, and Jordan.[21] There is no reason to confine "realism" or the "realistic" to a Coleridgean aesthetic any more than there is a reason to confine the "dramatic" to a simplified version of either personality or Freudian psychology. Finally, the alternative to a Coleridgean view of Chaucer's poetry or to a reductively

Freudian view of tale and teller is not ineluctably a textual formalism, whether rhetorical in character or mechanistic (structuralist or deconstructive). Chaucer grew up on rhetorical models of composition, but any mode of composition, any set of styles can be used to think about itself and to explore versions of human action and character. Chaucer inherits a rich entanglement of classical and Christian notions of character, notions that imply a Neoplatonic view of the world and an Aristotelian sense of character and action.

Given these classical antecedents, it is a lot to claim that Chaucer "democratizes" knowing in some way, bringing it down to the "lewd" and relatively unlearned individual. But although Chaucer may have gone this way reluctantly, he has never struck many readers as particularly philosophical (despite his fondness for Boethius). Indeed, study after study purporting to show Chaucer's debt, whether direct or indirect, to fourteenth-century theological ferment, has much enlarged our awareness of developments in logic, grammar, and physical theory without much illuminating Chaucer's mind and work.[22] In formal philosophy Chaucer is old-fashioned and highly deferential. He does not hold to new ways, unless perhaps the weak and unpredictable influence of a zeitgeist touches him from Oxford. He reads Boethius and translates Neoplatonic theory insofar as he translates the *Consolation of Philosophy*. Thus he knows Boethius's theory of truth, and he may indeed embrace that theory: Chaucer's longest glosses in his translation of the *Consolation* occur in a deeply Neoplatonic context, having roots in the *Phaedo* and the *Meno*. These glosses concern the grounds for knowing rational truth, grounds situated in the deepness of thought: "This is to seyn, how schulde men deme the sothe of any thyng that were axid, yif ther nere a rote of sothfastnesse that were yploungid and hyd in the naturel principles, the whiche sothfastnesse lyvede within the depnesse of the thought?" (bk. 3, metrum 11, ll. 38–43). Judging the truth of something is possible, Chaucer might say, given forms hidden within us when we confront hints of external things. This is how we perceive beauty and come to know it, as well as why we credit ideas or claims that accord with our minds. Our feelings, of course, are not everything; indeed, if not inherently part of an open disposition—of belief extended but not become faith or dogma—then feelings will very likely lead belief and warp understanding, rendering judgment unstable.

Chaucer also translates parts of Jean de Meun's *Romance of the Rose* and all of Pope Innocent III's *De contemptu mundi*. He very likely defers to these authorities rather than place himself in competition. And that, I think, is good, since he is irrepressibly a poet. Otherwise, he might have written the kind of morally philosophical poetry found in Gower's works: a poetry that teaches, sometimes quite flexibly, but one that asserts truths or the good more than it searches for truth—good, rhetorical poetry that repays attention but that is rarely lively or profound. If this is correct, how then does Chaucer move from a rhetorical tradition that produced his friend Gower and that clearly influenced most medieval poets, including Chaucer, in far-reaching ways? How did he arrive at the affective and exploratory side of the search for truth in books, stories, and life?

To pose that question is to search for an autobiography, letters, journals, or the testimony of others (assuming that interviews are out of the question). After paying due homage to the differences that genius and temperament make (opaque evasion though that be), we can turn to the works and attempt a path, a line of development or deepening and complicating interest. In Chaucer's early poetry it is clear that he *has* gone his own way and where his way stations and stops are, several of which I have already exploited in this chapter. Those stops are especially evident if we look to his depictions of the perplexed reader. For in various poems he presents himself in changing images, distanced from his actual self, but in images that develop a view of himself as reader, versifier, and poet. Together, moving from the *Book of the Duchess* to the *Prologue to the Legend of Good Women*, those images concern an education of the reader, beginning with a melancholic who considers books better play than chess or "tables," and ending with the Chaucerian poet-reader summarily accused of having defamed Love. Indeed, to play seriously at books is at the center of what becomes a complex poetics for reading and writing, a poetics worked out through successive narrators who read and write and who would rather read than direct a game of strategy (the player of such a game possibly being an image of the magisterial poet).[23]

3 ❦ BELIEF AND READING
IN THE EARLY POEMS

In the *Prologue to the Legend of Good Women* Chaucer has the God of Love apparently misread Chaucer's intentions in making *Troilus and Criseyde* and in translating the *Romance of the Rose*. Why would Chaucer make those books in defamation of Love? Chaucer's defense is that he has been misread; that although he may have misread his authors' meaning, what he himself meant was only to champion truth in love. Thus to read well, to understand what one's predecessors wrote and why, is everybody's problem; the reader's misreading is not the point. Rather, when we watch other readers (writers and tellers), we need to see why a misreading occurs. We should then approach our own reading humbly, aware that our feelings and cognitions may be inadequate (even comically so) to whatever we confront, such as those contradictory depictions of Love that trouble the *Parliament of Fowls* narrator. We should also recall the mixed nature of tidings and of how books can become entangled with life as well as with each other, as in the *House of Fame*'s mixed rendering of Dido (switching from Virgil to Ovid).

Thus equipped, we might take flight if only we would further consider our own intrusiveness in order to see the otherness of books and respond in cognitive openness, both of feeling and belief, to the truths books offer us, recognizing that books and experience need to come together if there is to be a standard for true belief. In these early poems, what and how the narrator-dreamers know is always qualified by their circumstances. Apparently, a knowledge that rises above person, circumstance, and time is not often won from books and "gestes," however much Chaucer might believe in its possibility. Instead, beginning with the narrator of the *Book of the Duchess*, Chaucer develops some of the problems with a naive reader's reading, problems that become acute as the reader becomes entangled emotionally with the material, thereby failing to respond insightfully to whatever intimations of truth the material holds. In part, the dream vision poems present a survey of Chaucerian personae responding to books, developing a detailed sense of the kind of thing reading is, as well as what it ought to be.[1] We can begin instructively with the *Book of the Duchess* dreamer, with the reader whose normality and health have been impaired.

The narrator of the tale assumes that old clerks and poets put fables into rhyme for our perusal and for our mindfulness, so that those fables will remain in mind for as long as "men" love the "lawe of kinde" (l. 56)—a transcendental law subsisting everywhere and glimpsed through regularities seen in particular organizations of nature. Perhaps rhyme enhances delight and thereby encourages mindfulness. Rhyme as an inducement to read might also suggest both entertainment and emotion; a heightening of language might encourage readers to react emotionally to the situations dramatized. For the narrator as a Chaucerian projection, then, we can infer bookishness, reverence for serious subjects, and an interest in various tales concerning kings, queens, and less exalted personages or things ("thinges smale," l. 59). The narrator chooses a book of tales thought of as addressing mindful readers for as long as men love the law of kind. Reverence for natural accord and for the Love that binds the universe is a reverence for nature, life, and pleasure—all things the narrator has "lost" in his melancholia:

> And wel ye woot, agaynes kynde
> Hyt were to lyven in thys wyse.
> [ll. 16–17]

So the narrator has a book brought to him concerning a general subject—the law of kind—within which he hopes to find a tale to occupy or entertain him, perhaps even to speak to him in his present condition. That a book might speak to his circumstances, however, is entirely speculative at this point. All the narrator wants is to drive the night away, to occupy his melancholy sleeplessness. But soon, in coming across the tale of Seys and Alcyone, he finds a "wonder thing" and begins to read in earnest, rather than in the dilatory mood implied by his survey of the book's contents:

> This bok ne spak but of such thinges,
> Of quenes lives, and of kinges.
> [ll. 57–58]

Wonder here is more than astonishment; it leads to an inquiring focus on a particular tale, a tale the narrator credits, although not everything in the tale is taken literally. What is it here that is reasonable to investigate, to believe in one's mood and one's delight?

The narrator begins by summarizing the Seys and Alcyone story. King Seys drowns at sea during a storm; after some time passes, his wife Alcyone wonders what has happened to her husband, becoming mournful when King Seys does not soon return. The narrator says that she longed so

> That certes it were a pitous thing
> To telle her hertely sorowful lif
> That she had . . . .
>
> [ll. 84–86]

Feeling for her sorrow, he nevertheless does not tell that piteous thing. Indeed, he reports, not what he thought as he read the text word by word but how moved he was to read about Alcyone's sorrow—so moved that his already perilous condition only worsened. Here feeling is all, leading neither to an understanding of Alcyone nor to moral action for the disabled narrator. Although a deficient reader, he is not wrong to read feelingly nor crucially wrong in neglecting moral judgment. Rather, he fails to understand what he reacts to feelingly. This is a failure rooted in his "head melancholy" and in his comical self-interests (although that comedy involves a serious point: the right tale at the right time might be lifesaving and restore one's vigor, one's "lustyhede"). Initially without feeling, the narrator has awakened to the sorrow of another, albeit a person in a book. That sorrow is convincing, so true that it in fact intensifies the narrator's own sense of loss.

Nevertheless, it is good that Alcyone's weeping moves him. Despite the narrator-reader's impaired "root of judgment," Ovid's intentions are realized as the reader empathizes with the living sufferer rather than with the dead cause. Here the narrator reacts as a medieval reader should to affectively heightened language, to Alcyone's extended complaints, yet not appropriately in either cognition or action. This failure is more or less repeated in other depictions of reading in Chaucer's poetry, even when the reader in question does move to moral indignation. It is here, I think, that Chaucer begins to reshape medieval poetics, beginning an evolution away from a rhetorically magisterial and figuratively beautiful poetry that moves us to thought and feeling in ways doctrinally controlled by an already ideologically committed poet.

Instead, the focus turns to the moved reader, to what moves him, and what the experiences depicted in books mean. Chaucer's narrator-readers credit their books, even when perplexed by what they read and seriously wrought in the feelings they have. They continue nevertheless and frequently develop a positive wonder, which suggests that out of a much more comprehensive crediting, wonder, and fullness of feeling Chaucer turns to poetry, to an emotionally involved and intellectually open poetry of reading rather than to the poetry of a magisterial writer. Rather than undertake tasks of high persuasion, Chaucer would explore problems of understanding—an exploration, however, that requires considerable rhetorical skill if he is to make poetry from it rather than consternation.

Perhaps the afflicted, hapless, or perplexed narrator is Chaucer's first step in creating a readerly poetics. This poetics of reaction and attention, rather than persuasion, involves narrators who respond to something and then either have or retell a dream (from response comes production; from attention, some understanding). Then, too, these narrators and their dream comedies may also be Chaucer's way of seducing his audience into favorable attitudes (a classical move, rhetorically), so that they will not indite this nonmagisterial poetry. The hapless narrator puts us into a mild, tolerant, somewhat benign mood.[2]

The best part of the reaction of the *Book of the Duchess* narrator to the book is to the scene in Morpheus's cave. The narrator tells us that Juno sends a messenger to have Morpheus animate Seys's body long enough for Seys to reappear and tell Alcyone what has happened to him. The excited messenger blows a horn and shouts "Awake" in Morpheus's ear, in a voice that is "wonder hye." This noisy falsetto awakens Morpheus, who does what Juno wants. Learning that Seys is indeed dead, Alcyone swoons for three days, saying much that the narrator passes over, and then dies. The narrator enhances the comedy here by telling us what he found so worthy and so wonderful in this tale: the idea that a god of sleep might help him in his potentially deadly sleeplessness! Clearly reading according to his own needs, the narrator skips through Seys's "sentence" for Alcyone ("To lytel while oure blysse lasteth!") as well as Seys's advice: "Awake! Let be your sorwful lyf" (ll. 211, 202). He promises a luxurious bed for Morpheus if Morpheus or someone would help him sleep. The idea of such a bed and sumptuous room so pleases him (the first thing that has for some time) that he immediately falls asleep and dreams.

Although disabled and narrowly self-serving, the *Book of the Duchess* narrator believes in Alcyone as a person and, at least in hopeful play, he wonders about and credits the tale. Moreover, seeking diversion and hoping to restore one's seriously damaged vigor are not bad motives for selecting reading material.[3] What began as an insomniac's pastime soon leads to wonder, then to emotional involvement, and finally to humor.

Glending Olson notes the function of that initial wonder as the narrator comes across the tale of Seys and Alcyone: "From the sense data of the story Chaucer derives 'wonder,' the 'admiratio' which the *Tacuinum* says is involved in reason's contemplation of the most interesting things that the imagination presents to it."[4] In relation to the narrator's melancholy, reading has a serious, medical justification and a notably positive result in this case. The narrator's imagination has been invigorated, his pleasure in the tale has been restorative. But wonder as an inducement to knowing (Olson cites Aquinas *Summa* 1.32.8) has led to humor rather than to truth or to a significant discovery. This particular development is absolutely right; the deflection is understandable as the narrator's disabled reason reasonably focuses in "game" on the notion that some being could be petitioned by the offer of a featherbed and a medieval designer's dream bedroom. But the narrator could not have gone through the tale without his emotional involvement in Alcyone's sorrow, an involvement that is appropriately deadly and therefore inappropriate for the suffering narrator. His game is life enhancing if not truth involving. It is a necessary defense against Alcyone's sorrow,[5] although it is equally a revelation that the good reader must engage his books both feelingly and without seriously impaired health or narrowly formed interests. To assay what one reads requires normal, functioning powers of judgment and an openness to as much of the story as possible.

The narrator of the *House of Fame* wonders about the causes of dreams and suffers from ignorance about the doings of love rather than from mental affliction. Whatever they are, his powers of assessing truth are intact. How, then, does this advantage improve him as a reader in relation to the *Book of the Duchess* narrator?

Initially, it gives him an even-handed approach to the mute but expressive text he "reads"—Virgil's *Aeneid*. The text is engraved on a brass tablet, the tablet placed in the Temple of Glass presumably dedicated to Venus. The tablet appears along one wall and begins with a four-line preamble to a text depicting the Aeneas story in a sequence of images. The narrator-dreamer covers the story from beginning to end, almost. Thus he demonstrates an obvious way to work through a book or through a sequential story that consists of illustrations. But to what does he apply himself, and how does this story illuminate the mystery of love? Is the Aeneas story merely a fable, an entertainment, no matter how famous? The dreamer will never know until he reads the tale and appraises it, seeking whatever truth he can recognize, much as one would do with dreams. (This may be why reading Virgil follows upon a predream discussion of dream interpretation; questions about dreams can slip into questions about the interpretation of stories).[6] Could a fable be oracular, presenting a pattern for action? Or could it have a prophetic dimension, perhaps a surprising way in which it projects something in our life to consequences not yet reached? Whatever the case, the narrator as dreamer begins simply to report what he saw, in order.

Here Chaucer depicts a reader in an ongoing reading one remove from an actual reading with its initial musings. The reader tells us what he saw and thus rereads what he saw, complete with earnest responses to the still fresh story. By bringing an ongoing rereading of text into the retelling of the text, Chaucer further changes the poet's task. Conventionally, the reader's experience should result in an editorially cut or expanded, morally dominated text guided by the poet. But for the *House of Fame* dreamer-reader, the editing process, while a means to amplify selected parts of the text, comes to serve an emotional response rather than moral comprehension. The intellectual or moral response follows belatedly and at cross-purposes, allowing the dreamer little adequate expression for his emotion.

In this emphasis on the reader's experience, thought now follows feeling, or is about feeling, and emotional response becomes the high point in a reading that focuses on old-fashioned pathos rather than the gathering of facts and truths one will use to teach others. Already comically aroused about dreams and hostile toward those who would debunk his, the narrator enters his dream primed and excitable. Initially, he is all eyes, reporting what he sees in the glass temple (especially a portrait of Venus naked and floating in the sea). Sense impression is all so far, until he enters into the story he saw of Troy's destruction. He begins to respond to some sections more than to others, forming an understanding of what he sees, developing images, feelings, and situations. Nevertheless, he reads primarily at a naive and emotional level. And he reads with such intensity that he is largely perplexed by the Aeneas and Dido scenes and oblivious to how he slights the continuity of the story. That said, there is still something irreducibly valuable about his way of reading, even though we never find out just how Chaucer would read the *Aeneid*. Thus we lack an authoritative critique of the dreamer's misreading.

Chaucer never abandons the device of the naive, partially perplexed and partially wondering reader. Instead, he brings that device into the heart of his poetics, writing poetry informed by such a reader's experience, poetry that often depicts such a reader (or teller), and poetry that at its best turns around the wonderment of reading (or hearing), of understanding the stories one reads. Of course, one can always pull back here and emphasize

the rhetoricity of Chaucer's procedures, the self-reflexive character of rhetorical composition, and the rhetorical functions of characters. But then both
figure and purpose would be lost in the general embroidery of words—
something that does not quite happen even in the most metafictional of, for
example, Barth's story tellings about adolescence. Self-reflexivity, after all,
is a technique harnessed to one end or another, something few postmodern-
ist readers would deny in theory, even if they ignore it in practice.[7]

The narrator begins his rereading emotionally when he tells us that
Troy was conquered and won: "allas, / How Ilyon assayled was," and
when he looks upon Ascanius's frightened expression—"That hyt was
pitee for to here"—(ll. 157–58, 180). Perhaps confused, he sees the fright
and pityingly hears the pain. Willy-nilly he extends belief and feeling in an
excited progress scene by scene, reasonably impelled by previous readings
or hearings of the story, readings that instantly animate what he sees,
providing an aural immediacy to the images before him. His task of understanding, however, is still ahead.[8]

We can see this task in the dreamer's anguish for Dido, expressed in
questions that implicitly address the meaning of her pain and the why of
betrayal. Although disclaiming any ability to speak knowledgeably of sexual love—which ostensibly is why he barely dwells on Dido's sexual liaison with Aeneas—the "falsing" of Dido nevertheless becomes both the
emotional and the moral center of the story (this he paints elaborately,
rhetorically):

> Allas! what harm doth apparence,
> Whan hit is fals in existence!
> For he to hir a traytour was;
> Wherfore she slow hirself, allas!
> Loo, how a woman doth amys
> To love hym that unknowen ys!
> For, be Cryste, lo, thus yt fareth:
> 'Hyt is not al gold that glareth.'
>   [ll. 265–72]

Unable to cry "alas" enough or to conclude his feelings on a satisfactory
understanding of this terrible event, the narrator continues in his explanatory mode for twenty lines more, before pausing to say that now he will
relate how Aeneas betrayed Dido. This section, including the next hundred
lines or so, leads Robert Jordan to see a glittering surface rather than
"meaningful depths." He particularly notes the differing lengths of treatment accorded to a long list of women betrayed by men.[9] Jordan's observa-

tions require an a priori reduction of the narrator's voice to a verbal device on the ground that Chaucer does not develop his amplifications. But Chaucer does notably back us away from the stories listed to observations of the moved narrator, who is in fact "overwhelmed with sympathy for Dido."[10] We should also note the narrator's deviation from his initial, scene-by-scene retelling. In the scene that depicts how Dido made Aeneas her life, her love, her pleasure, her lord (l. 258), the narrator, with knowledge of the outcome, loses his way in the rhetoric of outrage and sympathy. Having warmed up considerably at Aeneas's expense, he elaborates the theme of outward beauty and inward vice, something he profits himself to think about:

> Ther may be under godlyhed
> Kevered many a shrewed vice.
>   [ll. 274–75]

This and other commonplaces, however, do not stabilize his understanding of the event. Indeed, his moralizing, always too appropriate, seems excessive. In trying to extract some profit from the terrible event of Aeneas's anticipated departure from Dido, he works hard but not happily.

Turning to Dido's complaints for seventy more lines, he finally breaks off to tell us that she eventually stabbed herself. If we want to know how she died, and what she said then, we can read Virgil and Ovid. Composing her complaints himself would take too long. The point of it all is simply this, the pity and the sorrow:

> But wel-away, the harm, the routhe,
> That hath betyd for such untrouthe,
> As men may ofte in bokes rede,
> And al day sen hyt in dede,
> That for to thynken hyt, a tene is.
>   [ll. 383–87]

He here asserts a mutually confirming parallel between books and life, a parallel that should settle our heads and hearts and allow both him and us to conclude well. But instead, his parallel only intensifies the pity and the sorrow, when we think upon it. Books and life confirm the truth of such experience in each; neither is an escape from or an understanding of the other. To think upon each only intensifies our anguish. Drowning in pity and lament, the hapless narrator tries to break away, to conclude his retelling and return everything to portraiture in the sensorily stimulating Temple of Glass. His attempts to understand, respond morally, and judge, have not been successful; but their failure hardly negates all possibility of understanding.

The dreamer cuts away parts of Virgil's text to emphasize his points. This is good, medieval practice, were it not for his emotional involvement. That involvement, basically, carries him from Virgil to Ovid and prevents him from considering seriously the explanation Virgil gives for Aeneas's actions, an explanation mentioned nearly at the end:

> But to excusen Eneas
> Fullyche of al his grete trespas,
> The book seyth Mercurie, sauns fayle,
> Bad hym goo into Itayle.
>
> [ll. 427–30]

He skips over this mitigation to concentrate instead on Aeneas as a villain, and by shifting from Virgil's Dido to Ovid's, on Dido's pathetic suffering.[11] In many ways the narrator is a victim of his courtliness: How, besides shifting to Ovid's account, is he to understand a noble queen betrayed? Looking at Dido through several centuries of the idealization and courtly enhancement of queens, he can hardly, reasonably countenance Virgil's maddened tiger, so crazed by despair that in her ravings she would dismember Aeneas and devour his son. But then he has not had much experience of love or of love's pains.

Affect arouses his emotions, as it should, but his feelings inform his moral understanding problematically. His understanding in turn guides him from one text to another as he seizes upon commonplaces of male treachery and female pathos, a process that disrupts the coherence of Virgil's text, displaces the important information about Mercury, and neither settles his feelings nor obliterates the story. For belatedly he somewhat haplessly acknowledges Aeneas's lack of blame, although the man was "fals" and a "traytour."[12] Additionally, he reads naively in that he fails to consider whether the scenes engraved in the Temple of Glass tell a true story or a mixture of truth and lie. He needs an education of some sort and a grip on his authors: that if different authors focus on the events of the story in different ways—indeed producing not only different versions but different characters and drama—then that is a fact to confront, not elide, to face as fully as possible rather than reduce to a deformed equivalence as if to say, whoever wants to know what Dido said, read Virgil or Ovid. No wonder he forbears telling us, excusing the labor because of its anticipated length. Who could *endyte* what Dido said after her betrayal when Virgil and Ovid compose her in profoundly different ways?

Returning to the series of depictions, he finishes the Aeneas story without much response and with little amplification, contenting himself with a prayerful hope that Jupiter, who favored Aeneas, should always save us and lighten our sorrows. From this prayer, he comes back to himself and wonders where he and this Temple are. Having structurally run through Virgil's account, his amplifications upon Dido's misery indicate where he invests feeling and belief—implying that Ovid's account of Dido accords better with his mind than does Virgil's. And here he sticks until, in Book 2, his dream experience verifies accounts of atmospheric turmoil, as found in some of his books. Those accounts are true, although the sight in Book 3 of tidings as either lies or mixtures of truth and lie, largely amplified and exaggerated in both cases, should seriously qualify that dream verification. All of this suggests that we can neither devotedly believe nor experientially discount what we read or hear, any more than we can quite disentangle truth from falsehood by any sure method. That learned, the dreamer might next face his own mind and feelings, trying to assay what is accordant there and what it is reasonable to think in relation to particular stories—something he does not do in what remains of the poem, with its anticipation of a man of great authority.

Although perhaps cautioned by the dreamer's emotionalism, a better reader and narrator would not eschew feeling. Rather he or she should see that in a retelling a story may vary considerably from the author's work and intentions. This is part of the issue between Chaucer and the God of Love in the *Prologue to the Legend of Good Women*. While clearly a step beyond the *House of Fame* narrator, this issue also suggests the problematic nature of old stories as well as the difficulties one can have with one's own readers. The *Prologue* is also where Chaucer has placed his argument for belief in the truth of old books, for reverence and delight. But before considering Love's accusations, we might first raise the problem of old books and stories themselves: what they mean in furnishing us with contrasting views of similar phenomena as well as with radically different views of the same event or character. Chaucer poses this issue prominently in the *Parliament of Fowls*.

Wanting to know something about love, the narrator of the *Parliament of Fowls* takes up books, only to find contradictions in them about Love's miracles and Love's cruelties. Not knowing love in fact, he has no experience to guide him in his encounters with books about love. Nor does he have an easy way of deciding the reasonableness of belief in relation to the accounts he reads. His motives for reading are conventional enough—for pleasure and knowledge ("lore"). But his fruit has been astonished feeling and thought, when considering Love's "wonderful werkynge" (l. 5), such that when he moves from "felynge" to thinking (l. 6), he does not know whether he is floating or sinking. Because the art of love is a sharp and difficult craft, and because the lord of love is dismayingly contrary in his miracles and his cruel anger, all the narrator can say is "God save swich a lord!" (l. 14). His unease recalls the *Book of the Duchess* and that narrator's opening predicament—a potentially deadly *felynge in nothyng*. Much as the right book serendipitously came to hand (concerning the law of kind), so now the narrator and dreamer-to-be happens upon a book, Cicero's *Somnium Scipionis,* which he reads eagerly all day in the hope of learning some particular thing. Perhaps he hopes it will give him a clue about love, that it will reveal the truth to him (despite its antiquity, it may contain a wisdom new to him and his age in general). Proceeding much as does the *House of Fame* dreamer, this wakeful reader summarizes the book from beginning to end, event by event, in verse paragraph after verse paragraph. Unlike the emotional dreamer in the *House of Fame,* our wakeful reader does not respond notably to any particular section. Instead that response is withheld, implicitly, until it becomes the dream in which Affrican appears to the reader.

We might suppose that all of this is an elaborate way of addressing different aspects of love (literary, cosmic, courtly, and natural). We might suppose that the book about Scipio, in which Affrican introduces the idea of "commune profyt" along with breakers of the law, lecherous folk, clear souls, and a blissful place (*PF,* ll. 73–84), might in some way promise truth about love, virtue, and the cosmos (seeing the big picture). However, what other books confusingly join, Love's miracles and cruelty, this book simply divides transcendentally while shifting the ground for discussion. Where does Courtly Love fit in a view that defines bliss-deserving virtue as that which serves "commune profyt"? Is there Love for those lawbreakers and lecherous folk who follow something other than what serves the common good?

While not resolving the narrator's confusion about love, Cicero suggests that a book, rather than experience, *might* do so, while the truth in books remains undecisive, even curiously suspended. Of course, the more one reads, the more delightfully confusing, or at least various, particular issues might become. Borrowing a prophetic and oracular guide from one book, Affrican, does not help when the narrator falls asleep and dreams that Affrican takes him to a park entered through gates sporting contrary verses about Love. The nature of love (and worth and "gentilesse") is indeed a perplexing, comedy-inducing business that escapes the harmonizing effect of a cosmic perspective. Books tell of such a perspective, and the narrator's sober account of Cicero's book suggests that they may well tell truly, but how to assay that truth in one's own mind, especially given a ridiculous lack of experience "in dede"? The best the narrator-turned-dreamer can do is have the unresolved dream he has, one that proceeds through Venus's temple, with Love's dualities clearly marked in many ways, to a natural amphitheatre containing the parliament of birds, their various contributions to a love debate, and the presiding presence of procreative Nature. Chaucer seems to say that, in such cases as this, given confusing or indecisive matter in books (whether old or new), the best one can manage is a response that in some fashion reflects and faces one's perplexity. The *Parliament of Fowls* narrator reads and relates his book comprehensively, but its cosmic truth does not resolve anything for him. Rather, it adds another set of scenes to complement the dream scenes of the Garden of Venus and Nature's Parliament.

Chaucer himself writes complexly about love in *Troilus and Criseyde* but not to good effect, according to the God of Love in the *Prologue to the Legend of Good Women*. There the dreamer-poet stands accused of defaming love and love's folk—an inexcusable deed considering all the stories and books about virtuous women that he could have taken up. The God of Love claims that Chaucer has at least sixty books, both old and new, that treat of chaste, virtuous women, so why translate the *Romance of the Rose?* and why make a book about how Criseyde forsook Troilus? True accounts of true women should occupy the maker who otherwise seems bent on defaming Love. The stories alluded to are not particular to Love's court. Is the insinuation that Chaucer, unable to do homage to Love, should then confine himself to forms of secular and sacred hagiography? Whatever, the truth of story is not in question here, rather the maker's motives are suspected:

> "Hast thow nat mad in Englysh ek the bok
> How that Crisseyde Troylus forsok,
> In shewynge how that wemen han don mis?"
> [G, ll. 264–66]

Is this why Chaucer made the book of Troilus and Criseyde? The dreamer-poet is not allowed to reply immediately. Instead, the Queen of Love intercedes on his behalf with an extended, somewhat hypothetical plea.[13]

She raises doubts about the truth of Love's accusation, given that he may have heard lies about Chaucer on the part of envious and flattering hangers-on at court—a point the God of Love does not accept as he later tells the dreamer that a sorer penance than writing about virtuous women would have been just, but pity runneth over in a "gentil" heart. She also proposes hypothetical, extenuating circumstances: that, if Chaucer did write books defaming love, perhaps he was overly, foolishly scrupulous—not out of malice, but simply because he used various books in his makings and paid no heed to the matter he borrowed. Or perhaps he was bidden to make the *Romance of the Rose* and the story of Troilus and Criseyde by some powerful person. These points are not offered as fact, but rather as casting doubt upon Chaucer's motives (although they also, amusingly, question his attention to what he does and his independence from demanding patrons). That he wrote out of innocence or under compulsion should excuse him, especially if the God of Love understands noble mercy and would not be a tyrant. Moreover, the fact that these books were written is not a capital offense. Indeed, Chaucer's canon contains much that should already be seen as reparation, whatever the current state of Chaucer's service to Love ("I not wher he be now a renegat," G, l. 401). Given his abilities, such as they are, Chaucer deserves consideration for having made the *House of Fame,* the *Death of Blanch the Duchess,* the *Parliament of Fowls,* the story of Palamon and Arcite of Thebes, and many songs for Love's holidays. He has been busy in Love's service, if not altogether skillful. Moreover, he has translated books by Boethius, Pope Innocent, and pseudo-Origen, and he has "made" the Life of St. Cecile. He has already served good love and spiritual virtue (which should satisfy the querulous part of Love's accusation). So do not harm him, but let him do a lesser penance and further love in the making of stories about women who were true all their lives. In that way he can do exact reparation for such missaying as he did in "the Rose or elles in Crisseyde" (G, l. 431). Her argument is ameliorative, her persona charitable and true. She moves the God of Love and receives his thanks as well as Chaucer's. Having raised the question of motive, in Chaucer's interest but at his expense, she in effect has raised a question about reading and the truth of a book, which is more than the facts as history. Truth concerns authorial intent insofar as it involves a view of love, a use of character, and action. One can use a true story to tell a lie, to slander and defame Love and Love's servants. Moreover, that true story might be in the class of chaff, not corn, a story about the husks of womankind, not the fruitful, fertile, and chaste.

To write about husks can only be the impulse of a diseased mind and a malicious will ("'what eyleth the to wryte / The draf of storyes, and forgete the corn?'" G, ll. 311–12). When given an opening, Chaucer replies in his own defense. Truly in his opinion he is not guilty in this "cas" of having "don to love trespas" (G, l. 453). For just as a true person has no party with thieves, so a true lover should not blame him for speaking shame of a false lover (a thief). He is in the league of true lovers, who should hold with him, even though he wrote about Criseyde and of the Rose. For his intent, his point of view, was to champion fidelity in love, the cherishing of faithful love, and the eschewing of falsehood and vice. That was his intent, whatever else his authors meant. Alceste silences his argument, exclaiming that the God of Love will not be counterpleaded. The God of Love, magisterial, is no careful reader, nor should Chaucer now plead his case; he has received Love's grace and must now understand what he must do.

Although considered out of place by Alceste, Chaucer's plea nevertheless is important for raising the question of authorial intention and motivation (meaning). Chaucer's truth is that love understood in certain ways is worth cherishing and furthering. That is the story he meant to tell, a story that goes beyond plot, beyond mere story, to an affective and moral understanding of fidelity in love ("trouthe"). This is in the making of books; seeking it out must be part of the delight, the reverence with which one reads old books—the terms in which one extends belief and seeks understanding. The outcome of that belief is not a proposition or even a verification in the world of experience (though it might be). Rather, belief terminates satisfactorily here in the furthering of faithful love and the cherishing of it. Any other outcome would be "draf"; it would constitute the world of love in a disturbing way, in a way that does not accord with the mind or involve reasonableness.

Sometime in the middle 1390s Chaucer, while deeply engaged in the Canterbury tales project, undertook major revisions of the *Prologue* for the *Legend of Good Women*. He modifies, among other things, a few lines to clarify why the narrator brings up the subject of books, reverence, and belief:

> But wherfore that I spak, to yeve credence
> To bokes olde and don hem reverence,
> Is for men shulde autoritees beleve,
> There as there lyth non other assay by preve.

For myn entent is, or I fro yow fare,
The naked text in English to declare
Of many a story, or elles of many a geste,
As myn autours seyn; leveth hem if yow leste.

[G, ll. 81–88]

Lacking proof, we are nevertheless invited to extend credence and reverence to old books, especially to stories of goodness (one supposes). This does not mean that men should believe just any authority; rather men should extend belief where no other assaying of truth is possible, where experience or sensory evidence is lacking. Having some "other assay by preve," of course, would help greatly in bringing felt belief to closure as well as in the search for worthy material. Near the end of the G prologue, the God of Love asserts that Chaucer writes negligently when he writes of fickle women, given that he knows the goodness of women "By pref, and ek by storyes" (G, l. 528). These twin proofs are irrefutable but rarely had.

Chaucer had been working on the tales of Canterbury, and he may already have composed the *Wife of Bath's Prologue*, with the Wife's famous assertion of sufficiency in experience, even though there were no "auctoritee" in the world. I think that we can see the influence of that "auctoritee" in the revision that is the G prologue and in the twin value of experiential proof and story, an influence that gives an invaluable clue to the Canterbury tales project. Here Chaucer has used variously moved tellers to assay truth in fictions not guaranteed by both proof (or experience) and stories. We have tales of good women (including the hag in the Wife's tale), bawdy tales, noble tales, tales about scoundrels, and tales that are moral or merry in one way or another. These are all tales that we should credit and revere for the inherent authority that their existence commands, there where we have no other "assay by preve." Unlike the legend of good women, the tales of Canterbury are highly various, of differing styles and genres, and effectively cover the world of story types known to Chaucer. His assay here is enormously complex and unguaranteed. The open crediting of these tales, it will turn out, is a deep affair that must include the tellers as well. Brought together by a longing to go on pilgrimage, the Canterbury tellers become a group of tale sharers by accepting with "ful glad herte" the Host's proposal for entertainment. By telling competitive tales, they will shorten the way to Canterbury and to whatever meed they need from the "blisful martir." Tale telling will speed them over time and space, each to his or her own penance or prayer. A space has been won, when they all heartily agree, for their merriment and for a Chaucerian search for truth in fiction, a search that presents the reader with numerous opportunities for extending reverence and credence, as well as for considering what a tale tells and what a reader knows from his or her experience. But to investigate feelingly, in open belief, is a prerequisite for approaching the question of truth in any tale. Having proposed this way of knowing in the *Prologue to the Legend of Good Women*, Chaucer seems to feel constrained by the project he undertakes, conceiving in its stead a collection of tales that is far from being a "legende" and to which he devotes much labor for the rest of his life (rather than to stories of good women, as demanded of his persona by Alceste). Moreover, he creates a company of tale tellers, thus bringing forward the device of the personal, narrating voice used in the dream visions and in *Troilus and Criseyde*.

The end to which one investigates tales is knowledge of some sort, knowledge, for example, about love or justice or "gentilesse." But in enormously broadening and complicating the collection of tales he would have us survey, Chaucer loses the almost noetic focus that the "legende" project gave him. There, in story after story, perhaps at Queen Anne's behest, Chaucer was to tell of good women who were true in love, thus (possibly) creating a pattern of truth and goodness that participates in truth more fully than any particular story could.[14] Seeking truths in particular fictions, very different in kind, requires a dispersal of attention that keeps one very near the level of sensory experience and image. The best one can do in this situation is to group tales together in some way (according to genre or subject) and thus intuit some fuller truth from them. Chaucer pointedly focuses such groupings by clearly pairing tales in ways that invite attention to their competing truths about subjects treated in common. He seems to want contextual attention paid to these tales in a reflective search for something elusive but not illusory, for whatever mixed reflection of truth is in them, and has actualized them as the particular tales or fables they are. He also wants the tellers to come into prominence in more cases than not, thus directly exploring the quality of felt belief, of credence and reverence in many cases. Having set forth feeling and belief as a way of exploring truth in fiction, Chaucer seems to have discovered another world, that of sense and experience-bound individuals whose feelings and beliefs can hinder their efforts at a perceptive response to the tales (in part, a world of monkish Bernards disposed to credit nothing they have not seen with their own eyes, whether in visions or in waking life).

In responding to the tales and their tellers, we find ourselves considering the presence or lack of compounded truth and falsehood in the tale and the mixture in the teller of reliance on sense experience, feeling, belief, and reverence (as well as the quality of these things). To follow a teller across his or her tale requires answers to these questions, then: What does the teller see? What does he or she feel? What does he or she believe? What reverence does he or she accord the tale? and, finally, What is the nature of those actions we call tale tellings (ranging as they do from the unobtrusive to the superobtrusive). A teller's shortcomings should suggest the more intimate views that Chaucer's readers can take of the tale's possibilities and of the greater world with which it participates, in relation to which it bears truth. Those tales that seem to bear no truth in this sense whatsoever, such as Chaucer's *Tale of Sir Thopas*, come nevertheless as pointed entertainments, essentially as literary judgments upon a poetry of "draf." When we do follow the tellers, especially obtrusive tellers like the Canon's Yeoman, we see that they tend to become at least as engaging as their tales, so much so that we could justifiably call this Work "the tellers of Canterbury" rather than the *Tales of Canterbury*. In creating complex postures for various pilgrims and inviting scrutiny through ironic and satirical portraits in the *General Prologue*, Chaucer establishes an affective field that keeps the search for truth in fiction an interesting one, alternately focused on tales and complicated by the presence of tellers who reveal truths about themselves.

The wondering and readerly narrators of earlier poems have metamorphosed here into relatively unperplexed but still problematic tellers and their tales. None is a wondering reader. Instead the readers are either confident or confused rhetors who think they understand their tales and who try to control our attitudes toward them as well as their tales. Thus Chaucer begins to manage a rich and complicated project that ranges widely over tale types and tale-telling characters. But altogether, no interesting closure for the collection of assayings seems to suggest itself. Indeed, Chaucer's tales seem less guided by an idea or form than to be in search of a form, or indeed of many forms (depending upon the subject addressed or exhibited), with fictions and frame looking for an elusive coherence but always collapsing around the surprise of characters and questions about, as well as raised through, the tales. Perhaps Chaucer believes that if the assaying of truth in fiction is always subject to the mischance of strong individuals, their experience, feelings, belief, and powers of reverence, then, within the secular space won for the merriment of tale telling, his task is mainly a comprehensive one: to organize a plot in which a cast of characters tells a wide range of tales so that the assaying of truth in fiction and of blindness and sight in tellers is as generous as life permits. A plot requires occasion and drama, a beginning, middle, and end. A comic plot requires ordinary enough characters (no high nobility here) and the safe working out of conflicts, as in the Knight's peacemaking role. Having a Host is a nice way of having a foil; having competing tales is a nice way of expressing, while deflecting, various conflicts among tellers. All of these arrangements Chaucer has clearly made in what can justifiably be called a festive comedy, a carnival-like telling of tales.[15] I will have little to add to the perceptive commentary of many readers on these matters of plot and arrangement.

But the assaying of tales and tellers must be dealt with, considering the way of knowing Chaucer announces in the *Prologue to the Legend of Good Women*. The truth function of tales, as reports about the world as well as intimations of subtending forms, of a sense of justice, order, love, accord, "maistrie," and so on—these matters have not been adequately treated by Chaucerians. Moreover, the mixture of feeling, belief, and reverence in each teller—and therein the quality of the teller's understanding of his or her material—has been overly simplified in too many cases. Careful focus is needed on the *way* tellers move across their tales and on the affective side of knowing well or knowing ill, which means that claims for what these tales tell truly and for the misdeemings of tellers have often been too narrow or too vague. Nor have surveys of the tales been done consistently to discover competing views of whatever they treat in common. These views, moreover, do not cancel each other out but tend toward a norm that no tale manifests fully. Usually tales have been thought to "quit" or compete with each other in a mutually canceling way or else a certain tale (or two or three) above all others is seen as the measure of justice, truth, "gentilesse," or whatever (which provides an ideal, not a norm). However, it is true that some tales on a given subject will more closely approximate the norm that it and its fellows can only intimate collectively.

With these things in mind, a comprehensive review of all the tales and tellers is needed—a herculean task for which this study is mainly a preamble. I will look at about half of Chaucer's production and analyze the tales of the longest fragment with an eye to its great variety and to the mix of tellers. This should provide readers with a representative sample of Chaucer's work and also suggest the fruit possible given my themes.

Fragment 7 has been brilliantly analyzed as a play on the theme of "sentence" and "solas," which theme it certainly includes (especially given the question about what a merry tale is and for whom).[16] But this is also a fragment focused on the status of tales, on the dual value of tales as entertainments and as containing sobering, edifying, or even amusing truth and falsehood. Here Chaucer puts together the most intricate string of tales in the collection and works with tellers who do not overtly "quite" (or compete with and answer) each other. In the ordering of chapters focused principally on tales and tellers, I begin with the Manciple and the Canon's Yeoman to raise the question of feeling and understanding in its extreme form within the tales: The Yeoman is a novel and highly erratic truth teller—a virtual stranger to the reader—whereas the well-introduced Manciple is an unusually self-conscious, "objective" teller. I then address the question of understanding tale material, although not truth in fiction specifically, through the Squire and the Franklin, moving from them to Fragment 7 and on to an extended discussion of tellers and tales.

I exclude the first fragment because it would oblige me to deal with the *General Prologue* portraits—a subject Jill Mann has covered well already—and would confront me with the monumental undertaking of the *Knight's Tale* and its fabliaux companions. I forgo discussion of the Physician, the Pardoner, the Wife of Bath, the Merchant, the Friar, the Summoner, the Man of Law, and the Clerk partly out of a need to limit this look at Chaucer's arrangements and assayings. I can better show the usefulness of my approach by concentrating on minor tales (with a few exceptions) where the issues I address seem relatively transparent. Such major figures as the Pardoner and the Wife would make that labor difficult, although my themes are profoundly present in each case. The rhetorical and affective complexities of those formidably confessional characters require a study unto themselves. I do include the Franklin because his self-conscious approach to his tale is highly revealing of its content and of his feelings and beliefs. The *Nun's Priest's Tale* and the *Prioress's Tale* are in Fragment 7, the one piece of the collection that I survey entirely. As the most highly varied fragment, it has a good chance of being representative of the whole collection.

Finally, the arrangement of chapters should not be construed as a claim for Chaucer's ordering of the tales. The arrangement merely reflects an approach to Chaucer's concern for tellers, tales, and the truths both implicate. My last chapter begins with the *Parson's Prologue* and moves on to a consideration of Chaucer's preparations for an ending, to the reformation of the group and its purposes that he intends. Throughout I will follow what I call a belief-and-feeling theme for the tellers and a truth-in-fiction theme for the tales. That necessarily takes me to notions of intention and gesture on the part of each teller, thus involving readings of characters as well as tales. Through it all I hope to indicate what kind of thinker exists in this maker of the collection. If we cannot decide what he finally would have said about truth in fiction or about the vagaries of individual feeling and belief, we can at least attend closely to what he does say in the fragments assembled for the discussions that follow.

4 ❦ WAYWARD TRUTH AND WAYWARD RHETORIC IN THE *CANON'S YEOMAN'S TALE* AND THE *MANCIPLE'S TALE*: FEELING AND BELIEF

C asual readers rarely turn to the last three fragments in F. N. Robinson's edition of the tales. Yet those fragments contain at least two brilliantly rendered studies of feeling, belief, and truth telling gone awry. Before proceeding to the Canon's Yeoman and the Manciple, however, I would like to point out a recent attempt by some readers to find a sense of closure in those fragments. A pastiche of that commentary suggests the following as Chaucer's ending to the tales: The *Second Nun's Tale* with its chastity and martyrdom story stands for the truth of faith; against that truth the Canon's Yeoman's altogether misguided and intellectually misbegotten faith in alchemy collapses. Essentially, a spiritual or true alchemy of soul stands against a false—because entirely materialistic and slippery—alchemy of passions.[1] Then the *Manciple's Tale* and the *Parson's Tale* settle the question of letter and spirit, of poetry, tales, and prose. The Manciple's advice that we hold our tongues suggests an adieu—if not Chaucer's own, then at least the Manciple's—to tidings of any sort, an adieu strategically placed at the end of the collection. That leaves only a mean view of language after which the Parson will tell no fables (though he will tell a merry tale, a *meditacioun,* in prose). Thus Chaucer's ending to the tales, moving finally to the Parson's treatise on penitence and the seven deadly sins, is a literarily sophisticated, but still essentially medieval, distancing from materiality, the letter, poetry, and worldly passions.[2]

This is certainly a culturally plausible ending for a medieval poem, as it is for a collection of tales that seems to be going into the Parson's *Prologue.* Chaucer now seems to end his most ambitious project since *Troilus and Criseyde* on a teasingly ambiguous but finally conventional note. Perhaps

48

Chaucer would now have us abandon poetry and the question of truth in fiction, along with all modes of earthly knowing, and turn us toward penitence, along with whatever else we need for salvation. This could happen, but the whole affair can seem doubtful. At least I do not think a resolution can be confidently projected for the tales beyond the seventy-four lines of the *Parson's Prologue,* even if the Ellesmere order and the *Parson's Tale* are seen plausibly to constitute an exit from the tales, prepared for in the *Parson's Prologue.*

An argument against the *Parson's Tale* as Chaucer's last tale might begin as follows: The Parson's stern manner in his tale is not Chaucer's style in the *Retraction.* A prayer for grace so that Chaucer can bewail his guilt and concentrate on the salvation of his soul contrasts notably with the Parson's emphasis on purchasing bliss in part through "travaille, and the lyf by deeth and mortificacion of synne" (l. 1080). Moreover, the *Retraction* seems odd if attached to the collection after the *Parson's Tale.* Does Chaucer doubt the power of his ending? Is the treatise on penitence and the seven deadly sins in fact what Chaucer has in mind for the *Parson's Prologue?*

Whatever one may think of the *Parson's Tale,* it is not the "meditacioun" promised twice in the *Parson's Prologue:*

> "But nathelees, this meditacioun
> I putte it ay under correccioun
> Of clerkes, for I am nat textueel;
> I take but the sentence, trusteth weel."
>
> . . . .
>
> Oure Hoost hadde the wordes for us alle;
> "Sire preest," quod he, "now faire yow bifalle!
> Telleth," quod he, "youre meditacioun."
> [ll. 55–69]

Overwhelming evidence for medieval usage indicates that a "meditacioun" is almost always a meditation on the passion of Christ.[3] The Parson's treatise is nothing if not a "predicacioun," something the Host earlier fears the Parson will tell. There, in the *Epilogue of the Man of Law's Tale,* the Parson chastises the Host for swearing. The Host's mixed senses perk up, and he smells a "Lollere in the wynd." Announcing what he senses, the Host asks the company's patience as, "for Goddes digne passioun," he predicts a "predicacioun": "'This Lollere heer wil prechen us somwhat.'" The Shipman (or someone) will not permit such a turn in the tale telling.[4] Such an exchange, whether later canceled or not, gives a strong indication of the impression the Parson makes on the Host and on another pilgrim. It sets up two possibilities for the *Parson's Tale*: a sermon or something on Christ's passion (the Host's swearing taken literally).

The *Parson's Prologue* seems to settle the issue in its reverence for Christ:

> "I wol ful fayn, at Cristes reverence,
> Do yow plesaunce leefful, as I kan."
>
> [ll. 40–41]

A few lines later he asks:

> "And Jhesu, for his grace, wit me sende
> To shewe yow the wey, in this viage,
> Of thilke parfit glorious pilgrymage
> That highte Jerusalem celestial."
>
> [ll. 48–51]

Many readers have noticed that the opening of the tale also invokes Jerusalem, "the righte wey of Jerusalem celestial; / and this wey is cleped Penitence" (ll. 80–81), a way that will not fail to lead us all to Christ and to the "regne of glorie" (l. 79). This seems a strong link; the idea of a way to the celestial Jerusalem seems more than coincidental. Yet, along with another phrase or two, this connection is all there is between the *Prologue* and the tale.[5] Moreover, a close look at the spiritual path invoked in each case further separates the *Parson's Prologue* from the language in the treatise on penitence and sin.

The "righte wey" to Christ is a corrective means to an end for those who have "misgoon" through sin. But there are many spiritual ways to Christ; indeed, there is a way that is Christ, perfect and glorious. This is what I think "the wey, in this viage, / Of thilke parfit glorious pilgrymage" invokes. Certainly something other than ordinary penitence is promised, although no one can enter the celestial Jerusalem unrepentant. To the point is that the light of that city is the Lamb (*Revelations* xxi–xxiii). The *Parson's Prologue*, then, seems to promise a text, under "correccioun of clerkes," on the mystical text of Christ's passion. Perhaps, then, the tale, which emphasizes right correction rather than a showing of the Way (given a wit sent through Christ's grace), is not properly part of the tales of Canterbury. The one would instruct us in the definition, distinctions, and species of penitence, beginning with Ambrose; the other would rise inspired through Christ's grace to a showing of something perfect and glorious. Therefore, I do not think the Pennafortean treatise can be read confidently as either a doctrinal exit from the tales or as a conceptual framework for them. As for the Manciple's tale, no conclusive evidence links it firmly to the *Parson's Prologue*. Indeed, some evidence points to a much earlier location, perhaps somewhere in the middle of the extant collection.[6] The status of Fragment 8 is even more problematical. How near any ending Chaucer would place the *Canon's Yeoman's Tale* and the *Second Nun's Tale* is simply guesswork on everyone's part, from fifteenth-century editors to current textual scholars. Moreover, what would surround it is also unknown. Therefore, in just what extended context of tales and framing links we should read it will remain a mystery. Given these conditions, and not positing a plurality of connections unnecessarily, the last three fragments should not be conclusively linked, supposing that Chaucer's intentions have thus been served.

The *Second Nun's Tale* and the *Canon's Yeoman's Tale* together explore relations between faith and perception. The thematic formula for these linked tales is that seeing makes the believer and that seeing confirms belief. Set into the play of tales, and paired with the surprising invention that is the energetic Canon's Yeoman, the *Second Nun's Tale* is a good place to begin the study of truth in fiction and of the tale-teller's faith in her tale. For here Chaucer addresses uncompromising truth, the gold-lettered book of faith and the teacherly fortitude of the saint, approached by a prayerfully earnest teller, while pairing that vision with a tale of con artistry used illustratively by an impassioned, unsteady teller. The characteristics of the Second Nun and the Canon's Yeoman are unknown to us before their fragment begins. And whereas considerable commentary reads them together in ways that deeply discredit the Canon's Yeoman and alchemy, it seems better to consider how they qualify each other and how each marks a place on Chaucer's map of knowing truth in fiction.

Unobtrusively, the Second Nun tells of a saint's life in which an angel holding crowns of lilies and roses appears to the tale's heroine, Cecile. Only the faithful can see the angel or crown or smell the flowers. Thus the angel's appearance marks true faith and purity of heart, at least that is the basic idea (although not always literally the case).[7] Because Cecile is blest, a vision of luminous Truth awaits the chaste believer converted by Cecile's wisdom: "Bileve aright and knowen verray trouthe" (l. 259). Her spirituality appears early in the tale and wins over her new husband, Valerian, who threatens wedding night violence unless Cecile either sleeps with him or produces her guardian spirit. Of course, through Cecile's purity, they remain a virginal pair, their consummatory bond becoming the vision of the angel, after which Valerian goes to Urban for a purgation of sins.[8]

Seeing, then, comes of someone else's believing, and believing of one's own seeing. Valerian's conversion is so momentous that he wants to share it with his brother whom the angel produces and whom Cecile then teachingly conducts to Urban, her spiritual master. From Urban the brother receives the faith, and then he too sees the angel. Thus sight and belief can be suggested to some extent for the pure of heart, whether pagan or not. Conversion is possible in a world of spiritual sensation that penetrates both the pagan and Christian. So far this tale, as is true of its continuation, is something to credit. Although it concerns events and conversations not witnessed, material proof of Cecile exists "into this day, in noble wyse" in a church sanctified by Urban.

The Nun approaches her tale in straightforward reverence, telling us what the life says about Cecile. She does not intrude, merely becoming a minimally present, tale-telling voice. In this case the tale is the thing we credit, revere, and in which we find truth, touched perhaps by the Nun's diligence and her faith in both Cecile and Mary. At least one reader has sensed a Chaucerian sympathy for the Nun and her tale, indeed, a kind of "comic" reception. But very little evidence exists for a Chaucerian view (aside from tone, a kind of sweet earnestness in lines like those that open the *Prologue:* the image of the gate of delight, the opposition of "bisynesse" and "ydelnesse," the bending of "al oure entente," so that the fiend does not "us hente").[9] In any case, the tale ought to be approached sympathetically, in delight, so that we may learn something from it. This is a tale that exists apart from problems of experience and understanding, especially in Cecile's clear faith and teaching. The triune God she would have Tiburce understand is likened to three faculties of mind: memory, imagination, and intellect (l. 339). But her Truth in God has nothing to do with human ways of knowing, transcending all the categories of things, their aspects, and our sensory and rational modes. Instead, along with Tiburce, we take instruction in Christ, and through Christ, we become perfect in our learning (l. 353). Not to believe this is impossible for the Nun and probably also for a poet who will eventually thank Jesus and Mary that he translated many books of morality, saints' lives, and devotion. Moreover, the life of Cecile is one of those works by which Alceste defends Chaucer against the God of Love's charges.

Yet equally impossible for Chaucer is the task of obedient acceptance.

Certainly we believe in Cecile's goodness and martyrdom, her fortitude, and heroic stance toward Almachius, because not to believe is to discredit a saintly life whose church we can still see today. This does not, however, require an embrace of Cecile's spirituality and particular world of faith, chastity, and instruction, a world that is in fact closed to us except as the story tells us about it. We never hear Cecile's teachings. We know only about some of the subjects, such as Christ's role and his passion. Cecile's world of faith, and perhaps the Nun's also, exists on its own terms, as a book of faith, lettered in gold like the one Urban uses to cleanse Valerian, but essentially a book unopened to our experience and therefore untested on our imagination and intellect, as well as the cognitions of memory as ordinarily understood (assuming that Cecile's conversions of others reflect their openness of soul rather than some noetic remembrance). Chaucer could be taken here as suggesting that the Nun's life and the tale she tells are closed to those Christians among them who have not chosen it. Each of us, Chaucer might add, must find his or her own way, given the particular sensibilities of each, because spiritual truths are no more immune to idiosyncrasy than are the secular truths various pilgrims would take as their own.[10] Of course, what Chaucer might suggest here is entirely speculative. As Donald Howard has well noted, the tale's narrative style produces a stark effect, while the story recalls an early Christianity, "presenting an ideal in the 'figural' style beneath which earlier treatments [in the tales, of marriage] seem to pale. Its effect is to alter our perspective."[11]

I suppose this is true enough of our experience, coming from other tales to the Second Nun's, but the tale itself does not refer us to any other Canterbury tale's treatment of marriage through stylistic or rhetorical reference. What Chaucer would have us do is take this tale seriously, of course, but with no indirect prompting from him. We can only assume that Chaucer takes the tale as true, that its spiritual emphases do not repel him (whether or not they personally suit him), and that he reads it in an openness of belief, with reverence and delight. More, we have no reason to suppose that he expects less from us, that we might scoff at this unreal, indeed ideal fiction, which nevertheless an actual dedicated church to Cecile attaches to this world. In a sense, in private, we are invited by the very fact of the tale to let our most comprehensive intellect look over the tale, that eye that sees, Neoplatonically, beyond the particulars of Cecile and her works, beyond the forms of imagination, beyond even the species of saint that she is to the divine thought that thinks Cecile in the first place.[12] The Second

Nun's is an ideal tiding, closed to the mind that would separate the true from the false. As such, it is a simple light beneath which Chaucer's way of knowing truth in fiction engages all the other tales.

We emerge from Cecile's bloody martyrdom (in which she does not sweat a drop) and find ourselves at "Boghtoun under Blee," watching a sweaty rider and a mounted companion gallop in a froth up to the pilgrims. Links such as this one support joint readings of the tales admirably, but do not especially authenticate the one tale at the expense of the other. Judging from critical commentary, the Canon's Yeoman, his *Prologue and Tale*, is far more fascinating and thereby attractive than is the private Second Nun and her tale. The Yeoman and his tales (his *Prologue* autobiography and his illustrative tale of alchemic con artistry) are accessible to us, invite assaying and delighted crediting insofar as what we read accords with our minds and with reason. In an untrite sense, the Canon's Yeoman is a shot in the arm and takes us headlong into all the problems of feeling, understanding, and tale telling that will befall any pilgrim. Along with the Host, we receive him into the company, as he undertakes a kind of confession (appropriately prodded by the Host). What soon begins to emerge is a sense of the Canon's Yeoman as a sorely frustrated believer whose rhetorical stances represent or reflect suppressed emotional commitments, commitments that repeatedly confound his several attempts at an unburdening exposé. He cannot tell much truth about alchemy, because he does not know the truth of his experience in that miserable science. He is a teller whose feelings direct his understanding, turning all attempts at truth telling into headlong confusion. The major truth that feelings do grasp here, however, is that alchemy is a bitter business for the trusting soul. Chaucer would have us assess truth in the Canon's Yeoman's autobiography as well as in his tale, while considering the warping effects of belief led by passion and of truth telling unstabilized by still lively commitments.

Whatever assessment we undertook in the Second Nun's case is private compared to the public scene of the Canon's Yeoman and his *Prologue and Tale*. Here we are strongly invited to respond to the dramatically entering character and his tidings. Thus the *Second Nun's Tale* and the *Canon's Yeoman's Prologue and Tale* could not be farther apart—the one devoted to saintly labor and heroism—as part of private devotion and "leveful busyness"—the other to secular energy and public confession. There is much worth believing in each case, including truth, and much in which to delight, although the performance of the Canon's Yeoman is by far the more interesting, because it is the more vivid and vexed. It is also the one that fully engages our imagination and intellect, becoming a prime object for Chaucer's readerly way of knowing, for that openness of belief, feeling, delight, and mental accord with which we should approach—that is, credit—any tale. Thus the *Canon's Yeoman's Prologue and Tale* is a good place to begin our direct engagement with problems of perception, feeling, belief, and understanding as reflected in the performances of various tellers.

Wonder as a perceptual and cognitive theme arises early in the confessional prologue of the *Canon's Yeoman's Tale*. Chaucer wonders in his heart just who the person is with whom the Yeoman rides, a wonder that springs from seeing great sweat on the Canon's horse, as on the Yeoman's. From the way the rider's cloak is sewn to his hood, Chaucer begins to consider before deeming him some kind of "chanoun." Wonder leads to a guess, to an identification, but with the Canon's Yeoman wonder is a perplexed and confused business (part pretense, part belief). The Yeoman, startled by the Host's question as to whether the Yeoman's lord can tell a merry tale or two, replies positively. Then, soon, he undertakes a confessional turnabout, with conflicted attempts to say the truth, attempts that become personal after the Host asks why the Yeoman's face is so discolored. The Yeoman founds his disclosures on direct experience of this business of alchemic groping, a grief-stricken, laborious experience that leads him to curse the lord who led him into that *game*. The theme of wonder gives way to an attempt, based on sore feeling, to declare all that one knows—to tell a true tiding thoroughly.

The Yeoman tells two tales, one a tiding of what he has experienced, the other a tale of devilish con artistry. Most of the commentary on these tales emphasizes a metaphorical richness that emerges when we read backward from the Canon's Yeoman's to the Second Nun's tale,[13] but a richness that works against the Canon's Yeoman's tales. The Yeoman is usually alternatively seen as either freed or in the process of freeing himself from the snare of alchemic groping. Minority opinion, however, convincingly shows his continuing ensnarement at some level of hope and desire, a level of belief that confounds his attempts to say what he knows debunkingly.[14] However the Yeoman is taken though, readers usually move to a Chaucerian level of implication: That alchemy is a soulless materialism; that Chaucer is indicting mindless, technological energy; or that we face issues of blind reason and Christian revelation or some other pairing of knowledge, materiality, and the spirit. No doubt these kinds of suggestions are appropriate, in a way. But they pull away from the Yeoman and his predicament all too soon, as well as from his tale telling and all the problems attendant upon that tale telling.

In noting the *parade*like character of the Yeoman's monologue, especially his lists of wares and operations, Charles Muscatine incisively concludes that nowhere "else in Chaucer is there such a solid, unspiritual mass of 'realism,' and nowhere is its artistic function less to be doubted"—in its "chaos of matter, refuse, excrement" [it] "represents the universe of technology."[15] Perhaps this is so, yet such an emphasis leaves the Canon's Yeoman behind as a kind of outcast, a would-be pilgrim whose story telling is more Chaucerian editorializing than a way for Chaucer to explore an extreme case of feeling, belief, and truth telling in relation to a story of a life as well as to a tale of con artistry. We need to stay awhile with the Canon's Yeoman in order to avoid transforming his extended appearance into either an illustration of nothing more than failure or a display of corrosive feeling.

It is fair enough to suppose that Chaucer would have us see latter-day alchemy as so burdened with desire that, even if its theoretical foundations were true, invariably practitioners would mistake the intention and "termes" of alchemic philosophers. They would, then, mistake their powers over Nature, even if they could reduce metals to primitive states. Chaucer implies that alchemists would mistakenly see a possible way of knowing as a technology for recovering truths available only to the Creator and to Nature—hints of which beguile the devotee, raising a great desire to know what is hidden and to profit handsomely. Given this, it would seem that any claim of immediate access to Truth is either mistaken or impenetrable to an outsider. By assuming extraordinary access, the alchemist's practice becomes one composed of material parts guaranteed to fail. Crucially, however, the problem here is more a case of presumption than materiality. The Canon's Yeoman himself faces an additional problem because alchemic practice proceeds from an obscure rhetoric—one that he mistakes for a way to truth, if he could only rightly understand the terms.

Unlike Chaucer, the Canon's Yeoman remains too close to his material, ironically reflecting his own maxim

> "That that is overdoon, it wol nat preeve
> Aright, as clerkes seyn; it is a vice."
>
> [ll. 645–46]

But he is ever an innocent and not deeply to blame. Caught up emotionally, his warnings and revelations, his exclamations and puns become a seeming—a play of ironic perceptions that masks his continuing vulnerability.[16] So when he warns us—"Whoso it useth, soore shal he rewe!" or "Lat every man be war by me for evere!" (ll. 729, 737)—his ensnarement is deeper than he knows. By revolving such alchemic terms as "multiplie," he also indicates a relation between alchemy and its rhetoric; both the work and the alchemist's terms cruelly mislead or *mis-mean*. Here alchemy implicitly becomes a failed rhetoric, its practice failing as much as the manipulation of its terms fail.

Continuing this line, the Yeoman focuses on the language of alchemy. He speaks of terms as "so clerical and quaint" that they confer a seeming wisdom on the practitioner. Apparently that wisdom, a wonderful seeming, enslaves the would-be practitioner so that, as the Yeoman tells us of himself, "I blowe the fir til that myn herte feynte" (l. 753).[17] Especially in their order and mystique, alchemic terms beguile the Yeoman into supposing that various processes help the initiate reach the desired end, as though the order and manipulability of language guarantee access to Nature's order and to the secret of secrets.

Initially, everything seems otherwise. Employing *occupatio*, the Yeoman seems to abbreviate his account in a controlled way, selecting from his memory all that is important for his knowing exposé. Instead of control, however, he launches himself onto a sea of paraphernalia, processes, and materials. His beginning,

> "What sholde I tellen ech proporcion
> Of thynges whiche that we werche upon."
>
> [ll. 754–55]

quickly becomes a dismaying list that evokes a hell's kitchen of frustrating processes and bewildering sinks. Eighteen lines later his *occupatio* formally ends, and he draws the moral: "For alle oure sleightes we kan nat conclude" (l. 773), which justifies the *occupatio*, although more lists follow.

Those lists tell us almost everything. The frequency of the pronoun "oure"—our elfish craft, our terms, our arsenic, our works, our labor, our craft, our urinals and distillation vessels—reflects his mixed attitudes: despair, frustration, and pride. Traugott Lawler calls these lists more "loving than satirical,"[18] while seeing the Yeoman at this point in his confession as less removed from his past than he will be later. However we read his affections here, clearly he is momentarily lost in these lists, as he loses a clear hold on his original purposes. He apologizes for not rehearsing everything in order and in proper classification, deviating from his earlier protestation that the terms of alchemy were impossibly clerical and convoluted. He says that he knows more than he will take the time to tell— again deviating from his opening promise to tell everything he knows as best he can. His lists, accordingly, take on new meaning as he vigorously recites substances, vessels, and processes. He lapses at this point into the old obsession, coming to himself only when suddenly scornful in his recollection of the occult names for the four spirits and seven bodies.

Recollection of those names sharply returns him to a partial recovery of earlier purposes. He moves from a display of knowingness to his original attack as a debunker. In summarizing celestial namings for gold, silver, tin, and copper, he rhymes "Juppiter is tyn" with "by my fader kyn" (ll. 828–29). The rhyme suggests disbelief in the seriousness of this, as though alchemists would call anything anything. His rhyme (implying a completed expletive?) brings us back to the homely and the home, away from the occult. It suggests passion directed foolishly:

> "This cursed craft whoso wole excercise,
> He shal no good han that hym may suffise."
> [ll. 830–31]

He puns now on "multiplie" again and rhymes "philosophre" and "cofre," "multiplie" and "folie." As a rhetorician who would indict something, who would move us to a judgment, he is most effective in his invectives because they usually return him to his original, debunking intentions—all too brief returns as he repeatedly concludes too soon. For Lawler, the Yeoman's many shifts "all seem to imitate the alchemist's jumbled and groping attempt to transmute his intractable materials."[19] This is right. Apparently the Yeoman has absorbed that dismal characteristic of alchemic practice— forever confounding his accounts and ending prematurely, he imitates the laboratory process that ends in a messy explosion. Both the Yeoman's confessional rhetoric and his alchemy form parallel patterns. Driven in what he does, the Yeoman never steps back and acquires a felt grasp of whatever truth his experience in alchemy might yield him. For example, when he urges that we let the philosopher's stone be—for as God is in heaven it will not come to us, no matter how knowledgeable or skillful we are—he simultaneously indicates the total futility of that craft, belief in the stone, and in another line or two, the good hope that nevertheless creeps into one's heart (ll. 865–70). Such hope is the mother of poverty, failure, discoloration, stink, and pretense, whereby the devotee lies about his wisdom and so betrays innocence. But let that be also; both his frustration and his deep belief are still too painfully with him for the tale of his life to come right. However, he does better with the second part of his tale, the illustration of con artistry, because his case is clear, unimpeded by contrary commitments. He knows the difference, at least, between a frustrated pursuit of "wisdom" and the successful pursuits of a thief.[20]

The proof that is in experience exposes the folly of the would-be wise. Likewise, he who seems truest is likely to be a thief. This is the Yeoman's headnote, in effect, for his illustrative case against an alchemic con artist. We have moved from the confounding effects of feeling and belief to an emotional argument designed to move the Yeoman's audience to righteous anger against an unnamed canon of religion who would, the Yeoman insists hyperbolically, infect any size town, were it as great even as Rome, Alexandria, Troy, or any three cities. This canon of infection is fiendish, in fact, in his rhetorical skills, although the Yeoman wants to reassure all "worshipful chanons religious" that he seeks no slander upon their houses. He will reveal to us only a shrew, a rare exception among canons. Moreover, he does not address only canons, but many others as well, for we know that even among Christ's apostles there was Judas. The Yeoman's is an honest worry here, a sign of callow anxiety perhaps, but nothing more. For his intent, his meaning, is only to correct what is amiss—a process that will involve considerable heat, rhetorically, as he verifies in story the canon's stinking favors, how the root of all his treachery is a glad desire to bring Christ's people to mischief (ll. 1067–72). Thus our false canon chooses to con an unsuspecting priest, yet a gullible and silver-loving one.

As chief witness and prosecutor both, the Canon's Yeoman would encourage righteous anger in his audience. Aristotle defines anger as "a longing, accompanied by pain, for a real or apparent revenge for a real or apparent slight, affecting a man himself or one of his friends, when such a slight is undeserved" (*Rhetoric* 2.2.1378b). Having moved to put his audience on his side and at their ease (not to fear slander or improper motive on his part), the Yeoman would make his case against this urban infector, the false canon, against whose falsehood he would revenge himself if he knew how (ll. 1172–73). But he says this false canon is here and there, abiding nowhere and thus suggesting that the canon may in fact be the devil in disguise (a point a number of readers have made). The Yeoman does not quite make this point explicit; he would suggest it whenever occasion arises as part of his damning of trickery. In this he takes the prosecutor's direct approach, as recommended in the *Rhetorica Ad Herennium*, (1, iv. 6–7), because his cause is not discreditable, and he would clearly move his audience to hatred and contempt (*odium* and *contemptionem*) for the person against whom he witnesses. Happily, the inherent order of the tale keeps his purposes straight as he colors the priest innocent and "sely," while characterizing the false canon as devilish, false, and foul. He wearies even himself with his denunciations as the canon's duplicity exceeds the strength of rhyme.

Aside from rarely mentioning the canon without a dark epithet, the Yeoman proceeds with few digressions, allowing himself only an extended apostrophe (ll. 1076–86), through which he sounds momentarily like the Nun's Priest lamenting the fox's approach, an aside that stresses his humble tongue and moral purpose. The apostrophe is a strong response to the false canon's invitation that the priest come and see how the canon can work in "philosophie." Earlier he characterized the canon as possessing infinite "falsenesse," a rhetorical figure he now elaborates just before the apostrophe into a characterization that includes the "root of all treachery," fiendish thoughts, and a gladness that delights in bringing Christ's people to mischief. He will, moreover, verify the canon's stinking nature in the extended account of the canon's flim-flam. The apostrophe focuses on the "sely," unknowing priest. It is an effort at pathos on the victim's behalf and thus a means of further vilifying the false canon. But the Yeoman cannot sustain pathos because he must also concede the victim's gullibility, a mind blinded by "coveitise." Thus he concludes the apostrophe with a two-part task ahead of him: to tell the priest's "unwit" and "folye," while also telling us about the other's "falsnesse" insofar as the Yeoman's wit and knowledge permit.

Obviously he has a personal stake in this indictment, using it as a way of dealing with his feelings, given the frustration and confusion of his experience. But the terms of the tale give him little room for catharsis, especially through the priest he invents as victim. The priest's innocence is really covetousness now, "sely" having become mere folly, a silly stupidity. Yet he sympathizes with the role the priest has as victim and as enlistee in the alchemic Work (like the Yeoman himself). The canon's sleights of hand outrage the Yeoman, who feels sorely abused considering his own labors at the Work. Therefore, it is here especially that he curses the false, fiendish canon and would have the foul fiend himself seize that tainted soul. The urge for revenge is strong, as is the hope of exciting it in his audience. But on whom would the Yeoman be revenged regarding his own life? His canon may have been a fool but not a thief. And the silly priest is hardly a victim with whom to identify strongly, glad as he is in the apparent gains he has made (so glad, says the disgusted Yeoman, that he calls him "sotted" and measures that gladness in the language of love and lusty spring [ll. 1341–49]). Those associations—singing birds, a caroling lady, a knight hoping to stand in his lady's grace—form a recipe of glad desire that at least reaches out in genuine ways, unlike the priest's desire for the canon's recipe. In contrast, the priest's desire is that of a gulled fool's. By implication, alchemy speaks to a dark desire for gain and transmutation, a sexual possession that the Yeoman can hardly fathom but that he feels somatically, abused in the flesh, and weary even of his own need to denounce someone or something. The best he can do now is conclude his case, which he does, with a resounding view of the priest's undoing and the canon's fiendishness:

> Lo, thus byjaped and bigiled was he!
> Thus maketh he his introduccioun,
> To brynge folk to hir destruccioun.
> [ll. 1385–87]

That done, he proceeds to encourage his audience to consider men, gold, alchemy, and God's will. The flim-flam plot is interesting in itself, but hardly the final point of all this. The tale has clearly served the Yeoman's purposes and his character. It removes him somewhat from a nearly hopeless entanglement with his experience and gives him an opportunity to pursue something to closure—to conjure up a clear evil, enlist our feelings while expressing his own, and by relating how it works, to judge a particular falsehood and its effects conclusively. With this success behind him, with this melodramatic truth prosecuted, he can now move to the greater question of alchemic science itself, apart from its all too wearying and painful, all too present failures. By going through the case against con artistry, he has vented feelings in a direction that removes him personally, to some extent, from the considerations he now undertakes. This much is salutary, but it is not completely successful.[21]

Although this movement—from a hoped for wisdom, collapsing always into folly—to a tale of thievery aforethought narrows the Yeoman's focus, it nevertheless strengthens his mind without resolving the great issue of alchemic science: something that is still a lure at the end of his tale. With more balance, the Yeoman might now notice that the alchemic enterprise is so difficult and consuming that some practitioners stoop to fraud for finances, that some are purely frauds, and that even earnest efforts can fail miserably and repeatedly, defrauded somehow by an intractable Nature. But thoughts of the stone still compromise his efforts.

Readers have rightly noted a shift in tone after the tale of con artistry, yet not entirely to the Yeoman's final credit. For the Yeoman still has faith in the science, if not in the efficacy of its practice. He tells us that philosophers speak so mistily about this craft that no one can come by it nowadays, no matter how long one prowls about in the alchemic wilderness. But this does not bespeak the inherent emptiness of the craft, just its thorough shrowding in the mists of ancient speech. If we cannot see this with our eyes, then we should look with our minds; alchemic *practice* will invariably fail us, impoverish us, and burn us. So meddle not! This warning given, and probably taken, he undertakes a coda in which he invokes various warnings from the pages of alchemic masters themselves. These old books speak truth, understand them as best we can. What they tell us is that we should not undertake this art unless we can understand the intention and speech of philosophers, for their science is of the secret of secrets. The Yeoman's manner here has steadied considerably as he concludes, finally, with a measure of pious wisdom—to wit, that because God will not have philosophers reveal the secret, we should "lete it goon"; no one will thrive who makes God his adversary, "Thogh that he multiplie terme of his lyve" (l. 1479). The language here recalls other moments of intense frustration and of unready conclusions. Marked deeply by his experiences still, he nevertheless does now conclude decisively. He has calmed himself somewhat and come to partial terms with an alchemic science whose principles are securely hidden from all but those to whom Christ would reveal them. The efforts of all not inspired by divinity will be futile. This is the Canon's Yeoman's final judgment and the analogical truth he sees in his tale: Without revelation, all of our efforts will be as though someone has fiendishly gulled us, the hapless but not altogether innocent victims that we then would be. Thus old, alchemic books are not inherently false. They can be approached with delight, perhaps even reverence, and certainly with belief in the existence of an unrevealed secret. But they cannot be understood by unaided reason.

The Canon's Yeoman has demonstrated both the warping effects of emotion confounded by suppressed belief and commitment and the steadying effects of a prosecutorial emotion given an unambiguous tale. In the one case, feeling precedes understanding; the reverse occurs in the second.

But crucially, some understanding is possible for the Yeoman only after narrowly construed circumstances, in an indictment against a grossly simplified, fiendishly characterized con artist. The Yeoman's pain undoubtedly produces that narrowing and so helps him end his tale, leaving behind more complex cases and the vexed issue of an alchemic science whose lure is truth, but whose unenlightened practice is inevitable failure. Moreover, that lure is not altogether innocent, drawing as it does upon dark desires rather than natural love or a love of God, and remaining potent in the thought, still, that perhaps one day Christ will reveal the secret of secrets to someone.

As nearly every critical reader notes, we thus have contrasting tales in this fragment about various themes, labor being one of them. The Second Nun tells us about the Christian work of instruction and salvation, involving conversion and martyrdom. The Canon's Yeoman tells us about a material work of failure and recrimination, involving desire and hope (an endeavor without Christ's blessing but not inherently futile). Together the tales are of the world, but the second one is more open to assessment, the assaying of truth, and a scrutiny of how feelings confound perception, intention, and understanding, while also grounding such conclusions as the Canon's Yeoman manages. The Second Nun believes in Cecile much as the Canon's Yeoman believes both that he is through with alchemy (and for good) and that the secret of secrets exists. In this respect the tales are curiously parallel rather than nested in a way that discredits the second in favor of the first; both involve what are held as true beliefs and are referred, ultimately, to Christ's keeping. For Chaucer's readerly poetics of belief, however, the books of alchemic philosophers are the more fascinating, as they are also the more perplexing. Not lettered in the gold of the spirit, they are open to men in their misty terms and strange rhetoric, yet forever veiling a truth that no activity of mere wit can comprehend. The Canon's Yeoman understands this only after he has purged himself somewhat of his emotional intensities, which is primarily Chaucer's point. For it is through his experience and upon his bodily shame that the Canon's Yeoman comes to any measure of felt understanding. He has to that extent foregone the "fires heete," as he distances himself from those who still, to their shame, cursedly play that "lusty game" (ll. 1402–08).

Compared to the Yeoman's largely troubled performance, the Manciple emerges more than half-well, at least it seems so. His telling faces facts directly and unequivocally. The facts in question are clearly witnessed and forcefully related. Thus, overheated passion is not his; nor do suppressed commitments cause him to stumble in the pursuit of his ends. Instead, he suffers as a teller (reader) from a palpable meanness (although he shows other attitudes as well), from a smallness of heart, and finally from a superficial notion of truth (the result of his emotional life). Unlike the Yeoman, the Manciple believes that what one sees is all the truth there is. The phenomenon is all, or almost all, for the Manciple will indeed insist too much. He goes out of his way to call a whore a whore, and he invokes numerous authorities in dubious support of his point of view.

A careful reading of the *Manciple's Prologue,* in which the Manciple verbally attacks the drunken Cook—mainly by telling truths about the Cook's besotted condition—raises several questions about words, feelings, and truth. Do perceptions exist independently of personal predispositions, feelings, and beliefs? And does wicked speech differ from merely indiscreet speech? The *Prologue* seems to say that wicked speech indeed differs from the indiscreet, and that truth (its perception and its telling) is related to feeling. These links provide a perspective for reading the tale itself, a tale in which the truth telling crow has often been taken as an image of the Manciple himself—crude, mean, and contrary to the crow in the tale's source, Ovid's merely dutiful but unfortunately tale-bearing bird. The Manciple's crow deserves punishment.[22] While it is true that both the Manciple and the white crow lack compassion (*routhe*), the Manciple's presence is mainly an effect of his amplifications and anticipatory digressions, rather than of any relationship we might perceive between the Manciple and one of the characters in his tale. The Manciple's tone is well enough established, anyway, by his overt intrusions. That tone betrays a lack of sympathetic feeling that prevents him from seeing any human truth informing or giving rise to the facts he would narrowly report. In this respect the Manciple is like the crow, for each is narrowly objective in the unsavory things each reports—perhaps each is a parody of the objective reporter.[23] For Chaucer, first perceiving truth and then relating it to others are participatory activities, requiring an openness of belief, the engagement of feeling, and a reflective thought that considers how one's story accords with the mind and with that which is reasonable to think. The Manciple altogether lacks a sense of this as he insists on the definitive character of that which is seen (the "unreality" of mere sight). Accordingly, he lacks both sympathetic feeling and any awareness whatsoever of possible defects in his own understanding.[24]

That elsewhere Chaucer presents the issue of truth telling with an emphasis on "routhe" is clear in *Troilus and Criseyde.* Indeed, as Robert Payne has shown us, Chaucer's rhetorical interests contain as a central issue the problem of understanding love on the part of a "bookish, slightly alienated poet-narrator."[25] Will he get it right? Will he understand what he has read? If moved by beauty, What does that beauty mean?[26] Frequently the narrator appeals to an audience of readers and lovers or both. In *Troilus*, he establishes a direct relationship with us, alongside the story he vivifies and to which he responds emotionally as well as comically. He usually defers to the lovers in his audience—to those who have "felynge" in love's art—asking for correction. Thus he backs away from the complicity of understanding that a courtly lover might have and relies mainly on a middle ground of fellow feeling for others obviously in woe or clearly experiencing earthly bliss. But when he must face Criseyde's infidelity, especially after having wished for just the smallest part of Troilus's earlier bliss, and perhaps anticipating also the sad cruelty of Troilus's wait for Criseyde, the narrator comes undone. It is instructive to recall his approach to Criseyde's infidelity before engaging the Manciple's treatment of female faithlessness. In his confusion, the *Troilus* narrator essentially raises the problem of truth and feeling, which the Manciple confirms by denying.

Doubtless the Manciple, in his reductive nominalism, would call Criseyde a whore.[27] However, the *Troilus* narrator can barely bring himself to refer to, let alone name, the betrayal. He will not even try to narrate the scene "whan that . . . [Criseyde] falsed Troilus" (5, l. 1053). He hurries along, fearing interruption from his audience, and he would speak "gostly" (gospel truth?). Finally, to tell the truth, Diomedes "refte hire of the grete of al hire peyne" (l. 1036). That oblique remark precedes two stanzas of textual refuge where the narrator turns for both authority and voice to his sources. He refers to tender, if betraying, incidents—all of which signify what "men seyn—I not—that she yaf hym hire herte" (l. 1050). He lacks heart for this, but somehow he must tell the story. He tells it, then, without deciding on how to understand it, almost, if he could, without believing what others say. It is on their authority, not his; they say or know that Criseyde gave her heart to Diomedes. For his part, there is mainly the claim that in her pain she succumbed. Curious doctor of the heart, Diomedes bereaves her of most of her sorrow. A truth is stated, but what about the heart, quite apart from unfaithful action? And how shall we understand this paradox of cure through bereavement—a loss of pain for Troilus? for herself in a hostile camp?

The Manciple would not trouble with such questions. He would see the *Troilus* narrator's problems mainly as lexical ones, a bewitchment induced by fine words.[28] Cynicism is the Manciple's bedrock, while the *Troilus* narrator must somehow tell a truth—presumably both a historical and a human truth—that he would rather evade because he neither understands it nor can think of it painlessly. This is tale telling and "routhe," the rhetor and reader at his affective best, emotionally and mentally open. For the *Troilus* narrator, there is nothing like whole truth in objectively known or perceived fact; and especially there is no understanding. In his lack of "routhe," the Manciple of course thinks otherwise. Because of his tale telling comments and asides and the choice of tale told (with pressures that seem to narrow the tale in relation to its sources), there is an expansive ethos first revealed in the prologue to the tale, to which I now turn. For there we first see the Manciple brazenly and cleverly shift his stance in the hope of adjusting us to him and himself to the Host, strategies he employs in his tale telling as well.[29]

Chaucer begins with a jocular Host and an unfortunate, drunken Cook—a humor established some time ago in the *Prologue to the Cook's Tale*. There the Host establishes the idea of speaking "ful sooth" in "game" and "play," a notion that Roger varies with a Flemish saying that a true jest is a bad jest. One can banter and speak truth, then, even full truth (presumably unblinkingly), provided that the spirit is one of play (and so with the understanding and use of the truth in question). That Roger will pass off stale cakes as fresh is a peccadillo, if sin at all. Roger, in response, behaves waggishly, promising to "quit" the Host at some point but not now.

So when the Host wonders if the Cook has been awake all night because of fleas, or drink, or laboring sexually with some prostitute, his humor continues the truth telling in jest of their other relationship. The Cook can hardly say what ails him, concluding only that he would rather sleep than have the "beste galon wyn in Chepe" (ll. 21–24). The need for sleep must be great for a drinking man to strike such a bargain, so great that not even the Manciple's ill-humor can quickly arouse the Cook, though finally arouse him it does.

The Manciple intervenes in courteous measure:

> "if it may doon ese
> To thee, sire Cook, and to no wight displese,
> Which that heere rideth in this compaignye,
> And that oure Hoost wole, of his curteisye,
> I wol as now excuse thee of thy tale."
>
> [ll. 25–29]

The Host has demanded a tale from Roger, in penance for falling asleep on his horse and for falling behind, hence causing worry that he will be robbed, and for now delaying the pilgrimage. A tale as penance, although the Cook's might not be worth even a small bale of hay, is an amusing idea, akin to Chaucer's worry in the *Complaint of Venus* that English does not have enough rhymes for him to follow Oton de Grandson's poetry word for word. Similarly, the Host may suppose that the Cook will have difficulty telling his tale word by word. By excusing the Cook of his literary penance, the Manciple adopts a priestly superiority to go with his initial courtesy. Thus our first impression of him is that he would nobly condescend to the Cook, while deferring to the feelings of the Host and the rest of the company.

His almost immediate turn to an unblinking characterization of the Cook's condition is then entirely surprising, requiring a significant adjustment in our nascent assessments. To note the Cook's pallor and his dazed eyes only continues the Host's observation of the Cook's sleepiness. But we are now getting down to detail, to precise evidence: complexion, eyes, *and*, the Manciple knows well, a stinking, sour breath; these show that "sire Cook" is not well disposed. Moreover, our sharp-eyed and proud Manciple will not gloss over the Cook's condition: See how he yawns? This drunken man would swallow us up at once. Energized, the Manciple has moved from inclusive social gesture to pointed observation and now to separation from the foul-smelling, open-mouthed Cook, from him (the *he*) who would swallow *us* in a hell-mouth smelling of infected breath and the devil's foot, a mouth that would infect "us alle." Having cast the Cook out for the nonce, the Manciple would now use him to warn others, pointing out a lesson against foul, stinking, swinish drunkenness ("A, taketh heede, sires, of this lusty man" [l. 41]).

Obviously he despises the Cook—not his condition—with a disdain that is the nasty side of superiority. Moreover, he has nothing to gain, which suggests that he takes pleasure chiefly in the insult itself. His spite suggests that he hardly values the Cook at all, whereas his references to "us" indicate that he would enlist the "compaignye" on his side (a note of uncertainty). Somehow the superiority of an act of absolution has given way here to an act of excommunication. More than condescending, the Manciple is too quick, too loud, and too little regardful of the Cook, who has begun to wobble agitatedly in his saddle. Those uncoordinated movements, however, only provoke further, heavy-handed insult: "Now, sweete sire, wol ye justen atte fan?" (l. 42). The Manciple guesses out loud that the Cook has had counterfeit wine and is now in the third stage of drunkenness (apish imbecility).[30] Apparently the Manciple's speech has now penetrated through the Cook's hazy drunkenness, for he grows wrathful and angry, violently shaking his head at the Manciple because he is speechless, a violence that pitches him out of the saddle, onto the ground. If there has been any jest in all of this truth telling, any play in the Manciple's saying of "soth," it has escaped the Host as well as the Cook.

The first thing to do is to raise this unfortunate horseman back into the saddle and steady him there, a task requiring much shoving to and fro to lift the Cook up and much care and woe, so unwieldy is "this sory palled goost" (l. 55). Chaucer the Pilgrim has cried "allas" over the Cook's inability to stay in the saddle, and his characterization of the poor fellow betrays some sympathy, some "routhe." Even the Host's dismissive phrase—he refers to the labor of lifting up the Cook's "hevy, dronken cors" (l. 67)—is less cutting than the Manciple's various remarks. That something excessive has occurred here even the Host, in contrasting reaction, confirms for us. Moreover, he becomes explicit as he both excuses the Cook from telling a tale (fearing that it will be told badly by the drunken, nasalized, sneezing Cook) and admonishes the Manciple (who obviously has not won the Host or Pilgrim Chaucer to his view of the Cook). He chides the Manciple for being "to nyce." Someday the Cook may bring the Manciple's preying flights to the lure: "Reclayme thee and brynge thee to lure" (l. 72). The hawking image indicates the Host's awareness of the Manciple's aggression, that the Manciple would prey on the Cook.

Is this, then, the Manciple's motive? Does this clever purchaser and keeper of accounts, he who is always on top of things and who cleverly cheats his masters, have something of the bully in him? Brought up short, the Manciple acknowledges wisdom in the Host's words. After all, the Cook is only temporarily helpless. When sober, and if still angry, he might very well cause vengeful mischief by easily ensnaring him, says the Manciple. But the Manciple does not apologize. Instead, he excuses himself as having spoken in his "bourde," a kind of playfulness that elsewhere in Chaucer has something suspicious or stupid about it.[31] Moreover, the Manciple has a draft of good wine and invites the Host to witness a good "jape"; he will have "this Cook" drink of that wine, upon pain of death. The Manciple's sense of superiority is well founded. He is intelligent, and he can backtrack nicely in a pinch.

Chaucer the Pilgrim cannot believe what he sees; that is, that anyone would quite do what the Manciple now does—give even more wine to a hopelessly drunk fellow, indeed, to someone who has enough trouble just staying on his horse. But certainly, "to tellen as it was," the Cook took quite a drink of the wine, allas! "What neded hym? He drank ynough biforn" (l. 89). But the Cook was wondrously eager for that wine, and he thanked the Manciple "in swich wise as he koude" (l. 93). The trick is not cruel, but there is something sad in this spectacle, despite the Host's amazingly loud laugh, a laughter that proclaims the wonderful powers of Bacchus to turn "rancour and disese" into "acord and love, and many a wrong apese" (l. 98).

The Manciple has wronged the Cook and played him for a fool as well. He has done so all on his own, out of a sense of superiority, disgust, and a despising of someone he values not at all. But he is intelligent, and he can size up a potential threat quite nicely, dealing with it efficiently, if a trifle expensively. Moreover, he even reinforces his sense of superiority in the process. This, then, is the Manciple who will now tell us a tale about Phebus and his white crow. His manner of telling further develops the sense of character we have from the *Prologue*, as he adopts a superior relation to his tale (in his commentary staying well ahead of the tale's development) and feels that he can overcome whatever difficulties he encounters, undo whatever lapses or betrayals he commits, and in general recall the force of his words if those words become somehow unsavory (which contravenes the mother wit he professes, that once out, "jangling" words cannot be unsaid or recalled).[32] This notion, that he can simply turn about on his words, is the Manciple's greatest delusion, although his gesture toward the Cook works.

The Manciple tells his small tale in a straightforward way, without much elaboration of the characters. Where he holds true to *Prologue* form, and thereby gives us more to conjure with in assessing his character, is in his anticipatory amplifications and digressions, which begin early in the tale telling, virtually as soon as we learn that the character Phebus would keep his wife jealously. The Manciple thinks that such keeping is foolish, for a good wife (one clean in work and thought) should not be so kept (the labor is wasted), and a shrew will make the labor in vain. Therefore, it is

> a verray nycetee,
> To spille labour for to kepe wyves:
> Thus writen olde clerkes in hir lyves.
> [ll. 152–54]

If we do not consider this as a response, a way the Manciple has of staying on top of his story, we can at least relate it generally to the Manciple's sense of superiority and even to his learned pride (reflected in his *Prologue* figure of hell's mouth and in his penchant for "ensamples," having turned the Cook into an example of the stinkingly "lusty" man). Stephen Knight hears "no special prosodic character that tells us about the speaker," nor does he think that any prior knowledge we have of the Manciple would suggest a "clerkly sagacity."[33] This may be so: Chaucer is not much given to creating human characters through an individuating use of "prosodic" characteristics (although he does exploit dialect and verbal rhythms). But, whether sage or not, the Manciple has shown moments of considerable smoothness, as in his initial address excusing the Cook. And the way to understand response as a mode of characterization is to see it as extending, developing, or adding dimensions to what we have seen before (if you will, a coherence rather than a correspondence test). It is characteristic of the Manciple to take control of a situation, even to override it, which is what he does with his "ensamples." He would control our understanding of the initial situation in the story, much as he has tried to lead everyone's response to the Cook. Moreover, his tone borders on the unsavory as he tells us that it is a waste to spill labor over the keeping of wives, with "keeping" subtly linking the shrew to wives in general. Still, the Manciple is not bold yet. He relies overtly on the authority of "olde clerkes," perhaps trying to unsay what he has just implied.

His second digression begins the process of actual self-betrayal as he notes that Phebus sought to win a wife who inclines in some other direction. The Manciple puts his observation on the footing of a natural principle, for no man may "destreyne a thyng" (l. 161). He then moves to a series of damning examples, the common theme of which is that caged or kept things naturally desire both their liberty and the satisfaction of their appetites. Most of his material here probably comes from the *Romance of the Rose*, but the Manciple's use blurs the differences between natural and lewd behaviors, differences that Jean de Meun seems intent on maintaining. True to form, the Manciple mainly adopts the attitude of a satirist, an accuser, perhaps inspired by de Meun's *le Jaloux*, a figure who cites Juvenal in support of the notion that a good woman is almost as rare as a white crow—that impossibility of nature.

In his examples of things that desire liberty and the satisfaction of appetites, the Manciple progresses downward from better to worse cases of desire. We hear about a bird in its cage that would rather eat worms and such wretchedness; we then hear of a cat and its appetite to eat a mouse; and then of a she-wolf who will always take the "lewedeste wolf" when she lusts for a mate. The Manciple's examples combine de Meun's lines from parts of speeches by *la Vieille* and *Ami*, with the dominant tenor being *Ami*'s remarks that a lewd woman who suspects her lover's sincerity will reject him and pick someone lower, much as a she-wolf is so degenerate "as to select the most evil of the pack."[34] Much as he would cast out the Cook, so the Manciple would condemn most women (paying little more than lip service to the idea of good women). The motive, as far as the Manciple implies it, is usually one of ungratefulness combined with intrinsic, vile lust. No matter how well one fosters *any* bird, or how gay its cage of gold, the busy and ungrateful wretch would much rather live crudely and shiver in a forest, eating worms and other dreadful things. In contrast, *la Vieille*, following Boethius ultimately, first puts the matter as a natural longing. The bird pines for freedom and for the natural life, no matter how well kept it is in its cage. A plush prison is still a prison. Boethius likewise treats the bird's longing as a natural good: Given a chance, the bird will skip out of her narrow cage and seek the agreeable shadows of the woods because all things seek their proper course and rejoice in returning to their nature (*Book 3*, metrum 2). The burden of wrong here is on the "pleyinge by-synes of men," not on the perverse nature of an ungrateful creature. The Manciple is just such a busy man, first with the Cook and now with his romance examples of appetite and degenerate behavior. He abuses the Cook, and now he would abuse most of womankind, ending his list of examples with a she-wolf who has "a vileyns kynde" (l. 183).

But he has already been drawn up short once, by the Host regarding the Cook's possible revenge. The she-wolf "ensample," with its reiterated "she," has displaced the grammatical "he" that controlled the appetites of bird and cat. Moreover, the she-wolf returns us to the initial point of departure, Phebus's wife, to whose eventual lewdness the Manciple has already applied that natural principle illustrated by his examples. In effect, his digressions lead the tale such that the wife, who has yet to be "dishonest" with her body, will become the fourth "ensample." He could, then, simply condemn most of womankind, but he pulls back suddenly to assure us that his examples refer only to those *men* who are untrue; they do not concern women at all. This disingenuous avowal gives him a chance to praise wives implicitly (so many are fair and true, whereas their husbands . . .) and to condemn men explicitly.

What began as a relative discrimination—against some men, those who are untrue—quickly and confoundingly becomes a blanket condemnation:

> For men han evere a likerous appetit
> On lower thyng to parfourne hire delit.
> [ll. 189–90]

As in the encounter with the Cook, one gesture quickly becomes something else. Consistently, the Manciple both reverses himself and moves from qualification to sweeping condemnation. Characteristically, he would observe, accuse, judge, and damn whatever he turns his thoughts to (out of a denigrating sense of superiority and control). Then, just as characteristically, he would try to unsay or undo what he has said (he lacks sufficient confidence), as he even includes himself in his condemnation of men:

> Flessh is so newefangel, with meschaunce,
> That we ne konne in nothyng han plesaunce
> That sowneth into vertu any while.
>
> [ll. 193–95] [35]

Yet, in returning to the tale, he must manage not a man's lechery but a woman's, that of a wife who betrays her "joly" husband. Moreover, the greater harm here is that such betrayals of husbands happen so often, from which comes much harm and woe. His gestures always stagger wildly, first one way and then another—this even in his shift from clerkish examples to the pose of the blunt, plain man as he characterizes the wife's lover ("lemman").

Having led us to understand the wife's act as lewd, as a natural inclination in she-wolves, and having added that it is like the lecherous performances of all men, the Manciple now summarizes the first act of this two-act tale: "and so it befell that when Phebus was absent his wife anon sent for her lover." But is she courteous and "gentil"? No, she sends for her "lemman," a churlish word, says the Manciple while requesting our forgiveness for having used it. This sets off a digression on naming and calling, the heart of a theme concerning words and the Manciple's character.[36] We have seen in the *Prologue* that the Manciple addresses the Cook courteously in excusing him and then begins to savage him. This shift in registers is reflected in his reductive awareness of words (from different registers) and deeds (the self-same lust). He tells us now, in characterizing the wife's act, that he will speak plainly. This plain speech is in character, of a kind with his observations of the Cook (who is certainly no "gentil" sir).

The Manciple is both certain and proud of his insight into the mystifications of language ("there is no difference, truly," he says), a mystification driven by power and social prestige. There is, he broadly reveals, no difference between a lady and a poor wench if they both work amiss; men lay the one as low as they lay the other (notice the shift from singular wife to plural seducers, from singular desire to promiscuous reality). In our mystified state, however, we might foolishly call the one a lady, as in love, and the other merely a wench (something the Manciple has already called her, indicating his snobbery). He continues with another distinction, that between the outlaw and his band and the tyrant "Captain" and his army. Call them what one will, power is the only difference between the highwayman and the invader of countries, a point the Manciple refers (textually) to the education of Alexander the Great. So now he has justified the application of language he considers churlish to a nobleman's wife. He repeats the sending for her lover, and has the crow witness their "lust volage" and report the cuckoldry to Phebus, which precipitates the second act of this fable— Phebus's wrathful shooting of his wife, then his remorse and his punishment of the crow now accused of having a scorpion's tongue, of having told a false tale.

That three-part action of report, wrath, remorse, and revenge, forms a final "ensample" for the Manciple, of a piece with his comments on words and deeds. Not to mystify things for us, he points out an inadvertently funny moral: never tell any man that another man has slept with his wife, and a warning: keep well one's tongue, as Solomon teaches us and as does mother-wit. He does not quote Solomon—remember, he is not textual (although he is clerkish)—but he does quote his "dame." Apparently what he means by being "textual" is stopping to quote exactly what clerks have written or said. He would rather simply refer to what they said (hedging his boldness somewhat), another indication of his sense of superiority, and instead quote everyday mother-wit (superior to bookish sorts anyway).

Superior to a world of fools, disdainful of any who would suppose that words are more than conceptual mystifications, the Manciple ends his tale with the teachings of his dame about a wicked tongue, jangling, and speaking truths or lies for which others will hate one. In final position, he remembers his "dame" saying that one should not be the first to spread tidings, whether the tidings be false or true: Keep well thy tongue and think upon the crow. Perhaps one should carefully assay the tidings one would repeat, whether one would lie or report truly what one has witnessed. Assaying then would not apply only to those tidings heard from others but to what one has seen oneself, the event one would report. Moreover, there is a subtle qualification here; do not be the *first*, the "auctour newe" (l. 359) of tidings. The Manciple is true to this distinction. He follows the Host in observing the Cook's condition; he follows others in the tale of Phebus and the crow; and he follows clerks in his amplifying "ensamples." But how he follows is how he reveals his temper, the tenor of mind that is his character. His speech is in fact ignoble, verging on the wicked as he follows where others have gone. Moreover, his tale telling has only extended aspects of character first set before us in the *Prologue* to his tale.[37]

Where his tale telling differs from the Canon's Yeoman's is in the notable ways in which he would command the tale, by which he invades it with a band of "ensamples." He does a kind of mischief, forming a thoroughgoing case of tale-telling appropriation. More, he differs again from the Canon's Yeoman in preferring sight to feeling, the observed to the emotionally registered (in line, of course, with a parallel narrowing of spirit, by which even truth telling can become false). Yet he does tell a tale that we can separate from his uses of it, doing so to a greater extent than the Yeoman does with his illustrative tale of con artistry. And although no human context complicates the Manciple's view of things—he offers us a fabliau of sorts devoid of festive comedy or of sympathy with any of the characters—we might still conjure over this fable of the crow, asking questions about mean-spirited truth telling, the spectacle of a prince gone murderous and mad, and a wife kept jealously by her husband, be he ever so reverential. What is true in this tiding, aside from the emotional logic of wrath turned into vengeful remorse? Does the tale teach us the silly extremes to which men tend to go?[38] Perhaps some such point is appropriate for the Manciple, implicit in his last "ensample," but the dialogue (which is most of the tale as story, rather than the text, which is the tale intrusively told) should take us further. First, there is the crow's harsh, reiterative truth telling ("'For on thy bed thy wyf I saugh hym swyve'" [l. 256]), which a remorseful Phebus will characterize as the false tale of a false thief; then, there is Phebus's lament—"'O deere wyf! O gemme of lustiheed'" (l. 274). Phebus laments roundly and at length, turning his own action into an example of "wantrust," of the lack of wit and discretion. Is this funny or is it potentially profound? Could he have reconciled himself with his adulterous wife, perhaps become other than jealous and help her redeem herself from the consolations of wantonness? Surely some such possibility is latent here (in Ovid's account, the wife is pregnant). Even the wife's infidelity could be handled as something more than sheer lecherousness. Such a literary alchemy, if you will, is not beyond the tale, however unlikely it is for our teller.

Exploring the human potential here would require a teller with some capacity for "routhe," for compassion. The Canon's Yeoman's emotionalism would even have affected the tale telling in positive ways; he would have lamented the duped Phebus and at least developed that character's innocence and suffering. This kind of possibility is important to the tales because it reveals Chaucer's sense of the absurdity of what so many critics hope for: a point of certainty, of medieval objectivity by which the truth as

Chaucer would have it measures the partialities and frailties of everything else. What Chaucer explores instead is the notion that truth is often more felt than clearly perceived, more a matter of apprehending the complex and the suggestive than of bluntly seeing something beyond doubt. Truth, moreover, coheres with the mind and with our sense of what is reasonable, provided our minds are generous, capable of reverence and delight.

To tell of love is the hope of characters treated in the next chapter, the Squire and the Franklin. Each is self-consciously a rhetorician who would say something about love, as best he can. Each speaks feelingly; neither is undone by suppressed commitments or by a meanness of spirit. But the one haphazardly feigns interest in his love story, and the other relies too much on masterly gestures to appreciate the nature of the tale he tells. Thus, in both cases, the feeling for love is more often worked up than not. The Squire, a youthful rhetor with little or no interest in love, dominates his tale material in a way that prevents him from even presenting the love interest intelligently (although he presents a case for simple "wonder" adequately); and the Franklin, an apparently masterly rhetorician, sacrifices attention to relationships among his characters for a resort to the handy formula or the cute dilemma (both in his opening paradox of married lovers and in his closing request that we decide which of the male principals behaves most generously). Here Chaucer primarily shows us tellers who can handle the tale material that interests them but who perform unevenly because they lack real sympathy for the emotional parts of their tales (in each case focused on the female victims, Canacee and Dorigen).

In looking at these tellers now, although both precede the *Manciple's Tale* in the Robinson edition, we can gain a fuller sense of the tale-telling task than is possible by simply looking to the Manciple's lack of "routhe" or to the Canon's Yeoman's emotional and rhetorical confusions. To their credit, both the Manciple and the Canon's Yeoman think that their tales as wholes tell a truth. Neither the Squire nor the Franklin seems to think this is the case for his tale. The Squire interests himself in the magical details at the expense of the love story, whereas the Franklin interests himself in the male contest at Dorigen's expense. Neither teller takes much responsibility for the affective content of the tale material. An insistence on simple, closed wonder prevents the Squire from doing so, and easy rhetorical command along with too much gentility prevents the Franklin. Wonder does not lead to speculation and knowledge for the Squire (indeed, he openly equates such wondering with jangling, with false, if not wicked, speech). And feeling does not lead to truth for the Franklin (Dorigen's complaints are simply peculiar to the oddity that is womankind). In later chapters, in an extended study of Fragment 7, I will explore these issues again and consider the effects of tale telling on others, thus completing, through a consideration of what makes a merry tale and for whom, Chaucer's attention to the prominent features of tale telling as a rhetorical act. Through it all, of course, there will be idiosyncratic tellers come alive in their tale telling as they construe their tales.

5 ❦ RHETORIC AND CREDULITY
IN THE *SQUIRE'S TALE* AND
THE *FRANKLIN'S TALE*

ith an eye for virility, the Host must turn expectantly to the Squire. For here, if Pilgrim Chaucer's impressions can be trusted at all, is a lively, accomplished young courtier. The Squire's locks are curled, he is of middling height, but he is quick and strong. To stand the better in his lady's grace, he wears clothing embroidered with white and red flowers. He can sing and he can make music. He dances, he composes songs, he draws and writes as well as riding well, jousting, and loving so hotly that he sleeps no more than does a nightingale. He is young, of course, and not proud. Moreover, he *hopes* to stand in his lady's grace, and he is courteous, humble, and serviceable at his father's table. Doubtless the Squire knows something about love and love's service, but his hot nights are more ones of longing and hope than of experience with women. The Host probably expects otherwise when he asks the Squire to say somewhat about love, an invitation the Squire willingly accepts, but a subject that does not seem to absorb the Squire given what he emphasizes in his tale.

Much commentary on the Squire and his tale is negative. The Squire is accused of rhetorical incompetence, intellectual confusion, verbal grotesquerie, and even spiritual sickness unto death.[1] For many readers, however, the Squire is mainly young and perhaps endearingly callow, although recently the tale has found defenders who see it as a good beginning for a composite romance.[2] The most interesting responses lately have been to the Squire as a narrative presence, with Derek Pearsall in effect retracting earlier impressions by arguing that the dramatic model of teller and tale has highlighted supposed weaknesses and lapses that are better accounted for by thinking of the dispersive tendencies of Chaucer's style in tales "that lack a commanding center of attention."[3] David Lawton has been even

more vigorous in taking to task critics who fault the Squire and the unfinished tale in their efforts at a dramatic reading. He admits that the tale
contains some tonal problems, but that a combination of dramatic and close
readings does not address them adequately.[4] Much of what other readers
find objectionable or see as lapses of taste or competence is unexceptionable
when seen as *rhetoric*. One might do well, in fact, to see the tale as fairly
skillful, as a kind of early epic in the style (Lawton adds) that becomes familiar to us in Ariosto. Lawton's is a fascinating review of the tale, complete with speculation about its place in the manuscripts and about the possibly non-Chaucerian authorship of the headlink.[5] Still, the dramatic model
is serviceable in a humble way, although Lawton's correction has merit.
The Squire tells his tale in ways that tell us about him, but he is hardly
responsible for the tale itself (which does contain tonal problems). Indeed,
although young, the Squire is quite workmanlike, humble and serviceable at his task of telling. But never does he say more than "somwhat"
about love.

His tale, which he recalls dutifully, concerns a king named Cambyuskan,
who has two sons, Algarsyf and Cambalo, and a daughter, Canacee, the
youngest child. Until he mentions Canacee, the Squire has proceeded
heartily enough, but now he backs away from his material for the first
time. He apologizes for not describing her fabled beauty, saying that he
lacks tongue and "konnyng" for that task; his English is insufficient, and
he is not a first rate rhetorician, someone who knows the "colours" appropriate to describing Canacee. This deviation from his promise to say something about love is not serious in itself, indeed, it is a rhetorically respectable form of abbreviation. But it is puzzling in that he has given the reader
quite a few attributes for Cambyuskan. The focus there, however, was on
qualities of mind and body; what he backs away from here is an evocation
of beauty, feeling perhaps that his skill at *descriptio* or *effictio* is too limited
even to gesture at the ineffable that he refers to in speaking of "al hir beau-
tee" (l. 34). His humility is endearing but not laughable: Because he cannot describe *all* her beauty, he will describe none of it. How does one describe beauty anyway, with what deep mastery of "colours"? He responds
to the problem by acknowledging its unusual demands—he dare not attempt, in his English, so high a thing—and by naively supposing that
somehow a deep knowledge of appropriate *descriptio* might suffice. He is
not yet much awakened to beauty, although he seems responsive to such
natural beauty as the early morning light, and he has not had enough experience to see that the capacity to invent images of the ineffable, *inge-*

nium, is a human gift that he can develop, for which fit *descriptio* is a kind of proof.[6] He may learn something of this eventually; for now, the important point is that he recognizes the sublime character of the task and his youthful limitations. There is both predilection and wisdom in his humble awareness. He prefers wonder and mystery to explanation, and he knows his serviceable limits (in this connection the Franklin's praise is exactly appropriate: for someone so young and so much a novice still, the Squire has done well—a satisfied master's praise of a student).

After this first apology, he picks up the narrative again in the twentieth year of Cambyuskan's rule, focusing on a feast day celebration of Cambyuskan's birth. The day inspires him to try an elaborate astrological passage, a display that shows his delight and practice in the telling of time and season (seemingly it has no other purpose than the exercise of the skill in question, which is amplification by *descriptio*). The tone is decidedly cheerful as he gives us a "ful joly" and clear Phebus (with an astrological positioning) and a spring

> Ful lusty . . . and benigne,
> For which the foweles, agayn the sonne sheene,
>
> .   .   .   .
>
> Ful loude songen hire affecciouns.
> Hem semed han geten hem protecciouns
> Agayn the swerd of wynter, keene and coold.
>
> [ll. 52–57]

Readers have sensed something parodic here, especially in the mixture of season and horoscope, although this day *is* a nativity feast for Cambyuskan.[7]

Nevertheless, a 'ful joly,' a 'ful lusty,' and a 'ful loude' in eight lines is a little excessive, and the pairing through end rhyme of "hire affecciouns" with "hem protecciouns" is oddly put and overly hearty, but the whole is exuberant and not bad, and the final line provides a deadly contrast and sobering reminder of change: "Agayn the swerd of wynter, keene and coold" (l. 57). He then moves on to Cambyuskan, who is sitting on his throne in royal vestments, although now he feels obliged to tell us what he will not dwell on—the array of the feast. Again, his gesture is rhetorically respectable *occupatio*, the art of abbreviation while still keeping an eye on the source story. Again he invokes an amusing standard: Because it would take a long summer's day to tell all, he will not. No man can report the entire array of that feast anyway; certainly then he will not attempt it. No fruit will come of it, and much valuable time will be lost. He is humble and wise in his sense of limitation, although he could occupy himself and us for a time with lists of broths, birds, and quaintly valued meats. He will not because that time spent would not be serviceable and, anyway, he is eager to get on with his tale of the stranger knight.

Because he does not feel able to tell the *all* of something, he will tell none of it in one case and only gesture toward some of it in the other. Amusingly, an impossible totality in each case justifies an emptiness, a passing over, by the invoking of an impossible height and an exhausting and wasteful lingering, respectively. This reflects a consciousness of self and of audience, while it also indicates his lack of real interest in these things. What he wants to do, and does, is linger over the magical objects the stranger knight brings to court, as well as whatever battles the magical objects will somehow figure in (as indicated by his outline at the end of the fragment).

Turning to that knight, the Squire begs off a third time, saying that he could not repeat finely enough what the knight said because his own style cannot climb over so high a stile as does the stranger knight's. The knight's speaking was the equal of Gawain's in word and performance, a height the Squire thinks of as taught by the art of speech to those who learn it (something he has not yet done). This is a callow view of rhetoric, a question of well-formed, stylish elocution and demeanor independent of subject matter or affective designs upon an audience. The Squire can be pedestrian and drawn out, even tonally clumsy here:

> Al be that I kan nat sowne his stile,
> Ne kan nat clymben over so heigh a style,
> Yet seye I this, as to commune entente:
> Thus muche amounteth al that evere he mente,
> If it so be that I have it in mynde.
>
> [ll. 105–9]

The pun on style is awful, and the Squire's protestation is well enough founded. But to laugh is not to condemn, for his confusion about the ease with which one can give the general gist of someone else's words and meaning is balanced by his attractive proviso—"If it so be that I have it in mynde." This sounds like appropriate humility, not a modesty topos, coming as it does after the pedestrian denials of skill and that bad pun.

So, he will not hurt our ears with a botched effort at courtly style. Instead, he straightforwardly has the stranger knight introduce the magical objects, and then he moves on for a few lines to the disposition of the objects in the hall before devoting nearly a hundred lines to all the murmuring and speculation about the objects and their virtues.

Beginning with the horse of brass, on which neither nature nor art can improve, the Squire indicates his dislike of speculation. People invoke poetical analogies in a vain attempt to comprehend the horse, yet no one can move it, make it fly, or have it disappear. He characterizes the speculators as wondering, deeming, with diverse folk deeming diversely. The horse seems to be "of fairy," like something out of poetry, or like the illusion magician-jugglers create. These murmurings greatly annoy the Squire as he likens them to the humming of bees and characterizes them as the crude and reductive deemings of people unable to understand something more subtle than their "lewednesse." The horse, the mirror, the ring, and the sword are things subtly made—beyond the comprehension of speculating, wondering fools. The Squire is not opposed to wonder, but he would have us accept the magical devices as marvels closed to the mechanical and analogical speculations of men, whose wondering is really a form of jangling even if they do hit upon the causes or mainspring of a thing (l. 260). For the Squire, beauty and the marvelous should not be subjected to dissection. These are high things that are better simply taken at face value, without an effort to recreate them in thoughts and words. Thus the Squire has a circumscribed sense of inquiry and a highly limited sense of wonder, but he makes his point clearly and forcefully in relation to each object. His attack then should "free" those objects for unexamined use in the tale, for automatic functioning as needed.

Part 2 focuses on a story of love and betrayal, told by a falcon to Canacee, who can understand the language of birds because she wears the magical ring (the brass horse flies, the mirror shows the future, as well as who is true or false, while the sword can both wound utterly and heal). Canacee's communing with the bird is narrated without comment, as unexceptionable given the magical ring. This is the Squire's narrative gain in mocking those who would try to understand how the objects work. But freeing the objects for wonderful operation in the world of his tale goes well with his attitudes generally, concerning beauty, the plenitude of a great feast, the discourse of a supremely accomplished courtier, or the "revel and the jolitee" within which Canacee dances with the stranger knight (an account of which the Squire cannot give). To describe such a revel requires someone who knows love and love's service, who is festive and fresh, and who knows all about the "lookings" and the subtleties of dances and dancing—in short, a veritable Lancelot, and he is dead. The

Squire is exactly fresh enough (as fresh as May, in fact), and he knows how to dance; but it would be a mistake to read these amusing lines ending on Lancelot's condition as reflecting the Squire's fatuous self-regard.[8] We should take him at his word. He really does not feel capable; he does not know enough, that much he knows. He also would rather honor beauty and the marvelous by simply accepting what his tale tells him, rather than undertake lewd and fruitless speculation—mental jangling, not real comprehension.

Part 2 opens with a famous depiction of sleep taking the dinner guests away to their beds. Sleep kisses all of the guests with a "galpyng" mouth and urges them to bed with the notion that they should cherish blood, nature's friend, now that blood is the dominant humor in their overworked and drunken states. The guests "galpynge" thank Sleep and go to their rest. Passages such as this support readings of the Squire's incompetence as a rhetorician—well enough, but perhaps such readings are mistaken in their explanations. The Squire's use of *occupatio* and his various protestations about narrating or describing something are given authenticity in this amplification, which nevertheless works well enough once the reader grants the conceit. To kiss while yawning (perhaps noisily), to talk yawningly and in a full-bellied mood—these are hardly courtly manners. But to say that the guests simply began to nod and yawn, and then took themselves off to bed, would be equally uncourtly. It would be good to get them to bed through an appropriate amplification upon sleepiness and thoughts of rest. Once begun, the conceit moves in a consistent and workmanlike way, with some decorum in the exodus from the hall: "'As sleep hem bad; they tooke it for the beste" (l. 356) But beyond getting everyone to bed, the Squire has no intention of going—certainly not into whatever dreams various head fumes will give people. Although at heart an amusingly bizarre conceit, the "galpyng" passage is not long, and it bears contextual fruit in allowing the Squire to emphasize Canacee's discretion and moderation: She retired early, before such a noisy, yawning sleep came upon everyone else, for she would be rosy and festive in the morning.

Awakening early, Canacee goes out into the garden and there encounters the stricken falcon. In Part 2, the Squire largely disappears as a narrator, intruding notably in only one passage as he brings Canacee to the tree upon which rests the falcon. We are told that he will not tarry to describe Canacee's early morning walk because that might cool the interest of those who so far have hearkened after his tale, lessening the appetite of those who would get to the point or heart of it all (the "knotte"). He never reaches that point because the tale breaks off in mid-sentence, remaining a fragment. The Franklin's praise of the Squire indicates clearly that Chaucer intended to have that praise follow a completed tale. It is not, as some readers have maintained, an interruption disguised as a presumption that the Squire has finished when he has not. Chaucer works in two interruptions in the collection that are unambiguous intrusions: the Host's interruption of *Sir Thopas* and the Knight's stopping of the Monk. Clearly, the tale as fragment is a Chaucerian object, but it is not designed to be so in the Squire's case.[9]

What we have is an unfinished tale in the telling of which the Squire appears youthful and inexperienced to some extent but largely workmanlike and appropriately conscious of his limitations. What he does not mention is feeling—for love or for most of his tale material as it appears. Canacee's stricken falcon brings up feeling and "routhe" in the "gentil" heart, something the Squire is too young and inexperienced to value. He has not yet loved and lost, although he has fought well in battle, in knightly combat. Given time and experience he may well move beyond the serviceable as a tale teller and try for some of those heights that seem so beyond him (and are). He will then have also moved beyond schoolbook notions of rhetoric and a plot-bound idea of tales (the "knotte" and his summary of the rest of the tale at the end of Part 2).

For his part, Chaucer does not finish this tale. Does he tire of it? Is it a product of his relative youth, meant to be finished and perhaps revised? We will never know. But I would like to speculate on ways in which Chaucer might have seen something fruitful in this material, especially considering the love focus and the magical objects. If they are not simply accorded a marvelous reality, what truths about love could they be used to illuminate?

The horse of brass can bear one anywhere one desires to go in the space of a day. The mirror shows truth and the future. The ring translates otherwise unintelligible language (that of birds), and the sword can first inflict an incurable wound and then heal that wound. Artifice makes these objects, and Ingenuity applies them. We need not strain to see them in their functional virtues as possible images, each reflecting an aspect of rhetoric: the power to transport desire; reveal truths of the heart; make intelligible an otherwise inaccessible language; and both wound deeply and heal (consider the Host's wounding words for the Pardoner and the Knight's healing injunction). Such powers, of course, require much more than the use of various figures and "coloures" in one of the three levels of style.

The falcon's tale in Part 2 is of a false lover who professes great feeling, and his words seemed fast and good. The falcon says, however, that her aspiring lover dissembled in speech and behavior, using rhetoric to mask his intentions and actual feelings; he groomed his intended mistress with words (ll. 560–61). This instance of negative rhetoric does not elicit a comment from the Squire. Apparently a tale of duplicity is unexceptionable and within his reach, his level of confidence. As the falcon depicts her false lover in baroque images of hypocrisy (like a tomb, he was outwardly fair but foul within), an important issue forms. Given powers of verbal duplicity, how do we understand the truth of what someone professes? Some such question could easily arise for a feeling narrator responding to his material.

The Squire, however, simply continues, never reflecting on the problem of interpreting someone's words, of knowing when someone speaks truthfully and with honest feeling. Nor does he wonder about "gentilesse" in love as a code of behavior, whether the falcon could have avoided pain, or whether her pain is anything at all. He simply moves to the quaint bed Canacee and her maidens make for the nearly dead, grief-stricken, and self-wounded falcon. The bed suggests a miniature Garden of Love, the outside walls painted with "alle thise false fowles," while the inside is covered in blue, signifying the truth in women. As a reader and tale teller, the Squire resembles the *Book of the Duchess* narrator in some interesting ways. He has trouble feeling anything at all strongly; he reads for entertainment; and he knows his limitations. The adventures and battles and great marvels coming up are what interest him most, after which he will return to Canacee and her love story. What Chaucer has done is give us a humble, workmanlike teller whose understanding of rhetoric, tale telling, and tales is underdeveloped, although not insistently shallow or willfully superficial. Were Chaucer to finish this tale for the Squire, I doubt that any of the questions posed earlier about love talk and truth in love would arise. Indeed, if any such themes were to materialize—and we should assume that *much* more will follow (giving the Squire many opportunities to respond to his material)—they would probably emerge as only a reflex of his memory. Feeling obliged at least to mention everything along the way, his memory, unallied to a wonder that might lead to knowledge and understanding, might serve us anyway.

What Chaucer may imply here is the limited value of sheer memory in tale telling: A teller with some feeling in love might have commented on the falcon's baroque images; someone with a sense of how to arrange material and generate a story line might have used *occupatio* and the modesty topos effectively instead of merely honestly; and someone looking for truth and falsehood in his material—not simply wonder and delight— might have wondered pointedly about those magical objects and perhaps focused them somehow on the problems of rhetoric and truth in love. Indeed, the magical objects might become more than instruments; they might become resonant images for aspects of love: the steed of love, love's stroke, the ring of love's language, and the mirror of love's truth. The falcon episode contains all this, with love's bitter wound eventually healed by the return of the then-repentant lover. Much is possible here, but not for the Squire, sturdy soul though he is. Seeing rhetoric as he does and understanding his task as mainly having a hearty will to work through the tale, his telling and the artifice of the tale remain a gilded cage that confines rather than opens up its material.

But with experience and more wisdom, with feeling and a sense of truth, the Squire can take his already developed sense of delight in stories and leave behind a dismissible view of wonder (that of loose supposing and mental jangling). He might then replace it with an inquiring, felt belief: a reverential mode of knowing truth in fiction. So in the Squire, unlike the Canon's Yeoman, we do not face suppressed commitments; nor do we, in the direction of the Manciple, have a youthful version of reductive cynicism. Instead, we have a willing teller whose delight in parts of his tale is at least the beginning of fruitful wonder and whose sense of himself and his powers is appropriately limited and authentic. He is young and can learn.

That, at least, is an attitude shared by the Franklin, who praises the Squire's tale telling. According to the Franklin, the Squire has acquitted himself well and "gentilly"; he has shown a good understanding, and considering his youth, he has spoken feelingly. Surely he will improve as he matures, then outstripping everyone in his eloquence. These are sincere appraisals from a fatherly man. They evidence the Franklin's openness and generosity, and they prepare for what is perhaps the Franklin's deepest disappointment in his gentlemanly life—his wastrel son, someone not inclined to instruction in virtue and gentility. The Franklin's remarks go without reply from the Squire, although they irritate the Host, who rudely urges the Franklin to end his talk of "gentilesse" and keep his promise to tell a tale or two.

The Host's words imply that the Franklin does not command the deference the Host shows to the Knight and the Prioress. But neither this nor the Franklin's *Prologue* status as Epicurus's own son is sufficient warrant for demoting the Franklin to parvenu status, something many readers have been inclined to do.[10] The Franklin is no aristocrat, but he is "gentle" enough and a concerned moralist. He prays that the Host not hold him in "desdeyn"; when the Host brusquely commands him to tell on, the Franklin professes his glad willingness, his desire not to thwart the Host but to please him. If he has wit enough for that, then he trusts that his tale will be good enough. This exchange suggests both the Franklin's patience with a rude man and his good-natured humor (with its possible dig at the Host's literary standards).

In a short prologue to his tale, the Franklin identifies it as a Breton lay, which he will tell as best he can, only excusing himself from rhetorical flights because he is a "burel" man. Of course, he protests too much here given the skills he shows us in his tale-telling manner, but the point should be taken: He is not "learned" in rhetoric, nor do rhetorical fancies of description and high style appeal to him ("'My spirit feeleth noght of swich mateere,'" l. 727). He is a far better rhetorician than is the Squire, but he is not deeply schooled (he does not *know* "colors," except those of the field or paints or dyes—a clever "colour" in itself), and he professes no delight in these matters. No doubt he also has politely adjusted himself to the Host's brusque treatment: Why, treat me so! Afterall, I am a "burel" man. By now he has linked feeling to rhetorical speech twice—in praising the Squire and in excusing himself. That he speaks feelingly enough will be clear in his tale, but the role of feeling in the working out of this story, in the turning of the tale, has been seriously underestimated by most readers, who focus, rightly enough, either on the Franklin's definitions of "gentilesse" (involving "trouthe," "honour," and "fredom") or on various oddities— for example, that Dorigen's playful words should bind her or that Arveragus should send her to Aurelius in defense of "trouthe," an illicit assignation that neither Arveragus nor Dorigen desires. These are very important matters, but they are better approached through the Franklin's tale telling (which, as with all Canterbury tale tellings, is not comprehensive in its understanding of the tale). His commentary does not resolve oddity; rather it ends up highlighting the "utopian" cast of his thinking about marriage and "trouthe," an "unreality" that reflects nostalgia for older values and a sentimental view of the harmonies possible in love and marriage. But neither that nostalgia nor that sentiment is entirely misplaced. Both offer a maturer alternative than is found in the Squire's delight in storybook marvels, however much their objects are marvels of human arrangements. The Franklin's marvels, after all, are not magical toys; they involve noble sympathies and feelings.[11]

Much of the commentary on the Franklin's presentation of marriage and on Arveragus's decision to send Dorigen to Aurelius becomes entangled in the commentator's own views of a good marriage.[12] The effects are not necessarily baneful, but they tend to emphasize notions of patience and integrity that pull back too soon from the Franklin's labor, to which I now turn.

The Franklin opens his tale with the theme of accord in love. A noble lady so pities her worthy knight that, namely for his meek "obeysaunce" and for his "penaunce," she fell privately into a vow

> To take hym for hir housbonde and hir lord,
> Of swich lordshipe as men han over hir wyves.
>   [ll. 742–43]

The "pitee" here is appropriately "gentil" and a semireligious generosity for the knight's "penaunce." But feeling is important to the otherwise utopian formulation that follows: More than noble perception, a response to one's similitude in the other, "pitee" establishes a relinquishing of bad feeling, of "maistrie" and "jalousie," such that the knight will obey his lady in everything, as a lover, except for the shame of losing honor. In return for such "gentilesse," the lady promises to be his humble, true wife: "Have heer my trouthe—til that myn herte breste" (l. 759). At this early point in the tale, the knight and lady stand in an anonymous perfection; they become an emblem of marriage without "maistrie" or "jalousie," sealed by vows and emphasized by a full commitment of the heart. In such an arrangement, they subside into quiet and rest.

Now how does the Franklin read this emblem? His explanation runs on for more than forty lines, becoming a gloss that both belies the transparency of this arrangement and shows the Franklin's struggle to credit the marvel that is this marriage. He begins by invoking the equality of friendship, if the friendship is to last. Then he moves to Love and states the self-evident truth that love will not be constrained by mastery. In the *Romance of the Rose*, the Ovidian wisdom of similar remarks concerns sexual bliss and the avoidance of jealousy, the knight having forgone the latter already. But the Franklin emphasizes the freedom of spirit:

> Whan maistrie comth, the God of Love anon
> Beteth his wynges, and farewel, he is gon!
>   [ll. 765–66]

Such is the fate of any, potentially unstable, alchemic arrangement. Is the absence of "maistrie," then, the philosopher's stone for love? It would seem so, as women, of kynde, desiren libertee,

. . . .

And so doon men, if I sooth seyen shal.

[ll. 768–70]

What do we call this absence of "maistrie," if not "pacience" joined with humility and meekness (a meekness that suppresses jealousy and a patience that abides external vexation)?[13] This looks forward to Arveragus's patience in abiding Aurelius's suit and Dorigen's promise, a patience that precedes bitter tears, but how does patience really express this mutual freedom in love and marriage?

Patience conquers all, vanquishing where rigor cannot. So patience is an active virtue, although it requires the passive suffering of missayings and misdeeds committed by others.[14] So far we are in odd territory in the explanation of a free-spirited marriage, although patience no doubt is a better virtue than many for approximating the harmony of quietly wed lovers. The Franklin finally sees patience as a promise of sufferance, that the knight will suffer her freedom. In exchange, she promises that there will be no fault or sin in her. This "suffraunce" is the central wit of their marriage, setting all else into motion. In a sense, it is a mode of knowledge and exquisite feeling both (compare *Boece*, bk. 5, metrum 4, l. 47). Through his own "suffraunce," the knight knows that he can secure a happy freedom in marriage for himself and his lady, much better anyway than might rigor, mastery, or jealousy.

The Franklin summarizes this knowledge in its effect: In this "humble, wys accord" she takes her servant and her lord; but he is not in servitude, for he has both his lady and his love, and thus he is "in lordshipe above" (l. 795). Humility subdues unruly passions, and patience suffers the freedom of others; but the knight is lord above, despite having surrendered "maistrie." The phrasing of servitude and lordship is rhetorically winning but conceptually revealing in the close. As others have noted, the Franklin cannot quite sustain the tension of this marriage remedy for strife, pain (consider the pain Walter's testing causes Griselda), and jealousy—effectively understanding the marriage as the husband's lordship. After a salutary year of undescribed bliss, the husband, now called Arveragus, decides on a year or two away, clearly not in accord with Dorigen's will, who mourns his absence deeply.[15]

The husband's absence makes a would-be lover's approach socially possible in this tale of social virtues. But readers have often reacted strongly to Aurelius's love suit and to his insistence that Dorigen abide by her *words*, not her intent, even though he knows that he has not in fact removed the grisly rocks from the seashore. He has been thought of as almost a blackmailer, a bully, a man of surfaces and appearances, as unsavory.[16] These reactions are extreme, I think, given the Franklin's characterization of Aurelius, who has virtue and who, in courtly terms, deserves a hearing and a response, something Dorigen appropriately acknowledges in her "pley" after she has insisted upon her chastity as a wife: she would grant him love, since she sees him so "pitously" complain, if he could remove all the rocks. He has asked her for "routhe," given his two years of pain, and she has denied him this. But she knows the protocol and Aurelius is worthy. He hears her demand and despairs. Her friends come and take Dorigen away in solace and joy, unknowingly leaving Aurelius behind with a sorrow bitter unto death. This is the emotional context within which we need to see Aurelius's plight—"For verray wo out of his wit he breyde." The Franklin, noting that Aurelius does not know what he is saying (hence excusing the pagan prayer), gives us Aurelius's address to Apollo, followed by the one to Lucina, within which Aurelius prays for a high tide lasting two years. He cannot remove the rocks one by one, but perhaps he can invoke natural forces so that they are buried for a time equivalent to his suffering. His fantasy about the rocks matches Dorigen's in having them out of sight, showing a similitude of desire between them; moreover, it is the extremity of pain that drives each fantasy and which the Franklin clearly credits enough to elaborate. Of course, Aurelius's pagan prayers are unavailing and so he falls into a trance, which attracts his sympathetic brother, who eventually hears from Aurelius the cause of such pain.

The tale of woe, fantasy, and "routhe" now takes another turn as Aurelius's brother introduces him to an accomplished magician, a worker of marvelous illusions and entertainments, a clerk, notably, who is a man of both inner sight and feeling (for he weeps when he hears that many of his schoolday friends are dead). But he demands a princely sum for working his magic on the rocks of Brittany, a sum that seems trivial to the suffering Aurelius, who gladly vows to pay it. The clerk is happy with his part of the contract, but he also moves to the work of illusion making with an energy and a perseverance borne of "routhe" for Aurelius's nearly suicidal pain (l. 1261).

The Franklin has little truck with all of the heathen superstition and magic making in his tale, but he does not disbelieve entirely, allowing that in those past days heathen magic could make the rocks seem to disappear. That done, we return to Aurelius who sues Dorigen for her grace, knowing that there is no obstacle now. Dorigen, of course, is dumbfounded and made miserable. She undertakes a long complaint, similar to others the Franklin has given us. Apparently in matters of pathos, his spirit feels much.[17] Readers have noticed that the structure of Dorigen's complaint reflects changes of thought. She is not characterized as out of her mind but rather as piteously sorrowful and fearful, suffering so that it "routhe was to see" (l. 1349), a canny and anticipatory articulation of feeling and perception. She may speak amiss—one does, in states of woe, according to the Franklin—but she speaks with deliberation and with some hope of remedy (thus appropriately moved by fear, rather than given to despair).[18] On the third day of her new woe, Arveragus returns home and asks about her sorrow. She tells him weepingly what she has said and sworn. He, in his noble "pacience," holds Dorigen to her "trouthe," to a comparable "pacience" given this bitter outcome to her promise. In effect, choice is taken out of her hands and she is commanded to submit to the very shame and defilement she has feared for three days now. It is better that she suffer Aurelius's lust than that she break her word.

Incredible as this may seem, it is a version of patience, of that virtue that triumphs where rigor cannot. The Franklin knows that this situation is incredible, indeed, problematic and possibly uncouth in its surprising turn, and he hastens to forestall the reactions of the reader by appealing to the next turn in the tale—to the wisdom of the tale, if not the believability of the moment. Truth here is a rare and feeling thing.

Aurelius has sounded unsavory in his insistence that Dorigen abide by her mere word, but he does so out of his pain and wretchedness, not out of a devotion to sexual gratification. When he meets Dorigen on the way to their assignation place, he questions her, having saluted her with glad intent. He obviously thinks at first that she comes willingly enough, not having stayed around to study her astonishment when he earlier announced that the rocks were gone. She answers him, half mad with woe, and cries out piteously,

> "Unto the gardyn, as myn housbonde bad,
> My trouthe for to holde—allas! allas!"
>   [ll. 1512–13]

Although unsavory in his own plight, Aurelius is more than noble when he *sees* the plight of someone else (as we approach the heart of perception and feeling in this tale). His own woe blinded him to Dorigen's intent, given her fantasy promise, but now the woeful woman herself strikes wonder and compassion in him. Feeling triumphs, if not patience, in a meekness perhaps that subdues his own lust. First he has great compassion for Dorigen's lamentation and also for Arveragus's insistence that she keep her "trouthe." This brings him to feel great "routhe" for both of them, so great that he would rather put his lust aside than do a churlish deed against "franchise and alle gentillesse." Great feeling brings self-knowledge, a change in perception.

But the Franklin at this point in his tale is less intent on the knowledge born of wonder and compassion than on a lesson: Let every wife beware of her promise; at least think of Dorigen and consider. The person to whom one promises something in play may not have Aurelius's virtue, but Aurelius has demonstrated that a squire can certainly do as "gentil" a deed as a knight can. For the Franklin, the tale teaches us that very truth about the capacities of a squire—indeed, it does more when we consider the expanding world generated by successive and responsive acts of compassion. For Aurelius now seems truly destitute: his compassion has lost him sexual gratification with his lady, and the illusion he purchased will surely bankrupt him twice over. He takes five hundred pounds worth of gold to the clerk and calls upon the clerk's "gentillesse," hoping to arrange a gradual repayment plan for the great remainder of his debt. When the clerk asks whether or not he abided by the agreement, Aurelius says yes and then tells the clerk what happened. In response the clerk, by God's blissful might, asserts that a clerk can certainly do as "gentil" a deed as both the knight and the squire have done. He accordingly releases Aurelius of his debt, and the Franklin turns to his readers to ask which of these three "was the mooste fre."

The tale has turned into a competitive arrangement for the Franklin, who does not comment further. Clearly, he understands words as one's bond, no matter the intent, and "gentillesse" as a potentially competitive matching of one deed with another. Moreover, he virtually overlooks the ways in which the supposedly unconstrained Dorigen has been acted upon, subject to the commands and releases of first her husband and then her would-be suitor. He does not credit magic very much, but he does credit a simple code in which words have a life of their own. Yet he is no Manciple, and his warning about promises is well enough taken in its way: through some humor or desire, we may well misspeak, be mistaken, and subjected to an awful, unforeseen duty later. It is better to suffer in patience than to speak promises, even in play, amid our woe and fear.

By attempting the opening vision of a utopian marriage and by dwelling on the final conundrum of "fredom," the Franklin is at least consistent in his glosses, for covenants are usually arrangements within which we serve, within which we are not free. To forgo a covenant is a wonderful act of generosity and "suffraunce," but attention to that distracts us from the tension of equality and freedom within marriage, as well as from the tale's insistence on the liberating functions of "routhe." The Franklin would devote much of his commentary to marvels of arrangement and gesture, paralleling the Squire's interest in marvels of a different kind. But for the Franklin, the result is different, though he does miss things in his tale. The Franklin is old and yearns for something he does not have: a son "gentil" enough to take instruction in values the Franklin holds dear. There is poignancy in the Franklin's nostalgia, not misplaced sentiment. For that nostalgia does embrace "pite" for suffering hearts through the tale he remembers, if not directly in his glosses, then in his narration of key turns (as in the great "routhe" Aurelius felt, caught in his heart). All in all, the Franklin is a man of parts; he would warn us about the binding power of mere words. He respects material gestures (including those involving wealth), but he respects virtue more and thinks of a world in which the heart saves one and all from shame and disaster, though he would give it all a social and competitive twist. But like the Squire, the Franklin has little feeling for rhetorical heights (although he has more ability and he goes in for extended complaint). Together, the Squire and the Franklin have an insufficient view of rhetoric, born of suitable candor in the one case and a posture of plain speaking in the other (nevertheless aspiring to "gentil" gesture if not "gentil" locution). On the one hand, they do much better than the Manciple does, but they do not consider their tales fully enough to go far in the business of sorting out truth and falsehood, although they do believe in parts of their tales. On the other hand, each is aware of an audience in a less leading way than either the Canon's Yeoman or the Manciple is aware. This deference to audience keeps them sociable as tale tellers and brings the business of crediting fiction for its mixture of truth and falsehood into a public world, away from the enclosed room of the solitary reader. The audience is invited in, rather than asked to judge, especially by the Franklin in his question concerning superlative "fredom."

So far I have looked closely at three Canterbury fragments and at five tale tellers uninvolved in vengeful relations with other tellers (such as the Reeve "quitting" the Miller or the Summoner and the Friar attacking each other). The tellers vary in their motives greatly and in their emotional commitment, with the Second Nun at one end of a scale of venality and the

Manciple at the other. But what do we learn from this grouping of tales about the status of Chaucer's fictions and the reader's education, along with the status of the various tellers? First, either the tales are readable in more than one way, or the subjects addressed are open to other points of view. The Second Nun's tale and the Canon's Yeoman's tale of con artistry are less revealing as they become more illustrative. Each asserts truth, the one closed to further elaboration without faith, the other only glancing off the complexities of the experience to which it in some way relates. Cecilie's martyrdom is inspiring, but her life can hardly resolve everyone else's, her story insisting absolutely on an ascetic view of marriage. The Canon's Yeoman's tale of a trickster is not the equivalent of alchemy or of the Yeoman's experience with that dismaying science. Both tales do assert the inherent status of fiction as a bearer of truth, as a true tiding, whether inspiring example or proffered warning. The Canon's Yeoman's tale as a text, however, shows the teller in an ongoing process of reaction and the finding of a voice or attitude that will allow him to conclude satisfactorily. That process essentially is a powerful mode of characterization.

The Manciple repeats that mode in the ways in which Chaucer introduces him to us in the headlink encounter with the Cook and in his various asides and digressions, most of them reflecting his anticipatory control of the tale. Both the Squire and the Franklin similarly respond to their tales, in each case showing us an aspect of character that we could not otherwise infer. The Squire is young, likable, and humbly serviceable; whereas the Franklin is old, complimentary, nostalgic, and concerned beyond real matters of words and money about virtue, especially patience in times of pain or sorrow.

The tales these three tellers respond to are not resolved by the tellers' closed points of view. In the Manciple's case, the reader can moralize in various ways over both the crow and Phebus Apollo. Phebus is an example of jealousy, tragic anger, or confusion; the crow talks too much, not enough, or in the wrong humor. In the Squire's case, we can see various lines of development for his tale's images and for the love material. In the Franklin's case, obviously Dorigen's needs might merit more attention, along with the role of wonder and compassion (rather than unanalyzed generosity or "fredom"). These and other considerations suggest the fertility of the tales and the many ways in which the tales explore something and confront us. Perhaps, after all, Chaucer is not an ironist in any medieval fashion, not a master interpreter who would lead us to a better and a surer view than his mistaken tellers possess. We are, perhaps, invited to attend to these tidings seriously, with delight and some reverence, willing to credit them as compounds of truth and falsehood in the most open ways we can. Wonder and felt belief can lead to knowledge, although we may, as with the narrator of the *Parliament of Fowls*, emerge from our considerations with something more complicated than "a certeyn thing," perhaps more than we looked for and less than we want.[19]

Given tellers who use their tales to argue a point, the tales are not arguments in some literary courtroom. They are arenas for the epistemological play of wonder, feeling, and belief. The variety that these five tales offer is only increased in the longest fragment of the collection, the series beginning with the Shipman and ending with the Nun's Priest. Along with increased variety, however, comes a tale that seems secure in its serious import: Chaucer the Pilgrim's tale of Dame Prudence and the noble Melibeus. With its stress on a prudent disposition for thought and action, that tale assumes a centrality in the fragment that reflects various orders of prudence, in the tale as well as in the fragment outside the tale. Prudence, one of the close relatives of patience, involves a subduing of anger and then deliberation, thought, a weighing of things. Like "suffisaunce," prudence is a way to galvanize thought and discriminatory powers. It may also be an answer to the *Prioress's Tale*, perhaps on the question of mercy toward one's foes.

That Fragment 7 also contains two interruptions of tale telling can be seen to combine with the fragment's concern for "sentence" and merriment, producing a questioning of audience attitudes and prudence, of the relation between one's deeming and the merits of a tale.

6 ❦ THE SHIPMAN AND THE PRIORESS: LOW PRUDENCE AND TRIUMPHANT FEELING

ome late medieval compilers may have wanted the *Shipman's Tale* linked to the *Pardoner's Tale*, given a theme of misgovernance.[1] Such a broad theme, however, would fit most of the Canterbury tales, especially those dealing with marriage and friendship.[2] The Shipman's tale of a merchant cuckolded by a friendly and cheerful monk certainly involves busy if not unruly behavior. The tale is told unintrusively, after the awkwardness of the opening lines about the cost of keeping wives, and it exploits a number of common, bawdy puns, in the spirit of which the tale and teller eventually merge.[3] Whether or not Chaucer knew the pun, the merchant in the tale is cozened by a would-be cousin, and terms such as plow, debt, and tally are amusingly linked with sex. Stephen Knight dwells on the mercantilization of everything in the tale, although that requires a greater reader outrage than the tale can bear.[4] Its characters are not complex enough to affect us greatly, given what happens. Moreover, though the merchant is likable, we are not appalled that he is cuckolded. Indeed, the bawdy logic of the tale (given the merchant's absences from his lovely and playful wife) requires a sexual liaison. What the fabliau does not require is truth mixed with its exploitative merriment, and yet Chaucer supplies this as well.

With his schemes for profit, his lack of scruples, and his love of freedom and pleasure, the Shipman seems an appropriate teller for a materialistic tale of sex and money. Thus he might identify with the tale's opportunistically prudent monk, although nowhere does he say so, confining himself at the tale's end to a choric approval of the wife's brazen recovery from near exposure. The text reveals very little of the Shipman's mind because he neither comments nor elaborates intrusively in relation to any part of the tale; apparently his ending approval of the wife's brazen wit sizes up this tale and the world as exactly suited to each other. So we should take the tale and consider the gestures upon which it develops and turns.

Simply by changing a few pronouns, a voice for the tale is established in the opening lines: there is peril in a world in which husbands refuse to support their wives' delight in clothes. Anything can happen if wives are forced to look to others for their costs (as does the merchant's wife in the tale). A practical contract appears in this situation: the wife wears her new clothes in jolly fashion, "al for his [her husband's] owene worshipe richely" (l. 13). If this contract should fail "by aventure" or choice, then the wife will assign its fulfillment to someone else. Thus the wardrobe contract serves the wife's interests primarily and is redefinable at any time. This self-interest and the essentially mutable nature of contracts are features in all the relationships, contracts, vows, and promises offered in the tale. Presumably the redefinable nature of relationships and contracts, all offered in good cheer and with either blind or blinding feeling, is one of the key subjects in this tale—becoming the ground for the Monk's movements in the tale, and presumably, for the Shipman's movements in his larger world of exploitation and cutthroat behavior.

In the arrangement between the monk and the merchant, those features become clear. A traveling monk, friar John, visits a noble merchant who has a worthy home and a beautiful, companionable, "revelous" wife. Master John claims "cosynage," by which he and the merchant are "knyt with eterne alliaunce" (l. 40). This cousinly accord, with neither one superior to the other, forms an ideal covenant by which Master John makes himself familiar and at home in the merchant's house, so that eventually he can have his way with the merchant's wife. Moreover, the monk claims this cousinship without contradiction from the merchant, who is as glad as a bird is glad of the day to be so knit with the monk: "For to his herte it was a greet plesaunce" (l. 39). Here good feeling is cozened. The merchant of "Seint Denys," blind in his glad feelings for the monk, never does acquire insight, neither into the monk nor the beautiful wife whom he similarly cherishes. He is bound to his senses and to his belief in the fair words of others. He has an open and generous nature, as some readers have noted, and his patience at the tale's end is a form of "suffraunce," one of the Franklin's virtues. In effect, his is a temperate, sanguine blindness, despite the anxieties that form a part of his business life.

Along with patience, the tale further echoes the Franklin's tale in its turn

on "routhe" and "trouthe" as part of the friar's maneuvering with the
wife. That maneuvering involves the redefining of relationships after the
wife complains about her husband, "al be he youre cosyn" (l. 147):

> "Nay," quod this monk, "by God and Seint Martyn,
> He is na moore cosyn unto me
> Than is this leef that hangeth on the tree!
> I clepe hym so, by Seint Denys of Fraunce,
> To have the moore cause of aqueyntaunce
> Of yow, which I have loved specially
> Aboven alle wommen, sikerly.
> This swere I yow on my professioun."
>
> [ll. 148–55]

Disavowing any familiarity with the merchant stronger than whatever a
man would have with a leaf, the monk happily asserts his love-devotion to
the wife. This strongly sworn love cannot mean much either, although it is
met with a rhetorically strong profession of feeling: "My deere love . . . O
my daun John" (l. 158). His words were spoken advisedly and so are hers,
as she emphasizes her husband's purported niggardliness, the contrary
value of "fredom," and her need of a loan (for which she is willing to do
whatever the monk desires). Characterized as "gentil," the monk calls her
his lady dear and promises to deliver her out of her care. For his reward, he
indicates his sexual desire by grabbing her flanks and embracing her hard.
As others have noticed, there is no courtliness here; neither is there much
parody, only roguish humor as the monk knows his lady (and she him).
There is here no mistake of perception or understanding in the knowledge
taken and the desires expressed. The monk and the wife share a bawdy,
coarse, and manipulative similitude, although the wife is slightly more vulnerable in not questioning the source of the monk's means. Correspond-
ingly, she is more verbally agile when maneuvering before her husband to
escape discovery at the tale's end. Thus it is right that the monk should
only seem to keep his word, having urged the wife to be as true as he will
be. That speech gladdens the wife for the moment, as she goes forth "jolif
as a pye." Again seeming emotion, but really a rhetoric of feeling, trust,
and companionableness, is cozened as the monk eventually brings to her a
hundred francs in the merchant's absence (borrowed in fact from the merchant) and then spends a mirthful, busy night with the wife.

We soon learn, however, that he tells the merchant when next they
meet that he has repaid a loan equal to the sum he gave the wife, adding in

clever honesty that he gave those francs to her, to whom the merchant should apply. Master John has happily incurred and paid various debts in this maneuver, leaving the wife with a problem when the merchant confronts her. She brazenly outfaces the moment by claiming that the monk said the money was for her use and so she spent it. The merchant accepts this explanation, without inquiring further into the wife's affairs and without wondering about her heatedness regarding Master John, whom she defies as false. Here patience continues the blissful feelings born of ignorance for the merchant, whereas insight and intense feeling arise simultaneously for the wife, who nevertheless cannot share the moment with her husband, except by further gulling him.

She offers to pay her debt in bed, such that the merchant can score it upon her "taille." If he does so, she will enjoy the moment. If he neglects to do so, she is free of her debt, having defined its repayment in terms that suit her, thus becoming, in her fashion, Master John's exact mate, his female similitude. The Shipman may appreciate this development inasmuch as he closes the tale in two lines that pun on "taille," thus winking at the cluster of words for spending, profit, money, and sex. Meaning slides back and forth between account, tally, and tail, with "taillynge ynough" also indicating either a limit or simply a sufficiency. Let God give us "taillynge" enough in our lives, and let that enough be more than an imposed limit (as it is when the wife breaks away from the merchant's embrace: "Namoore . . . by God, ye have ynough!"). Here the Shipman's benediction on the tale embraces its punning and its values. Everything is redefinable or remintable; rhetoric, feeling, and action are to be cozened, although those who are quick and fair of speech will have their way.

The Host laughingly assumes that the tale teaches us to beware of monks who would cozen us, punning in his turn when he warns us about monks who would put

> "in the mannes hood an ape,
> And in his wyves eek, by Seint Austyn!"
> [ll. 440–41]

The Host's punning accords him with the Shipman in understanding the joke on both the merchant and the wife. A moral critic might focus on the low and narrow prudence shown by the characters, sympathizing (as many readers nearly do) with the merchant, whose business prudence causes his home, his servants, and his wife to be open to "friendly" traducement and sexual invasion. Here as elsewhere Chaucer leaves us to our own devices, to our own crediting of this tale. But, in a way we have seen before, he incorporates significant audience response independent of personal insult or revenge. Yet it is different now because it becomes a feature that recurs in Fragment 7 regularly and concerns the ways in which pilgrims either anticipate or credit a tale: The Host thinks the Shipman's tale is well said; all of the pilgrims are wondrously sober in response to the Prioress; the Host considers Chaucer's *Thopas* not worth a turd in its hateful rhyming; the Host anticipates a *Daun John* tale of sorts from the Monk; and the Knight, made weary by the Monk's little tragedies, cuts them short. In all of these responses, the various tales are accorded a reality beyond entertainment. Much as the Cook does in response to the Reeve, the Host draws a worldly moral from the *Shipman's Tale:* Let no monks into your Inn, unless you have no fear of being cuckolded. The Prioress's tale is soberly and wondrously credited. Chaucer's *Tale of Sir Thopas* is not at all amusing to the Host, and the Monk's tragedies depress the Knight, who would rather hear tales of good fortune in the world.

These responses are simple and unattended by any inquiry or reverence (except, possibly, the unusually sober response to the Prioress's tale). But they are complicated by notions of pleasing and keeping an audience in relation to the "sentence" one hopes to tell. Here delight and merriment matter, as may reforming instruction (the Host wishes that his wife could have heard Chaucer's tale of Melibeus's wife, given her prudence and patience). This focus on audience response in between the tales of Fragment 7 shifts emphasis away from concern for the ways in which tellers read or misread their material and accordingly away from attitudes and aspects of character. Instead, the reader concentrates more on the individual tales and begins to consider them in terms of their effects on an audience, moving from considering primarily the teller and the truth the tale may tell to an additional consideration: the effect a tale's "sentence" or truth has on particular pilgrims, given their understanding of the tale. A repeated focus on tellers responding to their tales is not abandoned here (especially not in the Prioress's case or in the Nun's Priest's); but it is interestingly supplemented by introducing a plurality of readings in the device of audience response and thus, if this is a late fragment, suggesting that Chaucer eventually came to the idea of staging a complete consideration of the tale-telling act in relation to teller, tale, and audience. What a merry tale is, for whom it is intended, and in just what sense, are the overarching rhetorical questions posed in Fragment 7. That those large issues should begin in a fabliau way, with a bawdy and unprincipled entertainment—however much that fable reflects exploitation and amorality in the world—is perhaps Chaucer's greatest achievement in turning us to this fragment through the Shipman. If a tale of false love and lowly desire can introduce great issues, then no tale is to be despised on its face.

Thematically, many issues link the tales of this fragment, most notably the question of prudence or patience and mercy. But how the reader is to respond to a tale, rather than how a tale is told and thereby how it reveals aspects of its teller, is the key issue here, involving questions of emotional response, "sentence," and fruit. In this connection it is not accidental that the *Prioress's Tale* and the *Nun's Priest's Tale* should have long fascinated a multitude of readers (judging from the large body of commentary). But the *Tale of Melibee* deserves its share, as does the Monk's string of tragedies (leaving *Sir Thopas* as an interrupted interlude, a preamble, in effect, for *Melibee*).

From a well-said tale of sex and trickery we reach the Prioress and her glad willingness to tell a tale. The Host turns to her as an appropriate teller now, the "first of al this route" to tell another tale. He turns to her first and thinks of her as first in his deferential speech—responding to the success with which the Prioress pains herself

> to countrefete cheere
> Of court, and to been estatlich of manere,
> And to ben holden digne of reverence.
> [*GP*, ll. 139–41][5]

The Host addresses her as delicately and courteously as though she were a maid (sensing something fragile in her?), clearly wanting to change direction in the tale telling, to leave the Shipman's kind of merriment behind for now. In this turn to the Prioress Chaucer will present a tale to settle down with, where certainly, as with the Second Nun, we will hear of truth and good doctrine, however schooled and dignified its expression. From the Prioress's prologue, furthermore, we soon come to expect a fervently told tale through which the Prioress would "declare" the great worthiness of Mary. But, judging from reader response, few of us are prepared for the tale she tells.[6] Surely here the reader might expect religious morality, not play, not sober doctrine, and certainly not heated speech. What we get is earnest piety, the vile murder of a reverential and joyous child, concentrated pathos, a quick review of an appropriately severe justice for the villains, and a turning away from that to a Christian witnessing that culminates in notions of mercy multiplied for all sinners. It is a tale in which the characterization of Jewish villainy is intensified in relation to some of its analogues and in which the affective character of Chaucer's rhyme royal tales is most concentrated, approaching total decorum in the integration of pathos and cruelty.[7] The tale's depictions of Jewish villainy and justice are important to the teller's sense of truth, as is clear in the ending reference to Hugh of Lincoln, child martyr (also slain by "cursed Jewes").

But too much has been made, one way or another, of the status of the Prioress's anti-Semitic piety. Too little attention has been paid to the tale itself as the Prioress's repository for intensely felt and believed but largely unexpounded truths, although the many readers who find the Prioress somewhat off-putting are not necessarily un-Chaucerian in their points of view. She is a careful, naive, and surprisingly passionate character. Her piety is not calculated for broad appeal, nor is the stunning pathos of her tale.

In her prologue the Prioress prays to Mary and prays for herself, although in doing so she does not seem conscious of personal sin. Such a consciousness grounds Chaucer's "An ABC" but is largely absent from the Prioress's invocation to Mary. Admittedly, the Prioress at the moment is not concerned with her sins; instead, she calls upon Mary as a muse, and she uses the prologue as a way of setting up part of her tale. She says that even children praise Mary, some while still breast feeding, ending her prologue with the notion that she, much as a twelve-month-old child, can scarcely express Mary's great worthiness. These emphases are more than mere topoi of humility or inexpressibility: for the Prioress, they are the tale's guiding themes, themes that in the tale assert the superiority of the young and helpless over the adult and murderous—as well as the efficacy of pure song over intellectual understanding—both in the expression of and service to truth.

The Prioress's sense of unworthiness concerns her poetical powers of praise, not her sinfulness. Her worshipful rapture recalls a religion of meditation like Richard Rolle's, not a religion of works like the Second Nun's. The Prioress is our first ecclesiastic to speak as though she were on fire with love (hence *amor*, not *caritas*, in her motto).[8] Nearly every intense moment in her tale telling has a parallel in Rolle's *Incendium Amoris:* one passes through a sinner's consciousness to a state in which one is seized "by this taste for eternal sweetness, which is going to make . . . [one] sing joyously for God."[9] Rolle embraces praise of the Blessed Virgin; with heart ablaze, the singer is "transformed into the likeness of him in whom is all melody." Extremes meet in a loathing of unbelievers and of those who lust after the flesh; to be raised to exalted love is to be rare, like topaz. But there are those who go astray in their ignorance of the contemplative life and who enter therefore into a "sham and fanciful devotion."[10] How much, if any, sham and fanciful devotion is there in the Prioress? We can tell only by turning to the language in which Chaucer impersonates her and thereby to the teller who presents herself as needing divine inspiration to sing a song in praise of Mary.

Her prologue to the tale contains a type of word play, especially repetition and inversion, that attracts the ear but may only problematically fulfill the spirit. For the sober-minded, excess possibly maims her song; rhetorical balances may lead to an overdoing, and nearly, to inadvertent parody. "O Lord, oure Lord" sets up an emotional tone that characterizes her effect if not her aim. Repetition should emphasize rhetorically by clarifying meaning or by overturning one meaning and establishing another for the same word. Apostrophe, though a perfectly respectable means of amplification and intensification, does neither: it emphasizes the Prioress's ecstasy instead. As with the successful pun, the Prioress's figures seem primarily to display her devotion rather than underline new or more precise meaning, something outside and other than the speaker. But, of course, that is the mystic's rhetorical effect, whether achieved through sham or sincere intent.

In the prologue's first stanza, the idea of honor and praise varies "heriynge" (praise or worship), and the performance of either is for both men of "dignitee" and for suckling infants. The reference to suckling on the breast emphasizes innocence and the spirituality of the newly incarnate soul. But it is also an odd detail that suggests an aggressive orality on the part of the Prioress—an early hint of those details in the tale that reflect a possible psychological complex outside the frame of this discussion, except that it likely involves severe rectitude (or "anality") and righteous, dismembering aggression ("castration").[11] But whatever psychological intuitions Chaucer may pose here, the surface intensity, the rhetoric of this prologue establishes a punned-upon extreme: from infant completion to elevated praise. As we will see, the Prioress would complete acts of praise both in infant innocence and in social dignity. I think she is not sham in her devotions, but her spiritualism is at least partly aggressive, as eventually revealed in the tale's melodrama of heinous, remorseless crime and summary punishment—a level of aggression that could reflect a cultural breakdown in the church to which she belongs.[12]

The second stanza uses "laude" for a transition and amplifies it to praise as song. Having established a rhetoric of repeated words, the Prioress continues, but now she tries for a difference and introduces humility: "wherfore in laude, as I best kan or may" (l. 460). She will labor to tell a story in praise of the Virgin, not to increase the Virgin's honor, but simply out of praise. For the Virgin herself is honor and the root of "bountee, next hir Sone, and soules boote" (ll. 465–66). Here, in repetition with a difference (*adnominatio*), the Prioress would follow the lead of men of "dignitee" as well as of suckling children, emerging as both "gentil" and innocent in her self-effacing praise. The play on words, devout in itself, tends to identify the Prioress with sheer laud of Mary, that "white lylye flour," although why she would even think to deny a crass motive—that she might honor the Virgin to increase the Virgin's honor—is curious. Would she deny the social impulse, the "gentil" bestowing of honor by those with honor? Whatever, she continues, raising the pitch of her praise:

> O mooder Mayde! o mayde Mooder free!
> O bussh unbrent, brennynge in Moyses sighte,
> That ravyshedest down fro the Deitee,
>   the Goost that in th'alighte,
> Of whos vertu whan he thyn herte lighte,
> Conceyved was the Fadres sapience.
>
>   [ll. 467–72]

She learns more than courtly table manners and Stratford French in school. She has acquired a rhetoric that condenses the Marian symbol system of the burning bush, forcing opposites into paradoxical conjunction, such that a heated confusion emerges rather than a "brilliant, organic whole."[13] The Prioress heightens rhetorical effects by inverting phrases balanced against each other and by repeating words in different forms ("unbrent," "brennynge"). Her verbs heighten and obscure, rendering a symbolic action almost sexual ("ravyshedest").[14] The difference she makes here is one of style: emotion worked up rhetorically, producing a baroque song when compared to a straightforward, earnest, and largely unheightened style in "An ABC":

> Thou art the bush on which ther gan descende
> The Holi Gost, the which that Moyses wende
> Had been a-fyr, and this was in figure.

Now, ladi, from the fyr thou us defende
Which that in helle eternalli shal dure.
                              [ll. 92–96]

The Prioress's figure is intensely rhetorical but not controlled symboli-
cally as it ends in the "alighte-lighte" rhyme. Such wordplay, involving
the shortening or lengthening of a word and thereby transferring the
meaning of one word to another, fails to distinguish the exact meaning of
either "alighte" or "lighte." [15] The Prioress does, however, conform closely
enough to traductio as Geoffrey of Vinsauf uses it: the repetition of a
word, in any position, for emphasis. This is the practice also in the pseudo-
Ciceronian Ad Herennium, the basic text for Vinsauf's use of rhetorical
figures. [16] In effect, the Prioress has considerable skill in the balancing of
phrases, but less skill in direct wordplay and punning so as to control
meaning through antitheses.

Moreover, confusion appears even in the midst of her syntactical success. The Virgin Mother is not the "bussh unbrent" itself; that is only a
sign of her virginity. Neither is she a maid mother or a mother maid
(rather, mother and maiden, though the Host thinks of the Prioress as both
a maid and a lady). More, the burning bush does not ravish or snatch anything down from the Deity, despite its figurative role as God's spirit and
despite the Virgin's role in receiving the Holy Ghost. Metaphysical passion, scholastic explication, and psychological demands upon the Father
fuse strangely here. [17]

Having heatedly expressed herself, the Prioress now undertakes an inexpressibility topos. She now dramatically asserts the impossibility of expressing the Lady's virtues. Yet she names those virtues—"bountee," "mag-
nificence," "vertu," "humylitee"—and adds the Virgin's inspirational role.
The movement of sentiment here is essentially correct: for who does have
the science to express the Virgin's virtues, those qualities that transcend
earthly categories? So the Prioress disclaims wisdom, knowledge, and skill
either to express the Lady's virtues or declare Her worthiness. This is fine
in itself but now seems to deviate from the mystical heat of the burning
bush stanza. She does not now seem on fire. Her mode is one of right
gesture, although her sense of being privileged is something she can still
share with Rolle.

Her last prologue stanza returns her to the first. By comparing herself to
a twelve-month-old child, she both reintroduces the idea of infant praise
and strikes an odd note, for she does not actually fare as that infant does.

Unable, of course, to "declare" the Virgin's great worth, she can still express something. Her identification with very young children (and helpless animals) is an identification with innocence and superiority both, as well as with helplessness and succor—something that turns into brutality and evil when separated from the exalted Mother (compare the widow in the tale). She would, I think, have a spiritual superiority, understood as the child's innocence, and therein the superior worship as guided by the Virgin. This spiritual superiority would match her social "dignitee" in that she would be the privileged child and the skilled voice, another child saint (Nicholas comes to mind when she tells us about the child whose mother taught him always to worship the "blisful Lady") as well as be a denouncer of "cursed folk of Herodes al newe" (l. 574).

The opening stanza of her tale establishes the central contrast for a drama of villainy: in an Asian city, among Christian folk, a lord sustains a Jewish ghetto for foul usury and shameful profits. This "Jewerye" thus undertakes activities hateful to Christ and his company, if not in itself being hateful to Christ. We then focus on the Christian school for small children and on the "litel clergeon" who will become the martyr of this Eastern tale.

In his aural delight when first hearing the *Alma redemptoris,* the boy essentially becomes the instrument of language as pure song, although he also desires understanding. Understanding that the song was made in reverence of Christ's mother, the child vows all of his diligence in the conning of it before Christmas. He will memorize the song even if rebuked for neglecting his primer or even if threatened with three beatings an hour. This worry about child beating perhaps anticipates the later assault on the boy by a hired killer. But it is an odd way still of expressing the boy's devotion and determination, as though something were illicit here, further emphasized when we learn that an older child *secretly* teaches him the song, day by day, on their way home from school. It is tempting to pair this anticipation of child beating with the Prioress's intense, helplessly pained feelings of pity for her lapdogs beaten by men, but she does not respond to the stanza.[18] Instead she takes us to the boy's mastery of the song and to his coming and going through the ghetto, ever merrily singing *O Alma redemptoris.* Knowledge here and for the Prioress generally is more song than instruction, more unintelligent praise and prayer than matter expounded. It is in this spirit that she tells the tale and that the pilgrims will soberly receive it.

As we all know, satanically inspired Jews, conspiring to kill the boy because of his Christian song, hire a "homycide" who waylays the boy, holds him fast, cuts his throat, and casts him into a pit. The Prioress emphasizes this last point:

> I seye that in a wardrobe they hym threwe
> Where as thise Jewes purgen hire entraille.
> O cursed folk of Herodes al newe,
> What may youre yvel entente yow availle?
>   [ll. 572–75]

Derek Pearsall has seen her as steeling herself here in a "deliberate act of self-discipline, inspired by a determination not to be mealy-mouthed about the full horror of an event which must have been specially distressing" for a woman who pities the death agonies of trapped mice.[19] The general point is well taken, although the disparity between trapped mice and a slain boy requires more comment than this. However, the Prioress *is* steeled as she turns what could be an outburst of indignation into statements of God's certainty: that murder will out, especially there where the honor of God will spread, and that the blood cries out on that cursed deed. She addresses the conspirators directly—"youre"—and anticipates the discovery of their crime. We sense that she will be ruthless toward these murderers, much as the discovery of their bloodiness will honor God.

Her heart, however, goes out to the child, with whom she implicitly identifies in her next apostrophe, addressed to this martyr wedded to virginity (as she is). He now may evermore sing in Christ's company, he who never knew women in the flesh. Martyrdom speaks to her vocation and to her sense of helplessness, even as it rewards the boy for his devotion to Mary. Instead of the Shipman's profit and pleasure motives, there is what I call a martyr motive: one suffers the world and hateful men in it for a greater glory after death, a glory expressed in the imagery, finally, of precious stones (the boy is addressed as "This gemme of chastite, this emeraude, / And eek of martirdom the ruby bright" [ll. 609–10]). As though in exchange for the innocent's "performing" of praise, God performs a miracle and has the murdered boy sing *Alma redemptoris* from the privy into which he was cast, his throat carved open—a singing that breaks out as soon as Christ, of his grace, inspires the boy's distraught mother to look into the privy. Although cursed Jews conspired against this innocent boy, and although the Prioress's indictment is unstinting in its graphic detail, she does not swell that indictment rhetorically.[20] It is the reward of martyrdom that gets her attention and her exalted rhetoric. Indeed, the provost's secular punishment, with its Old Testament righteousness, contradicts only those analogues of the tale in which Jews show fear and remorse, first confessing their crime and then converting. To argue from analogues, of course, is no substitute for an interpretation of the tale itself, any more than is noting either the commonness of anti-Semitism in medieval Miracles of the Virgin or the general characteristics of such tales.[21] Such perspectives on the genre help in posing questions about the idiosyncrasy of a particular tale, but still that tale must be examined for its internal use of conventional (but not therefore univocally meaningful) material. The Prioress's lack of response to the provost's summary actions does not necessarily condemn her for little charity and no mercy. The tale can be thought of as a kind of melodrama, a fairy tale, requiring certain kinds of characters and a plot in which outrage meets punishment.[22] But even this is not nearly enough to resolve the issue of punishment, the justice and appropriateness of which is determined or not by the context in which that punishment occurs. Here is an interesting development: the guilty and *unrepentant* Jews are distinguished from all others—and a general slaughter does not occur. In that sense the punishment is already discriminating. Consider next how the boy's distraught mother operates in the tale, beyond the strong element of pathos that she provides.

First, the mother is characterized as given to a mother's pity and as half out of her mind (recall the Prioress's *General Prologue* portrait, with its noting of her charitable and pitying nature; perhaps she is too much so, too tender-hearted). She prays piteously to every Jew she meets in the ghetto for news of her child. To a man, apparently, "They seyde 'nay'; but Jhesu of his grace / Yaf in hir thoght" the idea of the pit (ll. 603–6). The piteously beseeching mother is summarily denied by pitiless Jews. Their hearts are hardened against her; in them there is not "gentilesse" deserving of "pite" and "mercy" in turn. This is an important development because it decides the affective case here. Mercy toward the pitiless and unrepentant would be a vice (recall that conversion of the Jews in some of the analogue tales *follows* confession and remorse). Moving from Seneca to Aquinas, J. D. Burnley suggests that Chaucer might well have thought of "pite" as conflicting with *severitas* in a judicial context only when right reason demands *severitas*, when clemency would be pusillanimous (*severitas* in fact is a middle term between the opposed *crudelitas* and *clementia*).[23] In *Melibee* Dame Prudence will recommend mercy toward Melibeus's foes, but they must first show remorse—otherwise judgment without mercy is fit for those who, like the murderers in the *Prioress's Tale*, show no mercy toward others (to neither the boy nor his mother).

The murder does come out, and the boy is discovered and taken out of the pit, singing all the while. A provost has been sent for who measures out an Old Testament justice: He orders those Jews who knew of the murder to be starved, beginning at once; he then has them drawn by wild horses and after that he hangs them according to the law. The exact punishment is set forth matter-of-factly in three lines, with the drawing and hanging given in the past tense, as though no sooner commanded than done. As noted before, the Prioress does not elaborate the punishment or castigate the punished.

The stanzas devoted to the boy's account of his miracle gather together and concentrate various motifs of praise, adding the boy's authority to the authority of tales of Christian miracles:

> "I sholde have dyed, ye, longe tyme agon.
> But Jesu Crist, as ye in bookes fynde,
> Wil that his glorie laste and be in mynde."
> [ll. 651–53]

So we are to believe and keep in mind (much as we do with the contents of old books) these Miracles of the Virgin, especially now on the testimony of this child. Such confirmation from within a story is matched historically by the truth of martyrdom cited in the last stanza, in the course of the Prioress's prayer to Hugh of Lincoln. The truth witnessed to here is the truth of reverence for Christ and for Mary, the truth of death overcome, martyrdom, and glory in heaven. This truth in story is now necessarily believed and demonstrated; indeed, to believe otherwise would be insupportable for the Prioress on all conceivable grounds—from the doctrinal to the deeply psychological.

The Prioress's closing apostrophe brings the historical truth of reverent innocence murdered from Asia to England by invoking "yonge Hugh of Lyncoln, slayn also / With cursed [that is, pitiless] Jewes, as it is notable" (ll. 684–85). She does this beseechingly, so that young Hugh might pray for us, we sinful folk "unstable," such that of his mercy the merciful God would, for reverence of Mary, multiply his mercy upon us. Mercy reiterated and multiplied for all who revere the Virgin—this stands in awkward but not inconsistent contrast to the righteous justice that obliterated the Jewish conspirators, lending credit to reader responses that focus in dismay on the tale's and the Prioress's anti-Semitism. Yet her righteousness is both brief and quickly left behind by the seven stanzas devoted to the boy's narrative of his miraculous life, in the telling of which mercy is invoked, first by the boy and then by the Prioress, a great mercy that excludes the twice pitiless and summarily destroyed murderers, whether Hugh's supposed killers or the little "clergeon's," but no one else.[24] Beyond this, Chaucer does not help his reader, although it is hard to think that he disbelieves this tale and the Marian intercession to which it witnesses. The *Tale of Melibee*, far from ironically qualifying the focus of the *Prioress's Tale* on severe justice, lends it support in the idea that those who lack mercy receive no mercy (a similitude of act and consequence). But, altogether, the spirit of the *Tale of Melibee* moves in a different direction—for which we can be glad. For it is truly better to think upon mercy and forgiveness than to stay with crime and punishment.

Chaucer has all of the pilgrims respond to the tale amazed; it was, Chaucer says, a wonder to see such sobriety. The telling of the "miracle" has worked a further miracle, bringing the entire company of pilgrims together in a moment of seriousness. Wonder begets wonder here in a surprising way, given a brief tale of pathos, crime and miracle, of punishment and then movement onward to an invocation of mercy. The tale is less a tiding of mixed truth and falsehood than it is a song analogous to the child's song of praise—its intense piety taken seriously. But not for long.

The Prioress, however we understand or criticize her, or even if we sympathize with her and find her endearing in her contradictions, is a fascinating character. To repeat, however, the tale itself as something other than a vehicle for encouraging the Prioress's responses confronts the reader. Surely we do not see or respond quite as the Prioress does, however much we may sympathize with aspects of her response. Do we find inspiration in the boy, in his joyful truth? Do we acknowledge the comedic power of a God who uses both Satan and cruel Jews to light the way for a saintly child? Chaucer will not answer these or any other questions. As elsewhere, the fiction is what we have, make of it what we will—credit it, revere it, believe that it contains truth as best we can. This is a hard tale for twentieth-century readers, a tale mainly defended as a testament to an affective piety that was sincere and moving in its time. Otherwise, the tale is often read as a satirical vehicle, undermining the Prioress by exhibiting hateful lore about Jews, a lack of mercy, a lack of operation by the New Law. Certainly the tale contains triumphant feeling and intensified language; a hymn of hard contrasts that praises the well of mercy and martyrdom while countenancing a severe justice. I think we are expected to be sobered along with the pilgrims, but crucially we know nothing about the content of that seriousness. Were the pilgrims awed, shocked, or dismayed? For a moment, were they rendered pious? All we really have is the wonder of their group seriousness, followed after a time by the Host's freedom to play. We do not have anything like the Host's response to the *Physician's Tale*, his sense of outrage and of the pity of it all. Instead, the *Tale of Melibee*, soon to follow after a burlesque interlude in the form of Chaucer's *Tale of Sir Thopas*, I think will turn from the Prioress's song to a prudential perspective, a perspective at best only nascent in her tale's references to soul-saving mercy.

These two tales form a pair of sorts: each shows a teller's concern for particular exchanges, as the Shipman thinks that "taillynge enough" is a good joke and as the Prioress would reward virginity and helpless innocence with martyrdom. Calculating bawdry is the ingredient of play in the one tale, with punning its rhetorical accompaniment, while piety is the earnestness of the other, with a rhetoric of effusion, of feeling, its accompaniment. As a virtue, prudence embraces both public and private spheres: it concerns relationships within the family, marriage, the community, and the kingdom.[25] Only a low prudence governs the action in the Shipman's tale and apparently prudence is no issue at all in the *Prioress's Tale*. We need to wait for the *Tale of Melibee* to see how crime might be treated and so how a large design can work out a greater law through even the cruelest of events.

7 ❦ *SIR THOPAS* AND *MELIBEE*: CHAUCER AT PLAY

lthough little more than an interrupted fancy, effectively an interlude between the *Prioress's Tale* and the *Tale of Melibee, Sir Thopas* offers an instance of sheer play, sheer literary humor—a rhyme tale "lerned longe agoon." Throughout Chaucer's formulaically "true" account of Sir Thopas's love-madness we face mirthful parody: a laughing, abusive imitation and reading of metrical romances.

> And so bifel upon a day,
> For sothe, as I yow telle may.
>> [ll. 748–49]

The "solas" this narrative provides is largely literary, as it pleases one's taste for deft burlesque. Indeed, the tale is a concocted romance with a ludicrous, bourgeois hero for a knight, a melange in his own right. Surely the question of truth and falsehood in fiction can be taken too seriously, pursued everywhere. Perhaps some tales "lerned" long ago are empty of truth, only aping parasitically the conventions of similar tales (Chaucer's parody, then, could be said to show how empty and laughable are all of those metrical tales learned by rote—those foolish romances with their bastardized conventions). Unlike pious songs, *Thopas* lacks significant purpose, fulfilling Chaucer's obligation but paying reverence to nothing beyond the class of tales parodied.

With a comical vengeance, Chaucer has indeed answered the Host's presumptuous, if jocular, attentions to his person—that he seems elfish and that his tale will be a "deyntee thyng," given his countenance. Boldly, the Host has ordered a tale of mirth, and that anon. Moreover, he has insisted on a merry look and has had fun at Chaucer's expense. Fun on demand? Can one genially insult someone and then demand amusement? And what is merriment anyway, for whom? When Chaucer agrees to tell a tale, he offers a rhyme learned long ago and so strikes a kind of bargain. Demanding a mirthful tale, the Host settles for a "deyntee thyng," while retaining the presumption of fun. This dainty featuring a knight whose face is as white as "payndemayn" and whose beard is like "saffroun" is indeed edible play, but not, as we eventually find out, pleasing to the Host's ears. It uses the quality of littleness that has marks of pathos in the *Prioress's Tale* and spreads it everywhere in metrical and narrative play. As we settle down with the tale, what we do not yet know is what will follow it—that narrative of sober teaching Chaucer has paired with his burlesque romance.

Given that pairing, are we prepared for "sentence" after "solas" according to a rhetorical model Chaucer could have taken from Boethius's *Consolation*? Recall that Lady Philosophy pairs song and "sentence," with rhetoric as light medicine, as song, preparing for the heavy medicine of dialectic. In *Thopas* and *Melibee* we see a curiously distorted reflection of that kind of pairing. The two tales indeed form a radicalized pairing of mirth and "sentence," but the one does not ready us emotionally for the other, unlike the effect upon Boethius of inspired song followed by an explanatory dialectic. There the song relates in content to the dialectic that follows: beauty and reverence prepare the mind for that understanding fostered by the dialectic of definitions. In effect, Boethian song arouses that delight and openness of belief necessary to an awakened understanding of truth.

But *Sir Thopas* functions dramatically as something to be stopped, as an annoyance that the Host, by stopping, changes into a transition to something else. Thus *Sir Thopas* and its endlink become an extensive preparation for a tale whose serious mate is the Prioress's. A burlesque becomes an interlude between differently dedicated tales of justice and wonder, as well as a reminder that some—perhaps countless—tales survive through no serious merit of their own. They are merely the whims of minstrels standing in large numbers outside the House of Fame, who tell tales "both of wepinge and of game" (l. 1199).

The Host is not himself ready mentally or emotionally for Dame Prudence's teachings, but he is bodily set up in a comical way. His ears are so offended by what he calls doggerel rhyme that his head begins to ache. To end that pain the Host stops Chaucer's recitation and complains loudly. In a sense he is prepared negatively to tolerate one kind of glad tale if only another kind of mirth (foolishness) will end. Perhaps this comical reflection of Lady Philosophy's pairing of song and dialectic—an auricular softening up preceding what it is good to hear (matter enforced with proverbs)—is as close as Chaucer comes in any pairing of tales to Lady Philosophy's rhetorical program.

The tale we will soon hear is certainly moral, but it has been told in various ways by various people. Chaucer calls it a "moral tale vertuous," already emphasizing its moral character and perhaps distinguishing it from such moral tales told viciously, as the Pardoner's tale. Although told in different ways, using more proverbs than one perhaps is used to, *Melibee* is a tale told with virtuous intent. Chaucer then proceeds to apologize for the number of proverbs in "this murye tale," given less laden versions (such as the "tretys lyte" upon which it is based), by reminding the reader that the apostles also differed in their words, in how they enforced their separate accounts of Christ's passion.

> "But nathelees hir sentence is al sooth,
> And alle acorden as in hire sentence,
> Al be ther in hir tellyng difference.
>
> . . . .
>
> Whan they his pitous passioun expresse—
>
> . . . .
>
> But doutelees hir sentence is al oon."
>   [ll. 946–52]

How can we doubt the final clause? To emphasize this point is to undermine matter-of-fact certainty, but that is as far as one can go here. Chaucer makes an interesting claim altogether: that in expressing pathos ("pitous passioun"), individual tales or tellings are idiosyncratic—similarly with the rhetorical act of using proverbs to enforce the "effect" of one's matter. The analogy is the point here, not any oblique reference to the doctrinal sameness of the Canterbury tales.[1] The general intention can remain the same given idiosyncratic differences in emotional emphasis and the number of arguments. Of course such differences in the "telling" can mean only local differences in exactly what is expressed or argued, differences of pathos and force. A moral tale told virtuously does not make its own way, independent of the telling. More proverbs or fewer, and where they are placed—these issues matter, since too much ornament can be a vice.[2]

Chaucer approaches the *Tale of Melibee* seriously, both as pilgrim character and as poet, judging from his additions to the source. But that approach is circumspect all the same, something that becomes clear in considering the tale's internal concern for persuasive rhetoric. The tale's premise is as follows: Melibeus goes out hunting one morning. In his absence, three enemies enter his house through the windows. They attack his daughter Sophie and his wife, Prudence, stabbing Sophie in the nose, ears, mouth, hands, and feet. Melibeus returns from his "desport" in the fields and encounters all this "meschief," a sight that drives him to rending his clothes and weeping and crying. Dame Prudence, rather than join him in sorrow and grief, tries to talk him out of immoderate weeping and suggests that he gather a counsel of his true friends so that he can be advised on what to do next. Her stance, from the beginning, is to counter Melibeus's impulses, in the course of which she uses many arguments and proverbs to support her case for moderation, patience, and mercy—those virtues that in part define a Christian ethos for this world, a way to live with one's fellows in good times and bad and a way to have something good come from something hurtful.[3]

Dame Prudence "enforces" the effect of her counsel with proverbs. But that enforcing sometimes has a negative effect on her focus; her sayings exist partly as ways of compelling Melibeus's assent at each stage in her merry engagement with him. They usually support her main contentions within a rhetorical mode of argumentation, but their numbers delay us tediously. They weaken Dame Prudence's focus, and they sometimes jostle each other uncomfortably for attention, contributing to a discontinuous, additive style within each section of her discourse. But that she speaks in prose and that she speaks in the premises and conclusions of proverbs—these "enforce" a significant effect: closeness to truth and therefore to good profit.[4]

The *Tale of Melibee*, then, offers true counsel aggressively packaged in a rhetorical mode, not a mode of transcendence or deliverance but one that relies on the authoritativeness of a multitude of good reasons (perhaps to counter Melibeus's multitude of bad counselors). Melibeus gives way at each turn, as do we all: once Prudence's premises are accepted, contrary arguments have very little force, serving primarily to rationalize prejudice and unreason (as when Melibeus argues against accepting woman's counsel). But by looking closely at the progress of the tale, we see that Dame Prudence, a noble wife, has a better capacity for truth than for compassion, that she is a wise, not an ideally balanced figure, but that she would have Melibeus see the right thing to do—with sight uninjured, Melibeus can begin to perceive and understand that which is wise. But first in his "desport" and then in his grief and anger, he does not hear well, speak well, or feel well, nor can he nose out the truth unaided. These are the areas in which his Sophie has been wounded and to which Prudence must administer her cure.[5]

Like the *Pearl* maiden's, Prudence's perspective is transcendental in relation to the emotional addressee. She does not live in this world of injury, grief, and revenge; hers is a world of wise sayings, old books and authorities, true words, and good. But sometimes Prudence is hard to take precisely because she is of this world in all her force, advising action, urging an ethical response. She is not beatific, and her language, unlike the *Pearl* maiden's, is not that of visionary signs. Rather it is the language of ethical argument, variously inspired and variously pagan and Christian. Like Aristotle's maxims, her proverbs are concerned in general ways with "the objects of human actions and with what should be chosen or avoided with reference" to those objects.[6]

The tale was popular in its day and may have appealed to a medieval taste for copia and the compendium. But it is not a dramatic fiction of character and action, although it shows some lines of development. Thus the heap of proverbs in any section is not a distraction in itself from plot or character. The thicket of proverbs is mainly a demonstration of good words, true and profitable, for the troubled great man, as well as a reminder that true words do not win their way readily, through bare statement. The psychology of this is presented as a simple one of yielding, of giving up emotion, and giving way to prudential considerations. Melibeus finally admits that he does not know how to answer "so manye faire resouns as ye putten to me and shewen" (l. 1711). But that yielding does not occur quickly or easily, and perhaps the key turn in it is Melibeus's respect for Prudence's beautiful reasons in conjunction with an awareness that he has no good reasons of his own. Add to that shame a measure or semblance of anger on Prudence's part, and Melibeus becomes eager first to do Prudence's will and then, after an outburst concerning his honor and public worth (worship), to accord his heart to her will, considering her truth and integrity.

Initially, I think, Melibeus should have our sympathies: the mischief his enemies have wrought is maddening and grievous. But instead of crying, Dame Prudence is all calm reasonableness. She "as ferforth as she dorste, bisoghte hym of his wepyng for to stynte" (l. 974). This only increases Melibeus's woe, whereupon Prudence recalls an opinion (a "sentence," hence a true opinion) from Ovid's *Remedie of Love* that only a fool disturbs a mother weeping for her dead child. The Ovidian context concerns the lover's withdrawal from love, from worldly affections in the Boethian sense—for which no remedy is good until the passion ceases. The appropriateness of this is curious. Apparently Melibeus's love for Sophie must run its grief-stricken course before Prudence can draw him away. The few references to Ovid in *Melibee* follow a similar course: either the world and its pleasures will seduce Melibeus, or he will seduce himself. Still, pathos is on Melibeus's side as he weeps; the ethical Prudence suffers him for a while.

Ever timely, she eventually questions him: "why do you carry on like a fool?"—hardly sympathetic words. Hard truth is her strength, not "routhe," although she has Melibeus's interests at heart, and she is no Manciple of clear-minded objectivity. Essentially, the tale's thematic dilemma appears in that harsh question: when weeping is immoderate, it becomes foolish; but just how does one reconcile sorrow and turmoil with true and profitable words? Somehow one does so through "mesure," an all-important term linked through one equivalent or another to moderation in feeling, wise counsel, patience, and, most importantly, to mercy. But doing anything in an "atempree" and non-"outrageous" way is a problem for Melibeus, whose passionate self-esteem and self-importance require repeated jolts from Prudence. Although not mean-spirited, Prudence does begin her discourse impatiently and almost ruthlessly (albeit in a positive if literal way). She does so by holding a different man against the sorrowing Melibeus, a man both wise and stoical.

Provoked, Melibeus wonders what manner of man would stop weeping when the cause is so grievous? Prudence replies by conceding a place in her scheme of things for "atempree" weeping, this time with appropriate arguments from Paul as well as Seneca, ending with a reference to Job and to Job's blessing on the Lord, who gives and who takes away (anticipating thoughts of injustice and the anger-disarming argument later that Melibeus has already been punished for his sins).

In response, Melibeus does little, other than to concede the truth and profit of what Prudence says. But his grief is real all the same, so much so that he is confused about what to do. The tale, however, is not a consolation; rather it is advice on how to act well in this world, and so the focus shifts clumsily but irrevocably from grief (which is a melancholy weeping one simply must abandon) to revenge (a dark and destructive passion). Prudence urges Melibeus to gather together a group of true friends and wise kindred. Instead, Melibeus summons a great congregation of folk among whom the words of wise advocates go unheeded. Melibeus's initial deafness to Prudence's stipulation of true friends and wise relatives is only one of several essentially linguistic deficiencies Prudence labors to repair. They are all centered on rightly hearing and therefore on understanding what is said (Melibeus's wisdom has been wounded in the ears as well as the mouth). Moreover, saying what accords with one's passions is to "mis-say" and to fall short of deeming—a mistake Melibeus makes when he reveals his desires to his bad counselors.

From this early point on, although Melibeus's need for revenge is at issue, the tale concerns words more than anything else: wise words, sweet words, words of honey, mistaken words and true, profitable words. By means of proverbs and other sweet words Dame Prudence triumphs in what becomes a case of "maistrye" through Prudence. She would restrain Melibeus's purpose and overcome him through reason. In response, Melibeus submits step by step: "And, wyf, by cause of thy sweete wordes, and eek for I have assayed and preved thy grete sapience and thy grete trouthe, I wol governe me by thy conseil" (l. 1114).

That submission comes after the first of two serious clashes between Melibeus and Prudence. She has counseled him, against the strong counsel for war of his parliament, not to proceed hastily—a key term, as we find out later, when hastiness is held up as one of the three deformers of judgment (along with anger and covetousness). She does not directly recommend against revenge, however, instead adopting a reverential posture ("in ful humble wise") that some readers have confused with pusillanimity.[7]

Melibeus answers her strongly, vowing not to work by her counsel, because doing so now, after the advice of his many counselors, would make him seem like a fool; because women are wicked; because he would not give "maistrie" to her; and because, being a woman, she would not keep his counsel secret. He leavens all of this with sayings from Solomon—to the effect that Solomon found a good man but in his search of all women no good woman—and Jesus the Syriac. Prudence takes all of this debonairly and with patience. She forbears what it "liked" him to say, and then she speaks, having asked permission. Her counters are several: that changing one's mind when the situation changes is no folly; that true opinion is the possession of the few who are wise and thoughtful ("ful of resoun"), not the multitude; that to say that all women are wicked is first to express a blanket despising, not truth, and then to fail one of the lessons of life in not humbly seeking knowledge wherever one can find it. Part of her response next is a brief meditation upon those words of Solomon concerning failure in the search for a good woman. She points out that it does not follow that all women are wicked. Moreover, she shifts terms and introduces a problematic, rhetorical dimension in suggesting that Solomon's intent may have been to say that of "sovereyn bounte" he found no woman (only God alone)—for everybody will be found lacking in comparison to God's perfection. Then she fields the issue of "maistrie" by saying that Melibeus retains free will in choosing to heed particular counsel or not, and that only women who gossip will betray secrets. Melibeus knows from frequent experience that Prudence is patient and keeps secrets, adding that the claim—which Melibeus did not quite make—that women through wicked counsel seek to vanquish men is inapplicable in the current situation. Here Prudence continues a rhetorical motif (what one might mean by what one says) by playing upon possible implications in the issue of "maistrie," as she would turn Melibeus away from a wicked purpose. Far from "vanquishing" him with wicked counsel, she would "overcome" him with "reson and by good conseil" (l. 1092). She says much more in the vindication of women and their wisdom, concluding that if Melibeus would trust her counsel, she would heal his daughter and bring him honor "in this cause." The appeal to honor can only be a calculated tribute to Melibeus's status as a nobleman.

When Melibeus hears all of this, he *sees* and understands something—how it is that sweet words, well ordered and discreetly spoken, nourish the soul and bring health to the body. Prudence's words do this for him, reviving memories of the many times in which he has assayed and proved her great sapience and integrity. For that reason, and because of her sweet words, he vows to govern himself by her counseling. Prudence's "song" has brought Melibeus to a recovery of his better knowledge and a staying of his wicked purpose. But rather than song preparing for dialectic and philosophy, here it prepares Melibeus for practical advice and considered action. Melibeus's truculence sparks Prudence's strong-minded reply, but she comes out where she wants to—staying Melibeus from his decision to make war. Now she will instruct him in what she meant initially in urging him to gather together true counselors and a wise kindred.

This brings her to an evaluation of judgment and of the things that warp one's powers of deeming, given her insistence that first one must seek God's counsel and then take counsel in oneself. Anger, along with ire and wrath, affects judgment badly. So does covetousness. The third misshaper of judgment is hastiness.

Anger disposes one to speak vicious words, to stir up others and, in general, to think of doing things one may not or cannot do. The angry person does not judge well, hence cannot well counsel himself or herself. This is true also of the coveting person, who can judge and think only in relation to covetous purposes—a greed that can never be fulfilled. The hasty person misdeems because he or she acts on sudden thoughts rather than deliberating, being affected by moods that in turn can radically alter a sense of what it is good to do. Here, clearly, strong and sudden feelings are held to affect thought and action, changing one's objectives, perceptions, and understanding. The immediate antidote is an inward searching and reflectiveness, based ultimately on hope in God's counsel and involving a moderation of feeling. If reduced to cool calculation, however, this moderation can lead to a hard-heartedness, an unwillingness to do more than is minimally required by the law, with one's enemies. We can see here the prosaic outlines of a generous, open "reading" of anything, whether the truth of a political situation and therefore what it is best to do, or the truth of a tiding and therefore what it is best to think.

But neither Melibeus nor the reader of this tale is yet free from the struggle in which Prudence is engaged. She must still lead Melibeus through several redefinitions and yieldings before his heart accords with hers. At the moment she undertakes a backward-looking account of the choosing of counselors—her eye clearly enough on Melibeus's many mistakes in his gathering of what could be called a parliament of folly. He did not listen to old and experienced men; he included flatterers, whose words of "sweetness and pleasure" are said to ensnare rather than heal (a set of restrictions that would narrow confusion over the different sweetnesses of words). And he did not eschew the counseling of old, now reconciled enemies, which does not contradict the good of reconciling oneself with repentant enemies, although Prudence goes on to cite Peter Alfonce against doing "bountee" with one's enemies, who will pervert one's kindness into wickedness (l. 1189). Her arguments seem jarring here because, ultimately, some kind of reconciliation with Melibeus's enemies is at stake. But rather than blame this on waywardness in the text or on the ill-assorted nature of some of her proverbs, we should note that her citations from Cato, Seneca, Solomon, and Peter Alfonce emphasize the "enemy" in old enemies and the seemingness of apparent reconciliation. As a class, reconciled enemies require wariness, although genuinely repentant enemies deserve mercy.

After covering the topics of would-be counselors who are servants, drunks, or hypocrites, Dame Prudence adopts a forward-looking view and addresses the issue of assaying one's counselors and their advice, arriving at a general rule that any counsel urged so strongly as to forbid being changed is wicked. Melibeus then interrupts her and asks her to critique his assembly of counselors—not having understood the implications in her discourse on untrustworthy counselors. She humbly begs his leave and his patience for what she is about to say; then she picks up each issue again, including

Melibeus's own deforming passions (anger, covetousness, hastiness). She leads him to admit that he has erred, after which he begins rightly to adopt the way of the proverb himself in arguing for the good of changing his counselors. He is partly healed, but still his understanding needs to be worked on.

Prudence undertakes that further healing by raising the issues of contraries curing contraries and of what it means to garrison one's house. She corrects Melibeus's understanding of these matters by emphasizing that "suffraunce" is the opposite of revenge and that a rich man's best garrison is the love of his subjects and his neighbors. This brings her to an important issue concerning Melibeus's continuing emotionalism, his continuing grievance. Basically, his anger is unwarranted because he has been punished in this affair for his own involvement in the senses and his forgetfulness of Christ. In this connection, the attack of the three enemies is likened to the successful assault of the world, the flesh, and the devil on Melibeus's senses, an assault that penetrates to his soul much as the attackers enter his house through the windows and sorely wound Sophie. Given Sophie's wounds, this is not a perfect analogy; and it is awkward when we consider that eventually Prudence will lead Melibeus to a reconciliation with his enemies. Donald Howard has solved the problem by distinguishing the three *sources* of temptation from the three *human* enemies upon whom Melibeus would revenge himself.[8] The idea of "source" here is inspired, for Prudence has given an Aristotelian reading of causes for Melibeus's suffering: the originating cause is God; the near cause is his three enemies. So, of course, the three human enemies are not literally the world, the flesh, and the devil. Moreover, to be reconciled to their repentance is also to be reconciled with God. This exegesis is crucial to Prudence's argument because it undermines Melibeus's righteousness absolutely. If his suffering is just, he has no right to be angry. This essentially Aristotelian point, however, does not yet reach Melibeus's consciousness, despite his claim to see well what Prudence is doing. Indeed, at this point he sees her principally as willfully trying to master him with her many words—not sweet words to his ears—so that he will not revenge himself upon his enemies. We are more than halfway through the tale and Melibeus is still very sick, especially as he now emphasizes the evil of leaving wicked men unpunished.

In line with her various redefinings, Dame Prudence responds by translating vengeance as the accomplishment of justice, not by individuals, but by judges, who sin if they do no vengeance upon those who deserve it. We are now back in the world of the *Prioress's Tale* and therefore of the prudence that works justice "by the lawe." But Melibeus does not care for this kind of vengeance; rather, he would trust to the fortunes of war, supposing further that with God's help fortune will help him to avenge his shame. This establishes a relatively brisk counterpoint in which Prudence counsels against reliance upon unstable, unsteadfast fortune, offering trust in God's power instead (seizing upon Melibeus's hope in God's help). Melibeus replies with a version of his earlier common sense in a brutal world: if one suffers one act of villainy, one invites more—potentially so much more that one may be unable to survive the onslaughts. Prudence then grants Melibeus a point: overmuch "suffraunce" is not good; but it does not follow that every act of villainy should be avenged. Melibeus has cited a writing that says that if one does not avenge a villainy, one will invite or summon additional villainies. Dame Prudence reinterprets this not as a writing, a proverb, but as meaning the self-traducement of judges, who then do not simply "invite" more villainy but indeed "commandeth and biddeth" sin. She sticks to her point about revenge left to the courts and then undertakes a long argument for the good of patience, beginning with the thought that Melibeus has not considered his adversaries well or their strengths.

Melibeus shrugs off her argument by admitting that patience is a great virtue but that he is no saint. Moreover, he feels that despite committing an "outrage" in taking vengeance, he will put himself into only a little peril. This provokes Prudence's reply that Melibeus is still willful and only seeks his pleasure, which is to sin. Melibeus counters with the notion that there is no marvel in what he would do, as he is going about his own business, having been grievously touched and discommoded. He will trust in his riches to see him through the war he intends to wage.

Prudence takes up that gambit by instructing Melibeus in the proper use of riches: they should be used by "mesure" and in an openness that recalls the Franklin's generosity; that is, one's goods and one's house should be opened "by pitee and debonairetee." As for wealth and war, the man who desires and wills war shall never have "suffisaunce," for the richer he is, the more expense he must undertake if he is to have "worship and victorie." This point is telling in that it both undermines trust in sheer riches and contradicts the definition of "gentilesse" given a few lines earlier—that a "gentil" man would see to his good name in a godly way, for real victory in this world lies in the will of God, not in armies or in the power of man. Prudence's transvaluation of Melibeus's thinking and her redefining of terms continues through all of this and completes the present exchange

as she asserts that war always brings great, not little, peril and that he who
loves peril (rather than God) shall die by peril.

This point stops Melibeus for a time, although he still sees Dame Prudence as opposing his will and desire with hers. The idea of war is not one
of her pleasures, but he would know what she would have him do. She
jumps at this chance to say what that is: he should accord himself with his
enemies and have peace with them, supporting her point with quotations
from James and Christ. Melibeus responds sharply, "seeing well" now that
she is no respector of his honor and worship. This seemingly angers Dame
Prudence, who undertakes a final redefinition—focused this time on what
Melibeus's true honor and worship are, which is the purchasing of peace
and reconciliation. Her apparent anger cows Melibeus, who now puts what
he should do into her hands, according to her desire. He rationalizes his
move by evaluating himself in her terms—that he is still an angry man
who therefore does not well know what he does or says. The troubled have
no clear sight, he says, so he turns the clear seeing and doing over to Prudence. This is good, as far as it goes. But as long as Melibeus is still blinded
and deformed in his judgment, he will have trouble with Prudence's advice,
even though he is now ready to perform her will.

She counsels him to make peace with God, who will then send Melibeus's adversaries to him, repentant. Moreover, she will go to his enemies
and speak with them, becoming an active mediator who works it so that the
reconciliation occurs. This is her finest hour, although she does manipulate
both the adversaries and Melibeus (the latter by misrepresenting to him his
adversaries' willingness to suffer "all peyne").

In a sense, Dame Prudence becomes a worldly wise Mary, an intercessor
between the enemies and her lord, Melibeus. Melibeus grants to her will
and pleasure the task of bringing his adversaries around, putting himself—
his honor and worship—wholly in her hands, her "disposicioun and ordinaunce" (l. 1725). He leaves the outcome up to her plan and to her benign
influence (as though she were an astrological sign). At an appropriate time
she sends for Melibeus's adversaries and in effect speaks to them about
peace and war, presumably, much as she has labored over these matters for
Melibeus. But instead of arguing for an accord and reconciliation only, she
urges repentance of the wrongs they have done to Melibeus, to herself, and
her daughter. Her showing and saying are so wise and goodly that the adversaries are surprised and ravished—so much so that their joy of her is a
wonder to tell. In that wonder-provoking mood, they praise Prudence for
having shown them the blessing of sweetness (Psalm 20.4), proclaiming

that now they "see well" how true is the wisdom of Solomon when he said that "sweete wordes multiplien and encresscen freendes, and maken shrewes to be debonaire and meeke" (l. 1740, translating Ecclus. 6.5). Joy recalls God's glorification of a king (often read as Christ's glorification after the Passion); but that joyful feeling leads directly to perception and an understanding of the truth of old words—words from Ecclesiasticus that concern the fruits of wisdom within a context of chapters devoted to the good of charity and the folly of relying on wealth and strength.

Much of Prudence's discourse with Melibeus is encapsulated in their sudden, felt understanding. They are ready now to put themselves in Prudence's hands, although they worry about Melibeus's possible anger toward them. Prudence admits that it is perilous to put oneself into the hands of one's enemy, but she can assure them that because Melibeus is "debonaire and meeke, large, [and] curteys," that therefore he is not covetous. She uses their Solomonic truth, reversing only the order of terms (debonaire and meke), and she then adds that Melibeus desires only worship and honor. They then put themselves fully into her will and disposition, doing as Melibeus has already done.

In the reconciliation scene, the adversaries, through the voice of the wisest of the three, sue for mercy and pity as they repentantly submit and ask for forgiveness. Melibeus benignly lifts them up, accepts their sureties, and has them return upon a certain day to receive what shall be done to them. Public contrition and guarantees accord the adversaries to Melibeus. Worship and honor have been preserved, so what is left? At this late point in the tale, Melibeus still wants to punish: he intends to disinherit and exile the repentant three! Apparently Prudence is not right to say that Melibeus has no covetousness left.

She upbraids him for that cruel judgment and inveighs against "coveitise," saying that it is against the earning of a good name (honor)— the earning of which requires continual renewal—and that Melibeus's judgment amounts to a misuse of power. Instead, he should deem more "curteisly," conserving his good name by showing pity and mercy: let mercy be in his heart to "th' effect and entente that God Almighty have mercy on yow in his laste juggement" (l. 1868). Her arguments now move him, now incline him to her will; he does something more than simply give her leave of some kind. In his heart, not simply in his mind, he conforms himself to her will and agrees to work as she counsels, thanking God for a wife of such great discretion. Yet this lesson of mercy, even taken to heart, is not joyfully internalized and acted upon. Melibeus does forgive his adversaries and he does receive them unto his grace. But he does so constrainedly, as though acted upon—"it constreyneth me to doon yow grace and mercy" (l. 1880). The heart can conform one's will to right thinking and doing, but the ways of mercy are not easy for the lords of this world. Such is the hard truth of Prudence's encounter with Melibeus, a truth that points simultaneously to the difficulties of human deeming, given human desires, and to the ineffable goodness of God, who

> is so free and so merciable
> that he wole foryeven us oure giltes
> and bryngen us to the blisse that nevere hath ende.
>   [ll. 1886–88][9]

Unlike the Parson's promised meditation, the Pilgrim Chaucer's little treatise appears in the middle of things, a merry tale that implicitly confronts the Prioress's tale of justice and miracle with a secular working out that is good to think upon. The *Tale of Melibee* also dominates the fragment in which it appears, explicitly raising the theme of prudence to a copious and weighty level. But where does this leave the reader in the game of tale telling and in the question of response to the tales? Does a virtue concerning how we should act in all of our personal, social, official, and spiritual affairs help in coming to terms with truth in fiction and with the problems of perceiving and understanding that truth? Clearly, prudence is a notable business and not without significant, affective content: the counsel of prudence can bring joy and understanding to the heart, moving the affected soul to act appropriately. But in itself, prudence does not dictate the content of thought; Prudence involves an appropriate readiness to seek the good and prepares the heart for understanding words that previously must have seemed to be simply opinion. Thus prudence is at the heart of that reverential openness with which Chaucer entertains truth in fiction, although it does not allow us to disentangle the true from the false analytically. Instead, prudence is a disposition to believe in the possibilities of reconciliation; its axis includes noble "gentilesse" and spiritual "suffraunce." As a meeting place of mind and heart, it takes in mildness, generosity, "pitee," and meekness; when applied to God as "debonairetee," it means a noble, generous mercy. Indeed, these terms might be reduced to two: to be prudent fully is to be "debonaire and meeke": generous and courteous, unafflicted in one's deemings by the vices of anger, covetousness, and hastiness. A fully prudential state of heart and mind is a prerequisite for any full understanding of whatever situation or truth claim one confronts.

The *Tale of Melibee* is Chaucer's because the poet wants to stress the noble end for all reading and tale telling—being moved to understand truth in a way that leads to something worthy and good. To read prudently is to read "debonairly," in an openness of spirit and feeling, not narrowly in a self-reflecting or self-serving way, not hastily, not angrily, not covetously; in short, not as the Host does in his parodic conjuring of domestic bullying.

Noisily, the Host exclaims that his wife is certainly no Dame Prudence, no benign or gracious lady. What follows is a characterization of his wife, essentially, as Dame Prudence's antithesis at a literal level and as a comical similitude at a figurative level. An intimidating physical presence, Harry's wife is the bully manifestation and the intellectual inversion of Dame Prudence. Goodelief masters Harry with her "earmes big," rather than with proverbs. Moreover, in her way she moderates Harry's temper, mainly because he dare not withstand her. I think Chaucer does not endorse this parody as his response to Prudence and "hire benignytee," but there is something lively in the flesh of this comical sketch:

> "whan I bete my knaves,
> She bryngeth me forth the grete clobbed staves,
> And crieth, 'Slee the dogges everichoon,
> And brek hem, bothe bak and every boon!'
> And if that any neighebor of myne
> Wol nat in chirche to my wyf enclyne,
> Or be so hardy to hire to trespace,
> Whan she comth hoom she rampeth in my face,
> And crieth, 'False coward, wrek thy wyf!
> By corpus bones, I wol have thy knyf,
> And thou shalt have my distaf and go spynne!'"
> [ll. 1897–1907]

Goodelief—her name perhaps a joke on wifely "benignitee"—appears here in a hurly-burly far removed from Prudence's sweet and wise words. For a moment, at least, our ears ring with the colloquial energy of quoted anger as the Host calls up a shrew who would turn his household upside down. This carnival moment threatens to eclipse Prudence and the treatise in which she expresses so many good "sentences." In the Host's voluble

confession of domestic shrewisness, Prudence and her words recede into a
version of unreality. Somehow the comical anger, covetousness, and hastiness that misshape the Host's deemings and those of his good wife are
more palpable and attractive than Prudence's "debonairetee," at least in
this world of bone and flesh. Having lived, by this point, with Prudence's
engagement of Melibeus for a long time, I think Chaucer the reader senses
that *his* readers have grown appropriately restless. They have been away
too long from the noisy world and from the problems of coping with
everyday passion and lowly confusion. Of course, it is best to form our
opinions prudently, not as the Host does in assuming that patience is the
truth Prudence incarnates or as Goodelief does; but it is attractive to be,
once again, in a world of energy and comical distortion. Having set his
monument to good reason and wise counsel into the middle of this fragment, Chaucer can now, perhaps even cavalierly, take us into entertainments for the eyes and ears. But he will not have us stray too far for too
long, although the transition between *Melibee* and the *Monk's Tale* is
more extensive than any other Chaucer provides between tales, unless we
count *Sir Thopas* as a link between the *Prioress's Tale* and Chaucer's
Melibee; or even more impressively, unless we see the *Monk's Tale* itself
as a link primarily between *Melibee* and the *Nun's Priest's Tale.*

8 ❦ THE *MONK'S TALE* AND THE *NUN'S PRIEST'S TALE*: DILIGENT ''SENTENCE,'' GOODLY PLAY

═══════════════════════════════════════

The last of three pairs of tales in Fragment 7, the *Monk's Tale* and the *Nun's Priest's Tale* are more closely related in subject matter than is the case with the other pairs, and each reflects the theme of prudence. The *Nun's Priest's Tale* plays on ideas of tragedy and fortune, punning structurally on such aspects of the Monk's conventional formulas as the fall from high estate and the blindness of the victim: Chauntecleer descends from his perch to the dangers of the barnyard and blindly argues an interpretation of his dream that he later fails to heed. Figures in particular tragedies reappear in the Nun's Priest's obtrusive rhetoric—Nero and Cresus directly, Adam and Balthazar implicitly—and the Monk's ubiquitous rhetorical device, the ''ensample,'' reappears in Chauntecleer's reply to Pertelote's humoral theory of dreams.[1] Prudence enters each tale as a theme within this context of blindness and fall: the Monk's tale is a series of briefly narrated tragedies in which the central figure often does not act well (or ''see well,'' to use a key phrase from *Melibee*); the tragedies themselves are meant as warnings against trusting in blind prosperity; those warnings apply equally to Chauntecleer—who may be the Nun's Priest's lively answer to the Monk's ''ensamples,'' much as Pertelote, with her advice and laxatives, seems a parodic response to Dame Prudence and her medicinal words.

But before considering the two tales in full, the Monk's tale should be seen in relation to *Melibee*, especially so given the Host's bawdy expectation, as voiced in a prologue that becomes his most extensive performance in the collection. Half of that link begins with the Goodelief passage and moves to speculation about both the Monk's name and his sexual prowess.

The Host comically laments the departure from human breeding stock of such brawny, masterful roosters as the Monk:

> "Religioun hath take up al the corn
> Of tredyng, and we borel men been shrympes."
>
> [ll. 1954–55]

His conceit of the monk as a "tredefowel aright" is energetic and pointed, if not calculated to offend. That it might offend, however, is a thought the Host anticipates and would disarm:

> "But be nat wrooth, my lord, though that I pleye.
> Ful ofte in game a sooth I have herd seye!"
>
> [ll. 1963–64]

The immediate point of this in the context of the tales is to highlight emotional response to verbal aggressiveness; unlike Melibeus's response to his adversaries, the Monk indeed does not respond angrily, but patiently— promising to do in all diligence as the Host has commanded. He will tell a tale, or two, or three, thus passing over without comment the Host's thirty-four-line speculation on the Monk's manliness and sexual prowess. By addressing the Monk initially as "my lord daun John, / Or daun Thomas, or elles daun Albon" (ll.1929–30), the Host perhaps anticipates the Shipman's Master John come to life. But Chaucer's Master Piers resolutely elects to disappear somewhat into *Melibee* rather than to reincarnate the sexual spirit of fabliaux. Instead of sexual comedy, there will be tragedies of fortune, partially brought about by sexual contact and corruption.

Prudence offers a section on fortune in which she counsels Melibeus against assaying fortune and believing that she will help him avenge his shame. She quotes Seneca as saying that things done in folly and in the hope of fortune shall never come to a good end; for the more clear and the more shining fortune is, the more brittle and sooner broken is she. Fortune is an unsteadfast, unstable woman, who plays the man she nurtures for a fool. Instead of trusting in fortune, then, one should have recourse to God, the Sovereign Judge, and to the vengeance that is his.

This should well suit the manly abbot, although putting one's faith in God's protection and justice is not quite his solution. His wariness of fortune is prudent, but his analysis of causes for the fall of the powerful and the wealthy is personally revealing, such that where he places trust becomes a mistake and therefore exceedingly imprudent.

The Monk's definition of tragedy is conventional. Chaucer glosses tragedy in the same way in his *Boethius*,[2] but the Monk's view is too restrictive and without significant affect. He neither places these tragedies within a philosophical framework nor interests himself in the wretchedness and pathos to which the noble can fall, although he frequently laments their loss of strength, power, and glory. His definition of tragedy reflects the activity of mindless fortune, although the Monk does proceed in most cases in a personally revealing way.

Both in apostrophes and in some of his phrasings, especially for such manly figures as Samson, Alexander, and Caesar, the Monk reveals attitudes that may explain his devotion to riding out rather than staying in the cloister. He neither ennobles any of the tragedies he tells nor understands them empathetically as part of the human condition, perhaps seen finally as serving God's divine comedy.[3] As he says, he would warn against trusting blind prosperity; but what he says in his personal emphases often conveys the opposite—a way of life safe, in the Monk's opinion, against tragedy.

As he has warned us, he does appear to think of various tragedies in a scattered way: never taking an overview, he simply calls up story after story, confusing misfortune cruel and simple with divine punishment, and working associatively in a way that reveals his highly unreflective, imprudent sense of security. He seems to say that by not trusting in prosperity, lordship, power, or *women*, we shall be safe.[4] He of course reacts to *Melibee* simply in his choice of subject, but he also reacts to Prudence's championing of women. Prudence wants Melibeus to accept her advice, and so she attacks his antifeminist arguments, asserting that jasper is better than gold, wisdom better than jasper, and woman better than wisdom—with nothing better than a good woman (l. 1108). The Monk, however, depicts women who are treacherous and who cannot keep a secret (Delilah) and Woman as misfortune (Lady Fortuna). Moreover, and interestingly in light of the Host's speculations about the Monk's virility, we learn that sex may well disgust this Monk and that only chaste and manly women (Cenobia) win his approval. Perhaps this worthy Monk suffers the Host's lewd comedy in more "pacience" than is apparent.

Although the Monk does not progress in a straightforward way, themes emerge from his examples, and he does circle around key notions. In a sense, his "ensamples" are both neutral tales—with internal, teller responses (usually through apostrophe)—and rhetorical responses in their entirety, especially perhaps for tales that occupy only a stanza or two. To what are they responses? I argue that they are formulations by which the

Monk protects himself, in his "celle" and "cope," against disheartening meditations upon fortune and tragedy. Thus textual detail might in itself bespeak the Monk's character, although I will proceed and do little more than pose possibilities where the Monk fails to respond directly to any aspect of the brief tale he narrates.

The Monk begins with tragedies of will—sketches of Lucifer and Adam, neither one a tragedy of Fortune.[5] Lucifer falls because of his sin and is forever entwined with misery in hell. But perhaps in anticipation of later emphases, Lucifer receives a line of lament for the brightness he has lost. After the first rebel, the first man comes to mind—Adam, that man wrought of "Goddes owene fynger" and not "bigeten of mannes sperme unclene" (ll. 2008–9). Adam loses his "hye prosperitee" because of mis-governance, presumably in heeding Eve rather than God. But the Monk does not mention Eve, dwelling only on Adam's Edenic creation by God's finger. Although conventional enough, disgust potentially guides that otherwise matter-of-fact notion of unclean sperm, a notion that may have led the Monk to lordship in monastic chastity rather than to women and marriage. Perhaps Adam sets the Monk's pattern for most of the privileged: men who do not govern themselves well; men who heed women and fall into misery.

The role of women becomes overt in the next two sketches, devoted respectively to Samson and Hercules. The unblinded Samson is everything the Monk admires: "consecrat" to God, noble, strong, hardy, clever, and mighty in battle. But he begins his undoing, and falls to blindness and slavery, by telling his secret to his wife. This brings him to "meschaunce," and never mind that Delilah is his mistress as well as his wife. Sight, potency, and great power—these go together as a state of being independent of confidences with women. The Monk apostrophizes Samson's folly and warns us in direct address. The lesson is general: wives are likely to be wanton and untrustworthy, therefore no man should tell his counsel to his wife of such things as he would keep secret, especially if it concerns his life and limb (ll. 2091–94). In high pathos, the Monk apostrophizes twice over Samson: first when characterizing Samson as simultaneously noble, almighty, beloved and dear—a status superior to all others in the world, had he not told his secret to a woman; and again in lamenting Samson's blindness and slavery as a condition abjectly in contrast to his former nobility, strength, and glorious, wealthy governorship. The pathos here does not run to the conditions of wretchedness but in lament for the strength and glory lost because of a woman's treachery. In his first disagreement with

Prudence, Melibeus nearly anticipates this point when he quotes Solomon as advising that no husband should give power over his life to wife, child, or friend. Furthermore, Melibeus argues, to work by Prudence's counsel is to have his counsel secret sometimes and sometimes not. Prudence wins the moment with her various arguments, including her reminder that Melibeus has often assayed her and found her trustworthy. The Monk, however, has no wifely reminder to jog his memory. Indeed, when it comes to that, his "ensamples" of women betraying men are all the memory he has. By adopting Melibeus's position, he adopts an unprudential one, having heeded the narrow counsel of his bad "ensamples." But rather than misdeem out of anger and a desire for revenge, he proceeds hastily out of a need to justify his own disposition, his own sense of how one can secure oneself against misfortune.

For the Monk, plain truth is obvious in the case of Delilah's treachery. It is also apparent in the story of Hercules, although here one cannot with certainty know that Dejanira poisoned Hercules deliberately. In any case, she did give him the poisoned shirt, and he eventually died. The moral is that no one can trust in Fortune: again, in direct address, he would have us

> Beth war, for whan that Fortune list to glose,
> Thanne wayteth she her man to overthrowe
> By swich a wey as he wolde leest suppose.
>   [ll. 2140–42]

He is wise who can know himself, the Monk interjects, as he laments Hercules's downfall, that mighty flower of strength and hunter of monsters, brought low by a highly lamented shirt his mistress gave him, wittingly or not. The Monk, because some authorities excuse Dejanira, will not accuse her.

> Be as be may . . .
> But on his bak this sherte he wered al naked.
>   [ll. 2129–30]

She is the instrument of a female fortune that will flatter and deceive a man, waiting for the least likely time to overthrow him. In this context, knowing oneself can only mean not knowing women. Not knowing women and not accepting their possibly dangerous gifts can make one proof against Fortune's "glosing."

At least security against fortune can be had, if one also avoids pride, an issue in the next two sketches, devoted respectively to Nebuchadnezzar and to Balthazar. Mistress fortune recedes for a time as the Monk dwells on a Nebuchadnezzar so proud that he disdains God. That pride, of course, suggests Lucifer's sin and also implies a remedy after a pattern seen in Nebuchadnezzar's life. Although Nebuchadnezzar presumes that no power can deprive him of his own, God sees to his sudden loss of "dignytee" and consequent mortification: Nebuchadnezzar turns into something like a beast. He eats hay, his hair becomes like feathers, and his nails become like birds' claws. This terrible metamorphosis downward, however, does not last. God releases Nebuchadnezzar from grotesquerie, for which Nebuchadnezzar thanks God and lives forever after in fear of doing amiss. So in knowing oneself, the advice and company of women should certainly be eschewed and God dreaded and thanked, knowing that he has dominion over everything. That knowledge restores Nebuchadnezzar to his wits. Implicitly, both women and pride can become part of, or lead to, wretchedness and madness. Women would be the worst part of this bargain, however, since neither Samson nor Hercules recovers.

Balthazar not only never learns the lesson of pride from his father, but he becomes both an idolator and a blasphemous whoremonger, defiling God's sacred vessels with his wives and wenches and castrating the fairest children of royal Israelites, enslaving them. However, the pathetic misfortune is not the point, for the wise, young Daniel reads Balthazar's dream and predicts Balthazar's doom, given God's handwriting on the wall. As with Samson, a godliness in one's unmanly slavery can bring about a reversal. Sure enough, the following night brings the Persians and Darius. Darius occupies the kingdom and slays Balthazar, an event that brings the Monk to moralize on the uncertainty of lordship, "How that in lordshipe is no sikernesse" (l. 2240). For when Fortune will forsake a man she takes away his kingdom, his riches, his friends, and his life. The Monk's vision is not steady in many of these tales as he insists on moralizing them in terms of women or fortune. He does not see that in Balthazar's case God has punished a wanton and blasphemous idolator. And although God may act through Fortune, the moral should concern God, not Fortune's devastating whimsy. Instead, the Monk would teach us the well-known and proverbial truth that "Mishap wol maken . . . enemys" of a man and what that man has through Fortune (ll. 2244–45). The Monk believes in "sikernesse" in God, but his piety is that of the man who comforts himself with the thought that he has done the right things—avoided women, consecrated himself to God—and can therefore rest easy in his lordship, having taken on a monastic "cope" in eschewing the world's.

Perhaps the mention of Persians brings the Monk to his next example: his only tragedy about a woman. Cenobia, queen of Persia, is so keen in warfare that no one can surpass her in hardiness, nobility, or "gentilesse." The Monk seems to approve entirely of this woman, whose virtue in no way inclines her to lechery or pride or even to ordinary womanliness (the Monk does not claim that she is the fairest of women, but her shape cannot be "amended"). She is a man's woman from her beginnings until nearly her end; the Monk finds that in childhood she flees the "office" of women and undertakes the life of a chaste and virgin huntress. Like Hercules, she slays wild and powerful beasts. And like Hercules her undoing comes through the instrumentality of the opposite sex. As a woman she is an exception in the Monk's cases, but she also proves the rule: a man is undone by his wife or else by his "lemman"; Cenobia by her mate, Odenake.

After living happily for a time as a huntress, always keeping her maidenhood, she at last allows her friends to prevail such that she agrees to marry Odenake, a Persian prince. They settle down and live in joy and felicity, aside from one prohibition: that in no way will she sleep with Odenake except to procreate a child in the most parsimonious way possible: they will conjugate once; if no pregnancy ensues, they will do it again, repeating this process only until two children are born. She needs Odenake for this, but probably both she and the Monk would be happier if child bearing could occur immaculately. Although she has married, the Monk nevertheless asserts emphatically that in this world there was no "creature" who was more "worshipful," wise, generous, moderate, virtuous, hardy, martial, and courteous. She is Prudence's ideal vision of her own lord, the Melibeus she presents to his adversaries. But, in addition to her love of moral philosophy and languages, she conquers earthly kingdoms and cities also (in concert with Odenake). Had she never married, she would not have achieved a vast empire; had Odenake not died, she would have continued to rule that empire with him, unmolested. But Odenake does die, and she is now alone and vulnerable because of her many victories—having, in these mighty excursions, aroused Rome's attentions. For a time her hardiness prevails as she defeats various challenges. Then Aurelian becomes emperor of Rome and sets his legions against her.

Her husband's death left her weak compared to their combined strength and compared to her obscure singularity before marriage. But perhaps for the Monk the deeper tragedy is that Cenobia is not a man despite her ferocity and virtue. Certainly she is not a mere woman or wife, but her capture by Aurelian marks her fall from strength and rule to ordinary, womanly

weakness. However, the Monk does not dwell on the process here, referring us instead to "maister Petrak" if we want to know about her woe. The
pathos of undeserving suffering is not the Monk's strength, although he
dwells on the pitiable contrast between the queen she was and the woman
to which military defeat and capture reduce her. The Monk tells us that she
exchanges her sceptre for a distaff and her royal helmet for a woman's cap,
lamenting this change from great power to the object of plebeian stares.
She has been uncrowned, her power beheaded, much as Samson loses his
hair, his power, and his eyesight. Implicitly, the Monk is telling us that in
marriage, even as austere a marriage as Cenobia has with Odenake—one
without any regular paying of the marriage debt—one enters the world of
fortune, danger, blindness, and eventual wretchedness.

Robinson's text has the so-called modern cases next, a shift from
Cenobia and the third century that makes some sense associatively, especially if one supposes that these cases extend the Monk's lament for good
figures brought low through no apparent defect of their own. He focuses
now on men undone by relatives, friends, or corrupt bishops. All of the
modern figures are noblemen or kings, Christians if you will, but none is
monastically devoted to God. The Monk briefly laments their fates, en-
livening only the story of Hugelino from within. The imprisoned children,
all little, elicit the Monk's greatest pity, beginning with the first stanza in
which fortune is lamented for the great cruelty that put such "briddes" in
such a cage. The pathos is then dramatized through both indirect and direct
discourse in the stanzas that follow, as Hugelino realizes that they will be
starved to death and as his three-year-old son first wonders why his father
weeps, then wonders why there is no food, and then bids his father farewell
in his dying breath. Six stanzas of understated pathos end in a seventh that
seems sufficient to the Monk. For the full story, there is the great Italian
poet, Dante, who will not fail the curious in a single point or word. This
recourse to his sources, repeated several times in the tale, indicates his essential belief in the truth of his stories and in his own, editorial purpose: to
diminish the stories in the service of his repeated theme—from high estate,
Fortune takes one away, having, in Hugelino's case, grimly "carved" him
away much as he himself gnawed on his own arms. Pathos for the innocent
children, however, does not transfer strongly to Hugelino himself, who
starves to death and thus ends. The Monk reserves his feelings still for
those victims of Fortune who, without wantonness, enjoyed great lordship
and power, independent of women or lovers.[6]

Nero is not an example of such lordship, but his perversity delays the

Monk, who delivers one of the longest of his tragedies. The Monk wonders at Nero's wantonness and cruelty, especially toward his mother, moralizing that when might is joined to cruelty, the venom goes deep. This suggests that Nero was once otherwise, unbitten, uncruel, and so the Monk fashions this tragedy into a fall from supple, virtuous youth—led by the great moral teacher Seneca (unless books lie)—to tyrannical and vicious manhood. In the tragedies of Hugelino and Cenobia, the Monk has wandered away from Fortune as a lady or as a mistress who brings men low, but with Nero and with the following portrait of Holofernes he returns strongly to that theme. Nero's depredations upon his sister and his mother are terrible enough, but they do not lead narratively to his downfall. Rather, Nero's murder of his teacher brings the story to a point of nemesis as Lady Fortune no longer pleases herself to cherish Nero, thinking that she is too scrupulous to support a man fulfilled by vice. By God, she will trick him when he least expects it. This personalizing of fortune makes her into a personification of treacherous woman who laughs and has a "game" after Nero is beheaded. Nero's wickedness provokes a personal response from Fortune, who plays her own, wanton game so like a woman. Had Nero followed Seneca, instead of literally and figuratively killing him, presumably Nero's people would not have risen against him and Fortune would have continued cherishing him. That, at least, is the implication here when Fortune becomes something other than blind. Clearly the Monk puts the story this way because he believes one can avoid serious misfortune.

Holofernes repeats Nero's fall most luridly. For all of Holofernes's pomp and might, a lascivious Fortune kisses him and takes his head, righteously of course, through the woman, Judith. Here woman is a proper instrument for rebuking vice, but somehow in the Monk's language she becomes part of a lecherous scheme, the tone of which recalls the Monk's earlier warnings concerning women and their counsel. Women are treacherous, even if they slay one in their virtue. The next portrait, of Antiochus, follows from Holofernes in that Antiochus had nothing but spite for God's people and is sorely, bodily, punished for his cruel pride. He loses his body rather than his head, first through a horrible pain in his guts, then through delirium, and finally through a plague of worms creeping throughout his stinking body. This pitiless torment ends in death without mercy, in part repeating the Balthazar theme. Perhaps the Monk would say here that one should never presume on one's high prosperity. Pride, cruelty and wantonness follow quickly upon losing sight of Fortune. So one should keep one's head, one's mind, and one's potency by not trusting in worldly prosperity, by honoring God and his people, and by avoiding women. The Monk greatly respects power and strength, as is clear in his account of Alexander—the flower of conquering knighthood and "fredom." He inherits Fortune's honor and probably nothing would have diminished him had he not gone in for wine and women. The world was his, but his own people eventually poison him—a fact the Monk loudly laments when he considers this "worthy, gentil Alisandre" (l. 2658). He does not have tears adequate to this loss, to this change of Fortune's dice for the worthy man whose death is the death of "gentilesse and of franchise," for the man who ruled all the world and yet who thought the world was not large enough.

The Monk might finish now, having sufficiently insisted upon his point. But he still has something on his mind as he moves from Alexander to Julius Caesar—both well known stories but, unlike Cenobia's, the unfairest cases of all. Alexander is the embodiment of all "gentilesse" and Caesar of all virtue in manhood—so much so that he wraps his mantle around his hips when stabbed, so that no man "sholde seen his privetee" (l. 2715). But, alas, assassins do him in and the Monk cannot quite express the pity of it all. Caesar, after all, made his way from humble origins to royal majesty through "wisedom, manhede, and by greet labour" (l. 2671). He could thank Fortune that he subdued the entire Orient, defeating Pompey, but Fortune eventually grows into his adversary as the envious Cassius conspires murderously against Caesar. The moral for Caesar's manly end—in his fastidious "honestee"—is that we should think upon this conqueror, and upon Pompey also (who lost his head), and keep Fortune "in awayt for everemoo" (l. 2725). The moral is not that we all suffer misfortune and so need a broader or higher view of life and the good; rather, the moral is wariness: keeping Lady Fortune at bay; keep an eye on her else she blind, behead, or strip and castrate one quite. That this is wildly inconsistent with Fortune's whimsical rule in life does not bother the Monk. It is his advice for the manly man: keep a watch on Lady Fortune; avoid wine, women and envious friends; eschew pride and, one supposes, acknowledge God. But although despising God is cause enough for a wretched fall, God does not figure in these two tragedies at all—nor does He in the next, the story of Cresus.

After telling that tale, about the proud and mighty king who escapes burning only eventually to hang, the Monk notes that one cannot bewail tragedies in any terms other than those that tell of Fortune assailing the unwary, them "that been proude" (l. 2764). Moreover, it is a woman again who disabuses Cresus of his proud confidence: his own daughter interprets a dream of his as predicting his hanging. He will hang elementally, from a gallows, washed by the rain and dried by the sun. Certainly pride goes before a fall and a wicked appetite precedes sickness, but avoiding pride does not lift one out of this life of change. The Monk has never read the Book of Job or *The Consolation of Philosophy*—nor could he accept them given his views.

That he will not or cannot tell of Fortune in terms other than those we have heard does not settle the matter for other pilgrims. Presumably the Monk will simply continue, having given us only eighteen of his hundred or more stories, but the Knight has had enough. He remarks that the Monk's stories are right enough, certainly, and much more—but for himself he would rather hear of a man who begins in poverty, waxes fortunate, and abides in prosperity. Now that would be a story to bring joy and "solas" to his heart—a story with a "gladsom" outcome. The Knight would emphasize happy endings, in spirit joining with the glad outcome of *Melibee*. But he mistakes Fortune as much as does the Monk, emphasizing an opposite stasis. The Monk dwells on the kinds of wretchedness against which Prudence warns Melibeus; the Knight dwells on abiding good fortune, a thing which the opening of *Melibee* profoundly shatters. This mutable world brings prosperity and pain; we must learn both to enjoy and to suffer it in "mesure," never forgetting God in our pleasures or our pains. The Monk, while God-fearing in his vocation, is not God-centered in his solution to Lady Fortune's depredations upon the rich and powerful. But at least his is a partial wisdom, if also involving a partial imprudence in his belief that one can step outside of the cycle that forms more often than not—one in which Lady Fortune fondles and spoils one, raising one up, only to turn eventually in wanton play and have one's eyes, one's head, one's strength, or one's body.

The Host, agreeing with the Knight, offers partial truth and also considerable irrelevance as he notes that bewailing what is done is no remedy. Moreover, hearing of tragedy is a pain, and so no more of this, Sir Monk. Instead of concentrating on the subject and wisely considering its import, the Host claims that the Monk's tale annoys the entire company. He confers a kind of lone counselor wisdom upon the Monk in remarking that there is no "desport or game" in the Monk's tale and that only the Monk's bridle bells kept him, the Host, from falling asleep and perhaps pitching right over into the roadway mud. There is no point in giving one's opinions there where one has no audience (recalling the fate of the wise counselor at Melibeus's first parliament). Indeed, the Host insists, he knows that he has capacity for attention if any thing is well reported (like *Melibee?*). So he urges the Monk to switch over to talk about hunting (perhaps to a tale about some noble chase). But the Monk will not play, although he rebukes neither the Knight nor the Host.

We can infer that the Host would listen to tragedies if they contain some kind of remedy and are well told. The lengthy *Melibee*, after all, did not stupefy the Host, who virtually exploded in a lively application of the tale to his own domestic life. What the Host means by "remedie," of course, might be less thoughtful than whatever the Knight means. But the idea of remedy can easily involve something large and true: what the Host may sense but not realize is that he has felt no empathy, no enlargement of compassion, and certainly no increased understanding about what is stable and good and what is not. He invites the Monk to change the subject and at least play—an invitation the Monk declines.

The Host then turns to the hitherto undescribed Nun's Priest and de-mands a merry tale, something that may gladden the heart. The sweet, good priest, Sir John, readily agrees to avoid blame and thus to do the Host's bidding. And so begins the Nun's Priest's merriment—the tale of a cock and a hen, at the end of which the Nun's Priest invites us to take the "moralite" if we are otherwise disposed to consider it a "folye." Finally the Host will have some mirth—mirth that will face the *Tale of Melibee* as glad amusement faces glad earnest. From this point of view, the Monk's tragedies have been a preamble turned interlude, separating Prudence and Melibeus from Pertelote and Chauntecleer. The dreary tragedies have interposed heaviness between merry "sentence" and mirthful fable-exemplum, the Nun's Priest's rhetorical carnival.[7]

What is true and what is false in this tale of a "cok," his hen, and a fox has vexed Chaucerians for some time. Allegorical readings in an exegetical mold have seen the fox as the devil and Chauntecleer as the good Christian who comes to his senses. Variations on this kind of packaging all share a fatal weakness: they simply move to a great height above the letter of the tale and go their own way.[8] Overlapping areas for our attention in the tale have been suggested by D. E. Myers: the Aesopian cock and fox story, the narrator's rhetorical elaborations—which for Myers include the opening descriptions of farmyard, widow, Chauntecleer, and Pertelote, along with the narrator's concluding lines—and the tale's relation to themes in other tales and to their tellers (principally Knight, Prioress, and Monk). The sec-ond area, the narrator's elaborations, concern this study especially. Myers thinks of that area as an instructive and entertaining play for rulers concerning their duties. It does not depend on the character of the narrator; Myers would say that we need no prior sense of the teller.[9]

But those elaborations do lead us into a sense of the teller, given his responses and what he says in relation to particular details or moments, usually anticipated, in the tale. How far we credit the Nun's Priest with the language of the narrative, with the mock heroic texture especially, is something we will never settle. It may be best to keep to our practice and assume that there is a tale Chaucer constructs to which the Nun's Priest reacts in the telling of it, the whole becoming the *Nun's Priest's Tale*.

The tale's opening gives us a scene of "hertes suffisaunce" that does not seem ironic despite some readings that suggest that the good widow leads her simple life because she has been constrained to since her widowhood. The time indication—"syn thilke day that she was last a wyf"—really does not bear irony. The widow may have had to learn patience, but with patience is how she now lives. Her hooting at the tale's end in chase of the fox is not a break in her "pacience" so much as an outcry against the apparent disaster of losing her cock. Her poverty, moreover, is fairly rich in farmyard products, so in her temperate diet and in her "suffisaunce," she lives a materially pleasant life. The economy that provides her with milk, brown bread, bacon, and an egg or two sometimes is probably based on egg production, since there is a rooster and seven hens. She has already lost a rooster and a hen—Chauntecleer's sire and dam—to the fox, so naturally she would react excitedly to the fox's raid. The widow is prudent but not patient in dramatic adversity. She lives in this world but not spiritually.

The description of Chauntecleer is, as most readers happily note, a charming piece of mock-courtly characterization. An antecedent tone may well have prepared the way for this mock presentation. Stephen Knight notes a "mild note of mockery towards courtliness" in the opening account of the widow's country simplicity, and Charles Owen considers the possibilities for a gentle lesson in the opening comparisons with courtly life.[10] How does one live one's life? Not necessarily in rural simplicity but also not in courtly splendor, not in the repletion of rich sauces and dainty morsels. By not commenting on this opening valuation of the widow's temperate and sufficient life, the Nun's Priest might value it in simple terms and see its virtue as self-evident. This establishes the ground for his rhetorical elaborations and tale-telling responses elsewhere, primarily in anticipation of the fox's approach.

Leaving the mock-courtly and randy Chauntecleer in "his pasture," the Nun's Priest now promises to tell of Chauntecleer's "aventure," the "sorweful cas" (l. 3204) that will suddenly befall this prodigiously gifted character (a character filled with lore and extensive argument).[11] The Nun's Priest, however, delays Chauntecleer's moment of fright, his sudden awareness of the fox, for seventy-one lines of talk on tragedy, fortune, God's foreknowledge, man's free will, and woman's counsel. He elevates this tale in high style, adopting the rhetoric of apostrophe against murderers and traitors and including an aside on mermaids.

Although suddenly weighty, the Nun's Priest's tone is not easily resolved into either an unambiguous attitude toward his tale or an illusion weakly disguising a playful collision of voices and rhetorical postures.[12] He seems to accept the narrative details of Chauntecleer's dream and his forgetful sojourn on this perilous morning (ll. 3230–33). But in likening the fox lying in the bed of worts to an inveterate murderer lying in wait for men, he seems to make too much of a fox. He further apostrophizes the fox as a new Judas, a new Ganylon, a "false dissymulour" (someone who dissembles for evil reasons, I presume), and a Greek Synon, he who brought Troy all utterly to sorrow; in so speaking the Nun's Priest seems to heat up overmuch, as though he would mock this already mock tale of a cock and a fox. If he sees nothing serious or worthwhile in this tale, then playing with it rhetorically can become a way of dismissing it as utterly as Synon ruined Troy. Here rhetoric is a trojan horse: unpack it and it will destroy what it would seem to celebrate and adorn. But this view of the Nun's Priest is not forced upon us as self-evident. Indeed, various readers have seen the Nun's Priest simply as more hapless than dismissive, as unable to control the rhetorical dilations of his material in any way that speaks to appropriateness and decorum. That Chauntecleer would heedlessly descend into the yard, having been forewarned in his dream of a rapacious, houndlike carnivore is folly and so exercises the Priest that he envelopes his exasperation (if that is what it is) with talk of the fox as murderer and traitor and with talk of God's foreknowledge.

Heavy thoughts influence him. The first concerns the transience of worldly joy, and another is set off by thoughts of iniquity. He does not think of himself as a secular chronicler in the fair style of rhetoric, but he does think of his tale as being true or at least as true as the book of Launcelot of the Lake, which women hold in great "reverence." Here the value of old books as bearers of true "storie" is clearly proposed, along with the openness of belief required of the reader (women for Lancelot). His reader or hearer, or at least every wise man, should harken unto him, for his story of the cock and the fox is also true (no mere folly, one supposes, despite the animal matter).[13] Is the reference to women crediting stories of Lancelot a covert slander, one finding its overt expression in a shift of topic at women's expense (concerning their often cold counsel)? I think the most one can do with the Nun's Priest's comparisons and assertion of truth is to accept them at face value: the book of Lancelot of the Lake and the priest's tale of a cock and a fox are alike in being *unlikely* vehicles for truth—but that is exactly what they are. As women revere the Lancelot book, so wise men should harken to the Nun's Priest's story. That said, he now promises to return to his "sentence" (l. 3214), that is, to his opinion that "evere the latter ende of joye is wo" (l. 3205).

This opinion is kept in mind as he narrates the approach of a premeditating, sly, iniquitous "col-fox," who has burst into the yard through the hedge, under cover of night, and who lies in wait in that part of the yard where Chauntecleer and his wives are wont to sun themselves. The fox does this gladly, as do all homicides who lie in wait to murder men. This is the sentiment the Nun's Priest's rhetoric inflates, as for a few seconds he forgets that this particular homicidal creature is a fox, not an archvillain. The lurking murderer figure must be reproved as one of the most notorious types, assimilated to Judas, Ganylon, and Synon. The idea controlling the rhetorical figure is a deeply serious one for the Nun's Priest, who then for a time floats with his rhetoric above the matter of the tale.

That flight touches down in a serious concern for Chauntecleer's heedlessness, a concern that lasts all too briefly before thoughts of God's knowledge preoccupy the Nun's Priest (a sentiment anticipated in his earlier claim that God knows that worldly joy is soon departed). Pulling away from Chauntecleer, he undertakes a review of theories of God's foreknowledge and man's free will, in the middle of which he admits to not being able to "bulte it to the bren" (l. 3240). This is plausibly a reference to understanding divine or Platonic truth, an expression of deep comprehension, but an undertaking much better suited, he says, to the holy doctor, Augustine, than to himself.[14] He will not have much to do with such matter, although he seems to understand the basic positions. His tale, he reminds us, is of a cock who "tok his conseil of his wyf, with sorwe" (l. 3253) to walk in the yard on the morning he had his prophetic dream. Apparently the Priest has forgotten Chauntecleer's own defiance of his dream and of Pertelote's medicinal remedies for the choler and melancholia from which she supposes him to suffer. He needs an agent-cause for Chauntecleer's peril if he is not going to attribute the event simply to fortune and God's foreknowledge. Of course, "taking counsel" could mean Chauntecleer's own culpability, referring to his pride, defiance, and randiness. In this sense he first deliberated with Pertelote, then defied her advice and his dream, eventually taking randy counsel of her in the yard (twenty times). But what will not do here is to blame Pertelote within the general slander that women's counsels are often cold—this despite the truth that a woman's counsel first brought us all to woe. The Nun's Priest senses the malformation here and hastens to dissociate himself from the general remarks about women and counsel. He professes to have said what he said about women in his humour, adding that authorities treat of such matters, and so we had better go to them if we want to hear what they say. The words he spoke were really the cock's, he adds, not his, as though Chaunticleer's Latin, maugre the cock's translation of *in principio,* / *Mulier est hominis confusio*, were still ringing in the Nun's Priest's ears. This move indicates his sensitivity to audience response. He hopes not to be misunderstood in his tale telling, and so he professes to divine no harm of women and then continues with his tale. Repeatedly, what happens with our good, sweet priest is that topics move him to amplifications that are not earnest deliberations upon the tale's details. He is an emotional teller to a greater extent than many have realized in their scrutiny of his elaborations and in their search for pilgrim motives, dramatic or otherwise. The Nun's Priest's obtrusive elaborations are not rhetorical lenses turned upon his material so much as they are addresses to his audience or expostulations triggered by a given, serious topic when considered in its own right. In this way the Nun's Priest proceeds sporadically, detaching topics for a time and then recovering himself and the continuation of his tale. His rhetoric is not hapless in itself, but its relation to his tale of a cock and a fox is largely accidental, part of the "aventure" of his tale telling.[15]

For Chauntecleer, intense feeling in the form of heart-felt fear is a life-saving affair. It is when flattering rhetoric beguiles him that he loses that instinct and slips into jeopardy. The fox's success in this regard brings Chauntecleer to the trap:

> As man that koude his traysoun nat espie,
> So was he ravysshed with his flaterie.
>
> [ll. 3323–24]

This provokes a cry of concern from the Nun's Priest:

> Allas, ye lordes, many a fals flatour
> Is in youre courtes, and many a losengeour,
> That plesen yow wel moore, by my feith,
> Than he that soothfastnesse unto you seith.
>
> [ll. 3325–28]

This is good, prudential thinking, enforced a few lines later by a reference to Ecclesiasticus. The next lament is an apostrophe on "destinee" in response to Chauntecleer's plight, caught in "daun Russell's" mouth. The Nun's Priest laments Chauntecleer's flight from the beams and Pertelote's disbelief in dreams. These are accurate indicators of cause: Had Pertelote credited and heeded the dream, had Chauntecleer feared more and not been so pleased with himself, perhaps then his encounter with the fox would have followed native instinct or would not have occurred at all. All of this mischance, by the way, fell on a Friday, says the Nun's Priest.

That observation seems a non sequitur until the Nun's Priest apostrophizes Venus and wonders why she would suffer her servant to die on her day. He now pulls away from the plot line, initially saluting Geoffrey of Vinsauf in honorific terms, he who had the lore and the skill to chide the Friday on which King Richard died. A Friday can acquire somber, momentous connotations, becoming a day of cruel irony, betrayal, and death. This is the day for slaying a king and for seizing a virile cock by the throat. The comparison seems incommensurable, but actually it is no more so than the basic conceit of any animal fable. Consider the tones of these amplifications: Do they mock the tale and dismiss its characters and actions as mere folly?

Most readers favor mockery on the priest's behalf, in some sense at the expense of the tale. This is mock heroic, mock epic, rhetoric burlesqued in a general burlesque. But, as attractive as such readings are, one cannot be sure. The reference to Venus is to pleasure and the service performed is one of sexual delight more than a procreative one. This seems unexceptionable, given Chauntecleer's character and behavior. The reference to Geoffrey is honorific, a reference to the Priest's "deere maister soverayn," who complained expertly of the "worthy" King Richard's death. If the Nun's Priest only had Geoffrey's lore and "sentence" (whatever Chaucer thinks), then he would show how he could "pleyne" for Chauntecleer's dread and pain. One could simply see this sweet and goodly priest as feeling inadequate to the task; and so he turns to the outcry of Pertelote and the hens.

Their lamentation is such that certainly no such crying was heard from women at the sack of Troy or at Carthage. Is this because those women were not chickens and could not cluck or scream in the piercing way a hen can? Or is there something more exact and fitting at stake here? The Nun's Priest goes on to say that the woeful hens cried out exactly as did Roman wives when Nero had their guiltless husbands slain. So Chauntecleer's hens "out lament" epic but match the distress of history. The Nun's Priest feels pity for the hens at just this moment: he moves from a possibly ambiguous assertion of epic lamentation on their behalf to a direct and sympathetic address.

> O woful hennes, right so criden ye
> As whan that Nero brende the citee
> Of Rome cryden senatoures wyves.
> [ll. 3369–71]

In all of these references, the mock-epic fun is more Chaucer's than the Nun's Priest's, but even then the analogues are weighty and asserted straightforwardly. Unless we *assume* the mocking incommensurability of it all, the text will support its aptness as the Nun's Priest turns again to the action of his tale.

Given the chase and noise at tale's end, "in al his drede" Chauntecleer becomes inspired. Once more feeling is life-saving, but this time it also inspires cunning as Chauntecleer urges the fox to defy the "cherles alle," giving Russell the speech he should use. Russell readily agrees to utter the defiance Chauntecleer frames for him. In shouting it out, he opens his mouth enough for Chauntecleer to escape. This is truly deliverance by wit, inspired through fear. And it leads to truth telling, to a new understanding for the previously unwary, overly satisfied cock and for the previously confident, smoothly cunning fox. Keep your eyes open, says the cock (enforced by Ecclesiastes, allusively), and your mouth shut, says the fox. The fox even has a pun of sorts: he should have held his peace (piece of chicken) rather than jangled. The Nun's Priest sums up both morals by saying that here we see the fruit of recklessness, negligence, and trust in flattery. He addresses rulers and lords, but his point also comfortably fits Chauntecleer and the fox. Basically, Chauntecleer's ruse was to encourage recklessness and negligence by flattering the fox's sense that he had the upper hand against his pursuers. Russell exults too soon, counting his chicken before he has in fact eaten him.

As the Nun's Priest asserts at tale's end, there is truth here in this matter of a fox, a cock, and a hen. We, that is all people, should look to "moralite" rather than think of the tale as a folly. For even here in such a tale we can be edified. I think the Nun's Priest means this seriously, as he means seriously everything he addresses to us or to lords, turning from the action of the tale to do so. Moreover, the action of the tale supports him. Far from posing the ridiculous penchant for finding meaning or weighty morality in everything, the tale as handled by the Nun's Priest occasions a number of reflections that in themselves are sufficient.[16] It is also a hugely entertaining tale, the texture of which is far from allegorical. The Nun's Priest does not self-evidently register the tale's mock-heroic character. To have him do that requires a thought experiment on our part: Given that he might respond to the mock heroic, how would his doing so affect our estimation of his rhetorical expansions? We would have to maneuver him into position and then read his laments and apostrophes as ironic and mocking. The tendentious nature of such a maneuver is obvious on reflection, however beguiling it is to deal with the tale's mock-heroic texture in this way.

Chaucer has given a wonderful piece of rhetorical art to the Nun's Priest, a mock-heroic beast fable. The sweet and goodly Nun's Priest takes this merry tale to heart enough to find numerous occasions in it for reflections and addresses to his audience, as well as pointing a valuable if not awesome moral at the tale's end. Although the Nun's Priest does not seem to respond to the tale's mock-heroic texture, the reader certainly does; and almost universally readers have acclaimed that texture to be a triumph of literary art and imagination.[17] The Nun's Priest does not respond to the texture of his tale; rather he takes it literally, as plot and action, the moral of which he accurately notes. From Chaucer's point of view, the tale contains "man, distanced, visible, whole, under the species of a chicken." One might add mock heroic and make that plural—under the species of mock-heroic chickens and a learned, fable-quoting fox.[18] Given our delight in literary texture, the *Nun's Priest's Tale* has become a great favorite and more of a puzzle than it need be. We keep trying to see it as some kind of pointer, as containing a metafictional core inside its literariness, a core resolvable into a transcendent plot of Christian and devil or preacher and friar when not taken as reflecting the subjectivity, the self-referentiality of everything. For Chaucer here the mock-heroic is stylistic fun, and the tale in its plot is still the thing to conjure with. The teller shows himself to be an emotional if goodly and sweet narrator. Haphazard in some ways, counselorlike in others, he can unself-consciously pull away from the tale, given a topic that an incident or a turn in the plot suggests to him. In doing so, he addresses us, and then—either finding himself in matter over his head or in a quandary as to how he is being heard—he returns to his tale, clearly telling us that that is exactly what he is doing. He does not pretend to a general mastery of intellectual subjects or of rhetorical art; nor does he make more of the "morality" of his tale than it can bear, apostrophize and cry "Alas!" though he will. He is a sweet fellow, emotional, and taken to rattling on sometimes; but he does eventually lay hold of his tale's plot and bring it to an effective conclusion. As a counselor and a priest, he hardly believes that all human activity is meaningless. Neither does Chaucer, however much fun he has with this conceit of man as vain-glorious cock, finding deliverance through fear-inspired wit.[19]

So where do we stand? We have a mock-heroic animal fable ending on the subject of morals about prudence, telling us: Keep your eyes open and your mouth shut at appropriate times; do not act recklessly or trust in flattery. This fable stands in some relation to a serious treatise on prudence, becoming, in effect, the third and most extravagant version of prudence to follow the *Tale of Melibee*. In this connection, a "merry" tale is one that emphasizes the prudential in life in some glad way and to some good end. The tales of this fragment, even paired, seem "companionable" rather than "quitting" tales, which brings the sociable and public aspects of prudence into prominence. Prudent behavior, even in low and narrow confines, tends toward the making or keeping of community. Consider the Shipman's merchant who, seeing no "remedie" in the loss of his one hundred francs and that it would be folly to chide his wife, forgives her expenditures; consider Prudence's according of Melibeus and his enemies; consider Chauntecleer's prudent wit, which both saves his life and will end the bedlam his threatened loss excited, allowing the widow's humble community to reassume its previous sufficiency. At the level of pilgrim interaction, the companionableness of this fragment appears in audience reactions: in the Host's cheerful response to the Shipman, in the company's response to the Prioress—all wondrously as one in their sobriety; in the Host's energy after *Melibee*, forgoing any more comments on the elfish-faced Chaucer to concentrate on his own brawny and abusive wife; in the coming together of the Knight and the Host against the Monk's tragedies (the prudence in which requires a self-isolating and fearful view of the world), leading to the Host's articulation of a necessary community between tale teller and audience (lacking an audience, it does not help to tell one's "sentence"); and in the Host's insulting exuberance over the *Nun's Priest's Tale*. Merry tales inspire him to bawdy and virile thoughts, to animal images of procreative vigor—a potential he happily ascribes to the tale teller (in anticipation in the Monk's case and as a conferred honor in the Nun's Priest's case). Bodily, sexual activity here not only implicates an enlarged human population (expanding the possibilities of community) but also a strengthened and invigorated one. Comments about physical virility may be insulting play, the Host's mocking "exposure" of others, but it also has regulative dimensions, correlating as it does the successful telling of a thing with procreative acts and the merriness of a tale with animalistic, that is, innocent sexuality.[20] The Host's bawdy humour, aggressive and carnivalesque, is inherently a social gesture within the holiday world of tale tellings: however lewd and potentially damaging to the dignity of the celibate Monk and Nun's Priest and however cavalier in the happy promiscuity of the "tredefowel aright" image, the Host's comments would bring the Monk and the Priest into the community of heterosexual procreation as well as the community of "merry," even bawdy, tale telling. In addition, the Host's comments would award pride of place to these most manly of celibates.[21]

Of course the Host's ribald gestures of community are not universally embraced. His comments at Pilgrim Chaucer's expense are met with the annoying *Tale of Sir Thopas*; his ogling of the Monk meets with a didactic "pacience," and the Nun's Priest is given no reaction to the Host's blessings of breeches and "stone" (testicles). Among the tales, two stand out as singularly not about prudence of any kind: the Prioress's and the *Tale of Sir Thopas*. If we consider *Thopas* to be an interlude merely, a transition, then the Prioress is essentially answered by Dame Prudence in *Melibee*, which in turn, if we think of the Monk's tragedies as constituting a longer interlude than *Thopas*, is given a mock-heroic companion by the Nun's Priest. As this is so, prudence is a serious and pervasively necessary affair: the prudence of moderation and mercy, which builds an inclusive community, is preferable to the exclusiveness of community built upon harsh justice and formed around "miracle." Moreover, a wide prudence is higher or better than the narrow, worldly prudence of either the merchant or the cunning monk; and it is far superior to the fearful, self-protective prudence taught by the Monk's string of tragedies.[22]

At the level of the tales, Fragment 7 clearly presents questions of truth in fiction, the nature of a merry tale (and for whom), and Chaucer's continuing interest in the emotionally affected reading and misreading of tales, along with the emotionally funded changes of perception or misperception that occur at key moments near the end of all the uninterrupted tales. There is the matter of the teller's understanding of his material and the somewhat enigmatic nature of various tales, left as we are, having observed the teller's gestures, to a more syncretic attempt to discover the meanings of the tale. The tale upon which Fragment 7 breaks off neatly reflects all of these issues. As a fable, the tale asks us to make something out of it, to suppose that it contains some truth that can be separated from its falsehood. We are asked to consider the teller and his understanding of, as well as attitude toward, his material through what is an energetically and rhetorically inflated tale telling. We must consider this professedly merry tale that pleases the Host in relation to other tales called merry or mirthful in this fragment. Chaucer's merry treatise on prudence tells us that merriment is related to a prudence that sees and understands, to a softened heart and to right action. The Knight's response to the Monk's tragedies suggests that merriment also includes good fortune—or at least something pleasant to contemplate. The *Nun's Priest's Tale* in part indicates that merriment has a literary and playful side to it—a dimension that can either be exploited happily or so trivialized that it does little more than amuse many and irritate some (*Thopas*). If prudence makes for merriment in tales, the key effect of merriment in both the matter and the telling is the sense of community that develops. In Fragment 7, a sense of pilgrim community, of the forming of a group around various notions of merriment, is strikingly present within the carnival "grid" provided by the Host as master of the revels and the rules of his game. In effect, the Host's role and rules notably diminish in importance as a sense of group accord emerges, first in the Monk's patience, then in the Knight's interruption of the Monk and in the Host's concurrence. This diminishment continues in the Nun's Priest's sweet, good agreeableness, but it began in earnest in the extended "negotiation" between Chaucer and the Host (which is a way of reading the shifts from the Host's initial, mocking demand for a tale of mirth to his eventually energetic praise of Prudence and dispraise of Goodelief).[23]

How Chaucer would have us encounter a tale probably resembles the approach in which Dame Prudence instructs Melibeus: To consider anything, to judge what we hear or should do, requires driving ire, covetousness, and hastiness out of our hearts. The "irous" do not deem well, and they also speak incitingly, believing that they can do what they cannot. A covetous person thinks only about fulfilling his covetousness; and a hasty person, moved by sudden thoughts and feelings, may not deem for the best. Moreover, people are not always in the same state of mind or disposition; as mind or disposition varies, so does perception and a sense of what is good. Extremes of feeling can lead anyone astray, even though those feelings may allow the perception of things that fulfill passion's purposes. The prudent reader or hearer, then, should consider what he or she reads or is told in as untroubled a state of mind as possible. But, crucially, what is involved here is not acts of pure reason but dispositions of mind and heart. The prudent reader can avoid being abused by feeling but cannot avoid knowing feelingly; a softened heart is essential for any right understanding of a humanly or politically complex issue. So benign feeling and prudence involve each other and constitute a beginning. But they do not tell us what to think or just how to approach any particular affair, tiding, or tale. For this we need those Chaucerian notions of compounded truth and falsehood (in order to have the confidence that there is valuable truth in most things and in fictions generally), of reverence and delight, in effect, of the openness of belief.

That a prudential disposition of heart and mind will not give us exactly what we should think is perhaps why a merry carnival of sorts breaks out after the *Tale of Melibee*. We are pitched back into the world of pilgrims and their merriments, a world that captures our ears in the shrewish comedy of Goodelief's words and in the Host's sociable effrontery as he nearly accosts the Monk and later "studifies" the Nun's Priest. That merriment, to repeat, forms a sense of community that finds its essential statement in the Host's words to the Monk about how a teller's "sentence" is wasted if he or she lacks an audience, in spite of the Chaucerian worry in *Troilus* and elsewhere about how one's poetry is received or understood. Being understood or taken amiss depends alike upon an audience, moreover upon an audience that may have surprising capacities—an unlooked for "substaunce" such as the one the Host reveals in his acceptance of *Melibee* and in his claim to the Monk that he knows well the substance is in him to attend to any kind of "sentence" if the thing is well reported. This is the glad side of the problematics of reception: the surprise, not necessarily of understanding exactly, but of deeper reception than one might have hoped for.

The antithesis of this, while staying within the world of reception, is a tale telling that pleases only the ears, leaving the understanding untouched. Thus one's audience may demand either what one cannot entirely ignore or that to which one should not cater. The Host's best gratification comes in the form and manner of the *Nun's Priest's Tale*, although he reacts merrily to the Shipman's bawdry. The Host is not unregenerate without exception in his embrace of mirth: If he prefers bawdy mirth up front, he will settle for a dainty, and failing that, a narrative romance, or finally, something composed somewhat in prose in which there is some mirth or some doctrine. What he gets from Chaucer is *Melibee* and somewhat more in the way of proverbs, perhaps, than he has heard before. As Chaucer surely knows, the Horatian ideal is to please and profit one's audience, perhaps especially to please readers by giving them something profitable to read. Having forgone anything like Lady Philosophy's rhetoric of ravishing song in preparation for dialectical medicine, Chaucer settles into this pleasure-profit duality comfortably but with an acute unease about extreme cases—too much pleasure, too much mere "sentence" (or reductive and repetitive "sentence"). Here the interrupted tales match each other nicely:

Thopas is too much pleasure, and the *Monk's Tale* is too much of the same and narrowing "sentence." *Melibee,* with all of Chaucer's signaling about its load of proverbs, finally is a merry tale with which to reckon—or, if not as well reported as one might wish, still full of glad "sentence," a large thing indeed. However, nothing is formulated easily here in this fragment that embraces an astonishing variety of tales and an active audience. Perhaps in his poetical practice, Chaucer show us that the Horation ideal, fine enough as a formula, finally is too much of a schoolboy lesson to reflect the circumstances, problems, and successes of tellers, tales, and their communities.

That difficult tales are told for profitable and pleasurable purposes involves us and the tellers in estimations of truth and falsehood in rather explicit ways. Tales contain insights; they have a truth-telling function, if you will, here and everywhere else in the Canterbury collection. But nowhere else are so many explicit assertions of truth in the tales raised by the tellers so matter-of-factly. The Shipman objectively tells a tale about the folly of not supporting the wardrobe of one's wife, his tale being true to life. The Prioress invokes Mary's bounty and virtue as a muse for her miracle of a little boy martyr—a tale as true as Mary or the historical Hugh of Lincoln. Chaucer tells a tale urging prudential conduct as good and true policy. The Host claims to tell truth in play, and the Monk replies with an idea that tales should conduce one to "honestee," that he will tell tragedies as he finds them, as men have recorded them (historically true). Finally, the series breaks off with the Nun's Priest's claim that everything, including seemingly foolish tales, is written for our instruction: Take the truth where we find it, leave the chaff.

Broken down, we have semihistorical and historical truths, which may in turn prove or illustrate temporal truths; we have truths of behavior and experience; we have true miracles and marvels; we have exemplary truths (behave like this, Prudence says, and you will not only behave morally, but you will also cut down the possibilities of danger and disaster in the future); and we have morality in fables—truth defined, often, by its opposite or by a negative injunction. We have truths stated in play, the punch somewhat pulled, and we even have falsehood in the retelling of historical events given the Monk's narrow insistence on his "sentence." But through all of this, it is the inspiration of feeling, of heart that brings goodness with truth, that leads past the righteous world of justice to the community of mercy and the partly ironic accommodations of perception, wit, and deliverance. We should revere these tales as we revere audiences—for their surprising capacities, capacities that can gladden and, if only rarely, ravish us.

9 ❦ ENDING A "FEESTE"

In an elaborate telling of time, Chaucer begins to bring the tales to a close. Unlike a similar passage before the *Man of Law's Tale*, this telling by astrology and shadow is not pregnant with a sense of time passing, of time wasted.[1] Instead, now there is a sense of leisure and closure

> As we were entryng at a thropes ende;
> For which oure Hoost, as he was wont to gye,
> As in this caas, oure joly compaignye,
> Seyde in this wise: "Lordynges everichoon,
> Now lakketh us no tales mo than oon."
> [*Parson's Prologue*, ll. 12–16]

The "as" clauses give a repetitive and additive character to the statement; the Host's generous "Lordynges everichoon" roundly includes the entire company of all "degrees." Also, we will not hear one *more* tale, rather no more tales but one. A feeling of satisfaction, of near completion, imbues the Host's speech and gesture here, as in his wonted fashion he would direct the "joly" company.

The "grid" of tale-telling play, with the Host as governor of the game, is about to complete itself. The sundry pilgrims have been living in some sense by or through a revision of the rules of the game and the Host's decrees. He addresses the pilgrims and says that his "sentence" and "decree" are fulfilled in that he believes that we have heard from each rank or class of pilgrim. If Chaucer means to have the Host's Tabard Inn plan, to which all assented, meet a series of modifications to become a highly flexible ordinance, then the disparity between the Host's remarks in the *General Prologue* and here in the *Parson's Prologue* is not surprising. Indeed, many readers have seen some kind of plan in the various dramatic shifts of the tale tellings (beginning with the Miller's intrusion following the *Knight's Tale* and ending here with the one tale left and the last pilgrim to be heard from, who will now tell his first, not his second, tale, and with no return-trip tale telling).

The grid that constitutes the tale-telling game is obviously flexible and redefinable; it is not a strict set of rules tying the otherwise unrelated pilgrims to each other in reciprocal transactions. Instead, group dynamics—involving face-to-face relationships (consider Miller and Reeve, for example)—interfere with the social governance of the game, modifying its operations away from the Host's initial stipulations, which concern the number of tales and the right, as governor, to direct the sequence of tellers. Either because of what the Host wishes or because of some event, a particular pilgrim in effect alters the progress or even the rules of the game, such as in the Miller's churlish insistence that either he speak after the Knight or he will leave the pilgrimage.[2] What will happen now is that the Host will turn to the Parson expecting the fulfillment of "al" his "ordinaunce," of this play, and he hopes for a knitting up in a fable—perhaps a fable teaching a point of religion or morality.

The Parson bluntly refuses, thus asserting his freedom to change the local moment within this still-flexible "grid" of tale telling. Indeed, he rejects the telling of fables and seeks the agreement of the entire company for what he plans to tell. He is, as Alfred David has pointed out, the only pilgrim to turn so to the entire company.[3] But he is not the only pilgrim to negotiate with the Host. What would he negotiate here in this last tale-telling moment? First, he would tell his kind of "merry" tale, one of morality and virtuous matter. Second, he would tell it in prose, not in alliterative line or in rhyme. Third, he would not tell a fiction about happenings in this world, but he would do pleasure for his audience, within his abilities and with reverence for Christ.[4] Finally, he hopes that Jesus would grace him with the wit to show the pilgrims the way in this voyage, of that perfect, glorious pilgrimage called "Jerusalem celestial." In effect, he would reform the grid and take the Host's place as governor "of this feeste": for that he asks the pilgrims' thoughts. As governor, he would hope to show everyone the way, not to supper at the Tabard Inn, but to salvation in Christ. Hence, he would alter the competitiveness of the group, turning the pilgrims away from the fellowship of tale telling to the role of Christian souls contemplating the means to salvation. When everyone assents to this, and the Host gives him leave, the Canterbury game ends.[5]

What, in the course of this "greet mateere"—something the Host thinks can fittingly end on a fable—has Chaucer done? Given the preceding discussions in these several chapters, I think that in the tales and nearly everywhere else in his work, Chaucer presents the importance of belief. For the *Canterbury Tales*, especially, this becomes a poetics of reverence and delight. Its still center is the clear conviction that fiction has truths to tell, although not necessarily the truths of propositional assertion or logical demonstration. Those truths, and the proofs that become bearers of them, are not excluded from fiction in all forms; certainly not as statements along the way or in terms of plot and structure—the suasorial or argumentative terms of premises confirmed by the presentation and unfolding of a given tale.[6]

More important for Chaucer are those truths, as matters of report, that fall outside immediate confirmation; that are not affairs that have been witnessed or experienced but that nevertheless are entertainable and even deeply significant truths (disturbingly so if not true—as in notions of hell). For these truths, old books are our only witness, however doubtful we may be of their reliability as witnesses. But old books as keys to the recollection of these truths are only necessary, not sufficient witnesses. We must still bring our sense of what accords with reason and general human experience to our assessment of the things that books—and therefore their authors—claim about such matters as hell and the inhabitants of the heavens (not to mention the more mundane but equally puzzling subjects of Love, Justice, Order, and so on). Chaucer would have us do this in what I have called an "openness of belief," a cogitating informed by salient feelings and such attitudes as delight and reverence.[7]

Comedy, wry humor, ironical tones—these are not excluded from the Chaucerian poetics of reverence and delight. They are central to an approach that open-mindedly considers the truth of what is stated in fictions, without a narrow reliance upon personal and firsthand observation. Eschewing the necessity of eye-witness confirmation, however, does not preclude reasonableness as a rough criterion or harmony with other things that one believes. It does, however, require vision rather than narrow sight, something I call insight and understanding (the kind of prudential seeing that Melibeus comes to). As reverence shades into awe, it also requires a capacity for wonder; as delight becomes joy or great pleasure, that wonder takes us to a sense of beauty and the knowledge that comes with beauty. Old books, fictions, are something to rejoice in, to approach with awe, to believe in as witnesses to truths comedically beyond one's personal and immediate experiences—the extent and character of that "beyond" often generating a humor that is more amusement and acceptance than rejection and irony. Chaucer's notion of belief is of something both non-deductive and incomplete rather than incompletely deductive; it involves attitudes that neither reach for closure (toward either dogma or certainty, given sound inference from true statements) nor become seriously skeptical.[8] In the dream visions and in the tales of Canterbury, delight involving some degree of amusement, exuberance, and joy always marks an openness that is less speculative and less metaphysical than Keats's negative capability. Perhaps this is because there is no superiority for Chaucer in scientific fact or in philosophical certainty; indeed, there is no suspension of an irritable reaching because the world Chaucer countenances will never yield unalloyed fact or truth. Keats would have us adopt an attitude of mental experimentation, of thought experiment, in the expectation that something like fact or certainty can come of it—if only one does not insist. Instead, Chaucer conducts the assessment of truth in fiction as a form of amusive and inspired play—the play of exploration and of discovery, given an initial, de-bemusing certainty that truth rarely comes unmixed with falsehood in the fictions one hears or reads.

Approached prudentially, fictions are not to be read angrily, covetously, or hastily. When one's deemings are stable, when they are not led by passions that seek only their own ends (whether those ends are benign or hostile or else express some quick and risible feeling), then belief as a performance can begin fruitfully—leading, perhaps, to a merry overcoming of the self-servingly personal, to insight and the forming of community. The merry fiction is one within which and through which this overcoming either occurs or is dramatized. Fragment 7, then, the series of tales from the Shipman's to the Nun's Priest's, becomes the center of the extant collection of tales and fragments, given this view of Chaucer, belief, and the poetics of reverence and delight.

Whatever idea Chaucer may have had when he first undertook the Canterbury project, and whatever turns the making of individual prologues and tales involved, the centrality of Fragment 7 is where he ends up. His own *Tale of Melibee* is no elaborate irony or joke, nor is it a boring tale, unexciting drama though it is. All of the questions about disorder, love, justice, accord, and "maistrie" come together in this vision of merry prudence—a vision the truth of which dawns through feeling, through the "gentil" heart. This is not an easy vision, nor can it be held steady and focused upon the world as a whole. It always involves assessments of particular situations, claims, representations, and possibilities. Many tales are involved and many tellers, with all of their liabilities and subjectivities. But if even the most violent passions are susceptible to moderation and can, given deep mischance and shock, lead to significant reconciliation (as with Arcite and Palamon and Melibeus and his enemies), so can other perturbations of body and mind, from the ribald to the ecstatic (Wife of Bath to Prioress).

Indeed, this is dramatized in some tales and between tales in various prologues and links (consider the Wife of Bath's accord with Jankyn as a reformation of all those false accords between fabliaux wives and husbands, or
the Pardoner's kiss with the Host as a reformation of those antagonisms
that are proof against reconciliation—such as the Reeve's views of millers
or the Friar's view of summoners). In Fragment 7 the agreement between
the Host and the Knight brings literary judgments into an accord, considering the various instances of difference in the tales (such as the Host's disparagement of *Sir Thopas*, the different notions of a ''merry'' tale, and the
Miller's implicit preferences in relation to the Knight's or the company's
distaste for the kind of ribaldry a Pardoner might tell). Through these
headlinks, endlinks, and prologues, Chaucer's art shows how ''life'' re-
forms art prudentially and in the merriment born of reformed community.
In moments of accord, individual beliefs are shared, forming that community of interest and openness that is a variable microcosm of the community between Chaucer and his readers or hearers that his poetics of belief
inherently invites. This becomes a fellowship in merriment and sobriety
for his many readers, pilgrims all.

At the level of individual tellers and their tale tellings, this sense of community and relationship between teller and hearer is frequently called
upon, relied upon, and even presumed. Readers have undertaken various
categorizations of the tales: by genre, moral type, aesthetic criteria of internal design and complexity, relationship to other tales, and so on. But little
categorization has been attempted of the various tale-telling performances
given to the sundry pilgrims, aside from commentary on Chaucerian voice
or interpretation of the teller in relation to his tale. Chaucer has created
idiosyncratic postures for different tellers, if not realistically individualized
voices. He has elaborated character in each case through tale-telling intrusions, through the ways and moments in which a particular teller disrupts
the fictional illusion. As several readers have pointed out recently, too
much has been claimed for the presence in the tales of fully realistic and
individualized pilgrim narrators. But the move those readers then make
toward complete textuality is a universalizing one that simply ignores the
clearly marked, differentially variable moments of intrusion by various pilgrim narrators. That move also precludes by fiat any idea of characterization through imitation, based on Chaucer's sense of how people are, of how
human nature shapes itself differently in each pilgrim. The justification
usually offered is that notions of complex, realistic characters are anach-
ronistic in medieval literature. But clearly a complicated ethos is present in
many cases, and Aristotle provides warrant enough for many-sided views

of human passion—something Quintilian knew but decided not to include in his rhetoric. And when the reader does concentrate on the tale-telling performances, especially on those passages in which tellers comment or elaborate directly on the progress of the tale, considerable change occurs in the ways the tales are read.

In discussing individual tales, I have tracked those performances to an extent that goes far beyond most commentary and that depends upon a crucial supposition: That the tale as a paraphrasable story line, with its characters and conclusion, is independent of the teller's character; that character is developed or revealed in the moments of teller commentary upon story action, incident, or gesture and not inherently through the fabric of the tale itself. Chaucer's fictions are not pilgrim dreams. If we then step back and try to categorize the general direction of all of the tale tellings in view here, at least two categories of tale telling begin to form themselves: those that seek mastery of the material or a relation to the tale that aims for completion and consequentiality; and those that aim for closure in some convenient and plausible way.

By "consequentiality" I have in mind a rough analogy with ideas of deduction that seek every logical consequence of a set of sentences, whereas by convenient "closure" I mean a way of handling the tale that simply derives some plausible moral or point from it without seeking a full and complete account of everything in the tale.[9] This distinction seems especially prominent in cases of obtrusive tale telling, with the obtrusive teller usually trying to master or fully anticipate each turn in the tale (consider the Manciple). Contrastingly, unobtrusive tale tellings simply get on with the story and make some perfunctory point at the end, as in the Shipman's case. An interesting hybrid of these categories, or perhaps a movement from one to another, occurs in cases of "superobtrusiveness," with the pilgrim narrator first presented to us through a lengthy and usually confessional prologue.

The Canon's Yeoman comes to mind in this connection especially. The first part of his "tale" can be read as a confused, energetic, but well-intentioned effort at consequentiality regarding his alchemic knowledge and experience. This modulates into an obtrusively told satire that makes its point in a less than exhaustive way, followed by a meditative epilogue on the philosophical possibility of alchemic knowledge—that meditation permitting a closure unavailable to the Canon's Yeoman in either the confused first part of his tale or the angry and indignant second part (the tale of the alchemist as con artist). Tale tellings that move toward simple closure usually leave a wide gap between the teller's conclusions, the teller's view of the tale, and our own (for example, all of the commentary on the *Nun's Priest's Tale*). The *Tale of Melibee* is an interesting case in this connection, because it moves toward closure with Chaucer completely unobtrusive as a tale teller. The armory of proverbs and "sentences" is not consequentially mined or controlled, except within the general direction that Prudence goes with Melibeus and the conclusion to which she leads him. It would seem that prudence and prudential tale telling do not seek consequentiality and completeness, do not attempt mastery (another way of putting the difference between Chaucer and Dante and between the inquiring maker and the magisterial poet). The most notable exception to this rule is the *Parson's Tale*, where it does seem that consequentiality and completeness are appropriately driven toward, beyond the play of tale tellings and the deemings of individual tellers. In every other case, the attitude of tale-telling mastery involves misdeeming, confusion, hastiness, and even covetousness—distinctly unprudential attributes that deform the possibilities of knowledge through the openness of belief.

❦ NOTES

Chapter 1: Belief and Truth in the Canterbury Tales

1 The *Rhetorica Ad Herennium* (Caplan), 4, 5, 63–65, particularly advises vivid description, set before the eyes. The author tells a lively story about a rascal by way of illustration. This oral vividness is Chaucer's way of creating voice and thereby forming an energized sense of character that plays off of the *GP* portraits. That the pilgrims are not given to us as realistic personalities is a red herring in some recent criticism—see Benson, "The *Canterbury Tales:* Personal Drama or Experiments in Poetic Variety," and Lawton, *Chaucer's Narrators,* who want to separate the narrating voice of any tale from the pilgrim teller so that the tale provides no key to the teller's character. See also Pearsall, *The Canterbury Tales,* 148. I will argue later that many issues are confused here and that the power of an energized "voice" to convey a vivid sense of character, of presence, is much underestimated. Among the confusions are those of tale and text, of style and tale-telling manner, and the dramatic and the psychological. I will argue, however, that we err egregiously when we read any of the tales as though they were dreamworks emanating from their tellers. The tellers are more than narrative bridges to their tales; the tales are quite other than dreams of their tellers.

2 See Coleman, *Medieval Readers and Writers: 1350–1400,* 199–200. Also Pearsall, *The Canterbury Tales,* 298–301, for an account of the various fifteenth-century collections and anthologies of Chaucer's tales. But Cooper, *The Structure of the Canterbury Tales,* argues from some medieval treatments of the tales that Chaucer may have wanted them read in groups, even though he avoided directions and organizing devices common to the tale collections of other medieval poets.

3 Howard, *The Idea of the Canterbury Tales,* proposes memory and the labyrinth quite persuasively. Kolve, *Chaucer and the Imagery of Narrative,* sees Chaucer using iconographic images speculatively in exploring the possibilities for a collection of tales that resembles a wisdom book. Other books or studies I have in mind are Allen and Moritz, *A Distinction of Stories: The Medieval Unity of Chaucer's Fair Chain of Narratives for Canterbury;* Baldwin, *The Unity of the Canterbury Tales;* Brewer, *Geoffrey Chaucer;* David, *The Strumpet Muse: Art and Morals in Chaucer's Poetry;* Fyler, *Chaucer and Ovid;* Huppé, *A Reading of the Canterbury Tales;* Jordan, *Chaucer and the Shape of Creation;* Lawler, *The One and the Many in the Canterbury Tales;* Lumiansky, *Of Sondry Folk: The Dramatic Principle in the Canterbury Tales;* Owen, *Pilgrimage and Storytelling in the Canterbury Tales;* Patch, *On Rereading Chaucer;* Ruggiers, *The Art of the Canterbury Tales;* Spiers, *Chaucer the Maker.* Allen and Moritz classify the tales into four

categories inspired by medieval distinctions concerning metamorphoses and descents into hell. The tales then show "a unity of moral purpose and of general subject" (23). The subject is marriage in all of its personal, social, and spiritual implications—an ethical subject, essentially, and an idealizing thematic frame for the entire collection.

4 This has been well established, if not precisely or complexly enough understood. Recently Mann, *Chaucer and Medieval Estates Satire*, has convincingly explored the open-ended nature of that satire—in which our feel for many of the *GP* portraits depends as much upon what is not said, upon ambiguity, as upon what is said—and its debt to medieval estates conventions. Previous criticism usually focused on moral ironies as conveyed by details of person, dress, and speech.

5 Patterson, "The 'Parson's Tale' and the Quitting of the 'Canterbury Tales,'" argues that the *Parson's Tale*, composed separately, takes us away from the rest of the tales. Composition aside, the tale's separation from all the rest and the negotiation between Parson and Host do effectively end one kind of game and move us to something radically different—rather than enclose or resolve the tales in ways that Lawler, *The One and the Many*, and others would have Chaucer do. Lawton, *Chaucer's Narrators*, 36, thinks of the religious nature of pilgrimage as "conspicuously begged in *The General Prologue*," such that Chaucer needs "a penitential correction." Presumably Chaucer labors long over the fool's gold of tales and tellers (in most cases), so that he may defer strategically the final summing up and correction—a rebuke to sin and to the harlotry of fables. That laborious deferral would be difficult to understand if Chaucer were not as attracted to the world of tellers and tales as he is, in Lawton's word, "anxious" about his interest in and creation of such a world. Perhaps the pilgrimage frame is both license and safety net. In any case, the Parson simply negotiates to leave the play of tales behind and reorient the pilgrims to each other and to himself, replacing the Host as guide.

6 Howard, *The Idea of the Canterbury Tales*, 72–73, notes that during the "one-way passage *through* the world" that a pilgrimage was in "the traditional topos, and in practice," curiosity might lure the pilgrim—the journey could become a wandering by the way.

7 Howard, *The Idea of the Canterbury Tales*, 327–332.

8 The *Troilus* narrator sought understanding, but not by imposing himself, not by appropriation.

9 I have in mind a performance quite different from Lawton's notion of tale telling as Chaucer's way of drawing "discreet yet forceful attention to the narratorial presentation of the tale," which implicates an audience as a witness, and which means that the "I" "of narration is demonstrably not the "I" of the ostensible teller," *Chaucer's Narrators*, 92–96. That "demonstrably" should raise eyebrows, but Lawton's general point is sound: the tales in their textures are not dramatic utterances by individualized, psychologically conceived characters—a point Allen and Moritz, *A Distinction of Stories*, 11–17, also make. Nevertheless, the dramatic monologue theory hardly exhausts possibilities for characterization or for the psychological. The swing from a notion of realistic character psychology to an emphasis on stylistic formalisms is not the only arc possible—not in Chaucer studies now any more than in post-Bradleyan Shakespearean studies thirty years ago. The dramatic

monologue theory owes much to Kittredge, *Chaucer and His Poetry*, and to Lumiansky, *Of Sondry Folk*.

10 Fyler, *Chaucer and Ovid*, 22, sees Chaucer, like Ovid, as exploring how emotion "inevitably frustrates rational control," which in turn leads to "a view of the limitations of human reason and knowledge." Chaucer, I think, was not quite so ambitious or so pessimistic, nor does he split emotion from reason and perception. For a study of Chaucer's qualified skepticism, see Delany, *Chaucer's House of Fame: The Poetics of Skeptical Fideism*.

11 Kolve, *Chaucer and the Imagery of Narrative*, 82. Also, recent criticism has focused on Chaucer's pluralism (Sklute, *Virtue of Necessity*), on his reflexivity (Aers, *Chaucer, Langland and the Creative Imagination*), and on his hermeneutical interest in the hazards of discourse (Ferster, *Chaucer on Interpretation*).

12 Burlin, *Chaucerian Fiction*, 167.

13 David, *The Strumpet Muse*, 74–75.

14 Sklute, *Virtue of Necessity*, 114. This remark can apply partially to the truths Chaucer's tellers state for the tales they tell but not at all to the issue of tales as truth bearers. It may well be that attending to a limited teller's insufficient but not entirely blind claims can enhance, rather than diminish, our sense of the truth a tale may tell.

15 Using the terms of information theory, Bogdan, "The Manufacture of Belief," sees the content of belief as made up of the joint valuation of an entire configuration of things or representations—a configuration that specifies both the information believed and an active attitude toward (or an occurrent reading of) that information (especially 165–67). Thus I would not place Chaucer in the Pauline tradition that changes *pistes* (probable truth) to *fides* as a way of approaching intellection (see Hirshberg, "'Cosyn to the Dede': The 'Canterbury Tales' and the Platonic Tradition in Medieval Rhetoric," 115). Chaucer seems closer to Aristotle's probative balance of reason and appetite (Grimaldi, *Aristotle, Rhetoric I*, 354).

16 For a sweeping overview, see Nuchelmans, *Theories of the Proposition*.

17 The exemplum is something Chaucer nearly always fictionalizes within a larger frame and subjects to the use of a narrator. See Burrow, *Ricardian Poetry: Chaucer, Gower, Langland and the Gawain Poet*, 88–89.

18 In Pegis, *Introduction to St. Thomas Aquinas*.

19 See Gilby, *Thomas Aquinas Summas Theologiae*, 251–25.

20 For apprehension as a form of appraisal, which in turn involves truth as something recognized rather than proved, see Rodway, *The Truths of Fiction*, 99–101. The notion of characters and their voices as "constructed referents" comes from Martin, *Language, Truth and Poetry*, 92: "clearly 'Don Quixote' never had any corresponding referent in the real world. But of course this is a naively superficial statement. 'Don Quixote' is a constructed referent: he refers to a set of human characteristics that are very much a part of the real world. Thus . . . fictional referents do indeed refer, though indirectly. And we must add that this indirect reference allows a writer the freedom to recreate the infinite detail of experience, and hence to refer to the real world more fully and (paradoxically) more directly than any work of fact or reportage can."

21 For the idea of "circumlocution," I am indebted to Gendlin, *Experiencing and the*

Creation of Meaning (45–47, 135–36). In discussing "felt meaning" he suggests that when the symbols involved do not adequately symbolize the meanings we experience or know of from experience, then we try circumlocutions (if speaking) or attend to them (if reading) in an effort to build up the sense of felt meaning, which when experienced might lead us to an adequate symbolization or metaphor and thus to understanding (assuming we have relevant experience or knowledge).

22 See Nelson Goodman, *Ways of Worldmaking*, 19. On the truths of fiction, see Rodway, *The Truths of Fiction*, 99.

23 See Peirce, *Writings of Charles S. Peirce*, (471–95, 517). The triadic logic invoked here involves references to ground (or quality), correlates, and interpretant (involving a further triad of representations through either likeness, pointers, or symbolization). That Chaucer's thinking should in some categorical respects prefigure American pragmatism is not as astonishing as it initially sounds, once we note that pragmatism is a serious effort to overcome the difficulties in both realism and nominalistic materialism (especially concerning the participation of forms in the material world and the emergence of appearances from the world's deep structure, respectively). Pragmatism also tries to deal with such tensions between the two as the tendency to integrate laws and forms on the one hand and to reify backdoor guarantees on the other for why things appear or behave as they do. Perhaps it is Chaucer's version of pragmatism that in effect stymies our efforts to make him either Plato's familiar—however much he leans in that direction—or a wielder of Ockham's instrument.

24 Robertson, *A Preface to Chaucer*, 330–31, comes as close as anyone does, but even he turns doctrine into an illumination of something human—an "attitude" in the Wife of Bath's case. Robertson would have Chaucer scathingly denounce the carnal understanding Chaucer incarnates in the Wife of Bath—a carnality that Robertson would have Chaucer think of philosophically and represent iconographically. We still respond to the "feminine" in the Wife because Chaucer has accurately conceived carnal humanness in his rendering of her.

25 Both Quintilian and the author of the *Ad Herennium* think of historical narrative as largely true, distinguishing it from mythology and tragedy, as well as from comedy (which nevertheless has plausibility or verisimilitude and might be true). These distinctions in *Ad Herennium*, 1, viii–ix appear in the context of law court arguments, of presenting a statement of facts where plausibility is desired whether or not the facts in question are true.

26 Delany, *Chaucer's House of Fame: The Poetics of Fideism*, 24–25, carefully discusses this passage from the *PLGW*. At the least, she would have Chaucer say that we need to give fideistic assent to traditional literary and historical sources, having his narrator turn this into something like a leap of faith there where no adequate proof is available. We leap because otherwise we would court agnosticism. But this view mistakes the role of proof in Chaucer's narrator's statement: Proof, presumably from our own experience, might disconfirm something we find in old stories. Lacking such proof, belief (but not an assertion of dogma or faith) is best. Also see Karla Taylor, *Chaucer Reads 'The Divine Comedy,'* 40–46, for a view of "authentication" that reduces truth to something either authoritative or simply something that one says. By invoking an opaque sense of the imagination as a fabricating or

falsifying agency, Taylor too quickly resolves the hard issue of combined truth and falsehood in the nature of any "tyding," along with our relation both to the "tydings" of others as well as our own. To what in ourselves and in our experiences is a plausible tale conformable? Chaucer's answer, I am convinced, is enticingly Neoplatonic in its orientation if not in its actual commitments.

27 Howard, "Chaucer's Idea of an Idea," suggests that for Chaucer tidings make up poems and poems become things wherein we must search for truth without further directives. But finally Howard focuses on truths about tellers and on poems as seemings—not as bearers of various, including objective, truths.

28 For the idea of "grid" I am indebted to Douglas, *Natural Symbols: Explorations in Cosmology*. In her treatment, social groups form either around a sense of the group or around internal relationships or both to some degree. The Host would form a group with no strong, prior sense of group around himself into a tale-telling "grid," in which ground rules relate the pilgrims to each other on an ego-centered basis (competition). Kendrick, *Chaucerian Play: Comedy and Control in the Canterbury Tales*, 102–115, discusses the Host's role as master of the revels, emphasizing the Host's playful aggression, his seamy-side jokes at the expense of various pilgrims, but not well contextualizing that play in the Host's own losses of control at various turns (beginning with the Miller's trumping of the Host's first move toward the Monk). Nevertheless, Kendrick nicely indicates the Host's misruling preferences for fables and fabliaux from members of the clergy.

Chapter 2: The Poetics of Reverence and Delight

1 A notable and occasionally brilliant exception to relativized readings of Chaucer's tales is Lawler, *The One and the Many in the Canterbury Tales*. Our studies coincide most closely in our respective discussions of the Canon's Yeoman and of the *Tale of Melibee*, at the level of practical criticism. A formistic philosophical orientation might have led Lawler in my direction here.

2 Armstrong, *The Folklore of Birds*, 69–93. In the *Parliament* Chaucer names the crow with "vois of care" in the same line as the wise raven (l. 363). See also Trevisa's translation of Bartholomew's *De Proprietatibus Rerum, On the Properties of Things*, vol. 1, 620–21. Crows are clever teachers and warn about what shall befall. They appear in much folklore, mixed in with ravens often enough and betokening doom or bad weather or being messengers and speaking truth. Thus the multitude of "gestes" speak truth, however we understand their raucous voices, and apparently we need to remember that Chaucer's tiding-bearing crows (as in the *Manciple's Tale*) can lie as well as unknowingly speak falsehood with their truths.

3 For Kittredge's statement, see Kittredge, 155.

4 Leicester, "The Art of Impersonation," nicely dissects a naive view of persona and character revelation: "the speaker is created by the text itself as a structure of linguistic relationships" (217). But he does continue to think of the tales as texturally bespeaking the speaker they create. Jordan, *Chaucer's Poetics and the Modern Reader*, 122, finds little difference from tale to tale in the unfolding "now" of the telling, although he seems to be looking at rhetorical blocks, junctures, and phrases that move from one part to another. Lawton, *Chaucer's Narrators*, 7, distinguishes

between open and closed personae and narratorial voice, using characters sometimes in the usual way and seeing them sometimes as just unmarked narrators, as
dramatically neutral voices that mainly move the narrative along.

5 See Ferster, *Chaucer on Interpretation*, 50–51, for an ambiguous exception: In a
section on the dangers of will in interpretation, she notices that "will" includes
sexual appetite or "more general desire." But she ignores lines in the passage dis-
cussed (*Parliament of Fowls*, 4–13) on the narrator's astonished feeling as he confronts Love's wonderful workings. It is not feeling she emphasizes but helplessness, in contrast to the action for which one needs a will. Yet the narrator is not
"numbed" by desire; rather he is so astonished that his feeling cannot lead him to
an understanding of Love's contradictions. Will is not simply a matter of intellect,
nor is it a synonym for desire. That which is desired, which is good and fitting,
may move the will. Of course one can have intellection without moving the will,
without undertaking a choice (at least in Aquinas *Summa* 2.9.2).

6 For a notable exception to the phenomenological link between cognition and will,
see Merleau-Ponty, *Phenomenology of Perception*, 156. For him, sexually functioning human beings perceive objects with two resonances at once: objective perception has within it "a more intimate perception: the visible body is subtended by
a sexual schema, which is strictly individual . . . [without which] perception has
lost its erotic structure." For Merleau-Ponty, sexuality has internal links with the
"whole active and cognitive being."

7 There's a remarkable resemblance between the pleasures and anticipations of
Chaucer's early narrators and an aesthetic of purposive structure as worked out by
Pepper, *Concept and Quality*, 450–51, with its operational-correspondence theory
of truth: We perceive a claim of some sort; we understand the claim at an accept-
able, propositional level; we devise a way of verifying the claim that involves various, anticipatory operations; then we proceed with the pattern of anticipatory sets
until they terminate, whether satisfactorily or not. If we reach satisfaction, then
the proposition is true. Lacking a verifying reference, the best one can do is understand the internal coherence of the world from which the proposition comes, in
anticipation of eventually having a verifying reference and an anticipatory procedure come to mind. This is the lot of the reader-dreamer, awaiting some verifying
insight, lacking which he or she still tries to make sense of the old books in an
open-minded, felt way.

8 Burnley, *Chaucer's Language and the Philospher's Tradition*, 163, notes that
Chaucer "was among the first to use the words *felyng* and *sentement* in English in
their emotional senses." Nevertheless, Burnley's Chaucer adopts an ironic distance, remaining aloof as an investigator might from love and "gentilesse."

9 Burnley, *Chaucer's Language*, 136.

10 Eco, *Art and Beauty in the Middle Ages*, 81, sees Aquinas's sense of beauty as
something distinct from Neoplatonism in that light and clarity, the beauty and ex-
pressiveness of a thing, come from its heart, its substantial form, rather than de-
scending from above. Aesthetic perception concerns appetite, but appetite comes to
rest in the thing perceived, with perception being a kind of disinterested knowledge
that differs from the ecstasies and sensuousness of mystical love (Eco, *Art and
Beauty*, 72). Chaucer does not strike me as a follower of Aquinas in this disin-

terestedness. Nor is he a mystic. But his emphases on feeling, on delight, and on belief put him loosely in the company of such mystics as Hugh of St. Victor, Bonaventura, and William of Auvergne, given their intertwining of terms (especially in William's case) for cognition and for the affections (placere, delectare). See Eco, *Art and Beauty*, 67–68; also, Hyman and Walsh, *Philosophy in the Middle Ages*, 465, for Bonaventura's consideration of delight in relation to our physical, intellectual, and spiritual senses.

11 Cunningham, "The Literary Form of the Prologue to the *Canterbury Tales*," was one of the first to dwell on the similarity. Howard, *The Idea of the Canterbury Tales*, 155, asserts it unequivocally. Jordan, *Chaucer's Poetics and the Modern Reader*, 121, exploits it to undermine Donaldsonian treatments of the narrator, finding the GP narrator, as with the dream-vision narrator, to be little more than a "compositional device to establish the presentational level of the text and to effectuate narrative movement."

12 Leyerle, "Chaucer's Windy Eagle," 206, may have been the first scholar to link the House of Rumor with the tales of Canterbury.

13 Kiser, *Telling Classical Tales*, 30.

14 A hierarchy of sorts suggests itself here, with supposing and opinion at the bottom ("Men shal not wenen every thyng a lye") and a remembrance of truth at the top. In the middle we find the way of readerly knowing: belief intermingled with delight and reverence. Perhaps this is as close as Chaucer comes to a Platonic noesis, as we find it in the *Republic*, bk. 6: Socrates has Glaucon divide that which is seen from that which is intellected; he then has Glaucon further divide that which is seen and that which is intellected in the same proportion as the original division. This yields four divisions, with awareness of sensory images the largest area (cf. Chaucer's "seyn with ye!"), followed by two equal areas of intellection—that of things and the processes of thought (hypotheses, dialectic—cf. Chaucer's "thing is never the lasse sooth" and "in every skylful wise," *PLGW*, F, ll. 14, 20). The fourth and smallest area is that of the intellection of forms (*nous*). See Bloom, *The Republic of Plato*, 190–92, 464. Dialectic has beginnings and ends, using hypotheses and images. The intellection of forms begins with hypotheses and uses the forms themselves, being freed of reliance upon images. In relation to this scheme, opinion rooted in the senses is neither image nor thought for Chaucer ("For, God wot, thing is never the lasse sooth, / Though every wight ne may it nat yse"). It certainly is not pure intellection, something approached only through the openness of felt belief and that involves reason in the assaying of what we read and hear. Approached in this way, books become keys to a remembering, a knowledge the soul can have, of which the body may never have either experience or trust (either sensation or image)—although "imagination" in some sense is part of this view of knowing. Burlin, *Chaucerian Fiction*, emphasizes imagination as a way of knowing for Chaucer, but mainly by suggestion in the face of inconclusiveness and subversion rather than by an analysis of such Chaucerian passages as this one.

15 For Chaucer we would markedly change but still appreciate a similar orientation regarding Dante and his reader, at least as Colish, *The Mirror of Language*, 339, expresses that relationship: Dante would "reproduce in the reader a conversion similar to the series of catharses and illuminations which Dante the traveler under-

goes. . . . The traveler . . . and by extension, the reader, grows in knowledge as he grows in love and as his aesthetic senses are strengthened. . . . In this way he [Dante] underlines the notion that love and beauty are ways of knowing. Joy, for Dante, is not the consequence of knowledge, but its concomitant."

16 In Book 4, metrum 5, Boethius opposes the ignorance of impressionable people to a knowledge of causes. Wonder is the turning point, as one moves from astonishment about natural phenomena to an inquiring wonder about "the lawe of the heie eyr" (l. 9). Wonder as the beginning of philosophical inquiry and of knowledge is given by Aristotle in *Metaphysics* 2.982b.ll. 11–28. Chaucer exploits the sapient potential in wonder as his hapless narrators react to their circumstances or to aspects of their dreams: the *Book of the Duchess* narrator wonders greatly that he still lives, while the *House of Fame* narrator wonders about the causes of dreams and finds much to wonder at in the houses of fame and rumor (including Lady Fame's changes of magnitude, details of physiognomy, and the size and character of the House of Rumor). The *House of Fame* narrator also expresses wonder in his view of vigorous weather and its engenderings, its causes (ll. 970–78). And in the *Parliament of Fowls*, the narrator admits to astonished feelings as he considers the "wonderful" workings of Love (an initially ignorant wonder that then hopes for knowledge). But in the *Prologue* to the *Legend*, wonder has given way to delight and reverence, to an openness of felt belief by which we are invited, both wryly and otherwise, to believe what authors say in stories and "gestes," if we please (G, ll. 87–88).

17 Muscatine, *Poetry and Crisis in the Age of Chaucer* recalls the thirteenth-century "discovery" of the child and its role in the vogue of mother-child pathos. His discussion of pathos in the *Tales* is a ground-breaking suggestion for a mode of feeling that could operate as one of several alternatives to irony. The most notable text, of course, is the *Prioress's Tale*, not least in the universally sobering effect it has on the pilgrims and in its place just before Chaucer the Pilgrim's two tales.

18 I am reminded of a point Nelson Goodman makes, in *Problems and Projects*, 109: "In aesthetic experience, emotion positive or negative is a mode of sensitivity to a work. The problem of tragedy and the paradox of ugliness evaporate." Emotion is cognitive, no more so than when we would consider the feelings a work expresses, because the terms we use are "metaphorical descriptions of structural (or other) properties the work has and exemplifies. Only at the risk of overlooking important structural features of a work can a formalist ignore what the work expresses" (127). This is especially true of Chaucer's interest in tales of pathos, and it makes emotive knowing a form of reference—initially discriminating of aspects of the work and finally relating what is "experienced to what lies beyond it" (132).

19 Burlin, *Chaucerian Fiction*, 38–58.

20 Jordan, *Chaucer's Poetics and the Modern Reader*, 161.

21 A set of cards, each with a clue, and a blank card make up the test. The person tested invents a story based on the scenes or parts of scenes presented on the cards. Thus something is there to begin with, outside the viewer. In the case of fiction even much more is there, outside the reader, who reads more than he invents. That, I think, is closer to Chaucer's idea of teller and tale than is the notion that all the details of the tale relate to the teller as might the overdetermined details of a

dream or that mixture of fantasy, insight, and aesthetic control—the invented story.

22 See the essay by Wetherbee in *Geoffrey Chaucer*, which suggests the futility of precisely defining Chaucer's spiritual or philosophical workings in terms of four-teenth-century intellectual developments. For Wetherbee, Chaucer seems to share the "general lack of certainty of his characters"—because most of the Canterbury pilgrims hardly seem uncertain, Wetherbee probably has the dream-vision nar-rators in mind—and to emphasize obstacles to knowledge while dramatizing his characters' "inherent capacities for love and spirituality" (89). I am in accord with this statement to some extent, although crucially it either misses or only obliquely senses Chaucer's view of feeling, belief, and cognition. Chaucer may well be as much at sea as many late twentieth-century readers say he is, but he is not merely drifting. He has paddles and knows which way God is. See Leff, *The Dissolution of the Medieval Outlook*, for a history of fourteenth-century intellectual ferment. Also see Eldredge, "Chaucer's *House of Fame* and the *Via Moderna*; and "Poetry and Philosophy in the *Parliament of Fowls*," along with Sklute, *Virtue of Neces-sity*, 13–22; and Peck, "Chaucer and the Nominalist Questions," for reflections about various poems and fourteenth-century thought. Nominalist emphasis on what Duns Scotus calls the "thisness" or *haecceitas* of things would seem to corre-spond to Chaucer's interest in detail, particularity, and multiplicity. But I doubt that particulars interested Chaucer for their cognizable thisness, of which we can have direct intuition. Chaucer has an emotive theory of perception and will. For Duns Scotus on thisness see Hyman and Walsh, *Philosophy in the Middle Ages*, 631–32.

23 I am conscious of a growing body of theory loosely called reader-response criti-cism. Freund, *The Return of the Reader*, 1987) has conveniently surveyed that body of theory, especially in eventual relation to structuralism and deconstruction (with Culler doing double duty here in successive books: *The Pursuit of Signs* and *Structural Poetics*). For my purposes, Fish, *Self-Consuming Artifacts*, and Iser, *The Act of Reading*, seem more appropriate theorists of reading, but neither one attempts the kind of affective turn I think Chaucer emphasizes. Fish calls his theory of reading an affective stylistics, perhaps because he addresses the entanglements and internalizations of what I. A. Richards would separate as the emotive and re-ferential aspects of language. But Fish's idealized reader has a thoroughly profes-sionalized consciousness, interrogating the text virtually line by line given a set of aesthetic commitments that do not move far from new critical categories. This reader is both the stumbling boob and superintender of his own progress, primarily involved with cognitions, expectations, frustrations, puzzles, and solutions. At his most accomplished, he or she presumably manages to attend to the text's con-textual unfolding as well as to the unfolding of his or her own consciousness in engagement with the text. This is a neat accomplishment, if ever realized—a little like looking carefully at the surface of a pitted mirror while also attending carefully to one's reflected image. Iser, in contrast, offers little that is quixotic or exceptiona-ble in his presentation of the competent reader, except that Iser's reader is oddly affectless as she cognizes the potential of a text into actual communication. That cognizing mainly occurs, in the competent (rather than dilettantish) reader, in

ongoing processes of blocked "ideation," which concern expectations, frustrations, and readjustments as a "basic prerequisite for comprehension" (Iser, *The Act of Reading*, 189). The experiences a text forces upon us become our way of comprehending it. In this respect, Iser's competent reader resembles Chaucer's dream-vision narrators more than she resembles the Canterbury pilgrims (who in their turn resemble Iser's dilettante—someone who may be a garrulous ignorer of indeterminacies, but who certainly is habitually inclined to "degrade the knowledge offered or invoked by the text during the process of moulding the imaginary object" (ibid., see also 174). These approaches have something to do with any common sense attention to reading, but they crucially miss the Chaucerian emphasis on felt belief, on an emotive and cognitive openness. This is true, curiously enough, even of reader-response theory indebted to ego psychology, as in Norman Holland's work, and of course in the few applications to medieval texts derived from Fish or Iser. See, for example, Travis, "Affective Criticism and Medieval English Literature."

Chapter 3: Belief and Reading in the Early Poems

1 This seems Aristotelian in that we might ask what the form of reading is, drawing our intuitions about that from observations of actual readings. We might even consider these early poems as gestures toward what comes to fruition in the Canterbury project: a natural history of "gestes," of what they are, of the truths they bear, of how one should read and use them, and therein of how one should read. For Aristotle, the natural world is an object of knowledge insofar as forms somehow subtend the substratum of things, a substrate of potential, of process, out of which the actual world of material things and processes emerges. See Cherniss, *Aristotle's Criticism of Plato and the Academy*, especially chapter 3, and Owens, *The Doctrine of Being in the Aristotelian Metaphysics*, 366–77.

2 The *locus classicus* for some such move is Aristotle's *Art of Rhetoric*, bk. 2, 4–10. On manipulating the audience, see Frank, *Chaucer and the Legend of Good Women*, 11–36. Frank sees Chaucer as maneuvering his audience into accepting what will be uncourtly treatments of love in the various tales of the *Legend*.

3 See Olson, *Literature as Recreation in the Later Middle Ages*, 86.

4 Olson, *Recreation*, 87.

5 See Hill, "The *Book of the Duchess*, Melancholy, and that Eight-Year Sickness," 44–45, where I discuss comedy in the poem as both life-awakening and as displacement.

6 Delany, *Chaucer's House of Fame*, 36–47, notes Chaucer's skepticism about the truth value of dreams—a skepticism that spills over into his attitudes toward fiction, with dreams and fiction literally mingled and metaphorically interrelated. Delany notes the narrator's request that we judge dreams aright ("demen" rather than some word for belief), which opens the whole matter for judgment. Jordan, *Chaucer's Poetics and the Modern Reader*, 37–38, treats the entire, tactless, shifting, and comical discussion of dreams as Chaucer's way of here foregrounding verbal rendering and thereby dramatizing "the gap between experience and its verbal rendering." The story then becomes one of writing itself. Presented as "per-

siflage," the telling becomes crucial to the "ironic rhetorical mode of the poem." In
Medieval Dream-Poetry, 74, A. C. Spearing adds that in representing one imaginative product as an analogue for another, Chaucer escapes the judgment of fiction
as lie and links it to ambivalence (dreams being considered highly ambivalent). For
Boitano, *English Medieval Narrative*, 168, airy ambiguity, if not mere ambivalence, seems to be Chaucer's response to everything addressed in the *House of Fame*.

7 Jordan, *Chaucer's Poetics*, 46, would agree that the *House of Fame* is about or
treats many subjects, including its own composition. But his discussion over-
whelmingly focuses on the poem's rhetoricity, virtuosity, and lack, not of themes,
but of themes subordinated to one another within a consistent scheme. I would
agree that the poem is an assortment of amusing moments and that the narrator's
is not a psychologically coherent mind. But he is a persona, a speaker who reacts to
what he confronts in moments that are variously serious or funny (or both). We
are right, I think, to infer what we can on Chaucer's behalf from those fictional
confrontations. They are of the world of readers and books rather than constructed
according to some incomprehensible logic. See Heintz, "Reference and Inference in
Fiction," for a logic of inference in fiction that countenances both contradiction and
incompleteness.

8 Sklute, *Virtue of Necessity*, 38–39, attends to the narrator's activity and concludes
that mainly we respond to the persona responding to his story. Instead of letting us
respond to the story of Aeneas, Chaucer creates an "involvement with the persona
and his interests." This involvement becomes a way of raising "questions about
the nature and value of poetic appropriation." Sklute also sees questions here about
the possibly deceptive nature of human communication and artistic representation.
In pursuing inconclusiveness—an outcome that many readers have registered—
Sklute does not stay long enough with the responding persona to estimate what
those responses imply for readers and reading.

9 Jordan, *Chaucer's Poetics*, 45.

10 Delany, *Chaucer's House of Fame*, 52. Here she follows Bennett, *Chaucer's Book
of Fame*, 38. For many readers, however, that sympathy is separate from the possibilities of understanding. Fyler, *Chaucer and Ovid*, 40, for example, sees Chaucer
reacting to more than differences between Virgil and Ovid or to variations within
Virgil's work itself: Beyond the difficulties of truth and falsehood lie enigma and
the impossibility of understanding. Facing the incomprehensible, all one has left is
a "pious hope."

11 Which he must do if he is to adopt a courtly attitude. See Delany, *Chaucer's House
of Fame*, 56, who argues further that in the shift from Virgil to Ovid we see Chaucer facing conflicting versions of the same story, with no rational means of choosing one over the other (for truth value). This is so, but reason is not a controlling
element in Chaucer's theory of reading. In an emotional and cognitive openness—
felt belief—that is how we should approach both versions, insofar as both are reasonable and accordant with our minds. Instead of *remaining* open to Virgil's story,
the narrator reacts so strongly to an undeniably troubling part of it that he translates it into Ovid's—a version that accords better at this point with his mind.

12 McCall, *Chaucer among the Gods*, 50, sees all of this as part of a madcap world in
which the point is simply "that fame, supported by literary records, is entirely irra-

tional and unfair." Fame may be capricious, but sometimes those who deserve fame receive it, and the intermingling of truth and falsehood in some tidings is not something to feel hopeless about.

13 See Kiser, *Telling Classical Tales*, 87, for a perceptive account of Alceste's intercession, for which both Chaucer and the God of Love thank her. The God of Love responds well to Alceste's "eloquent comments on mercy, justice, and good kingship." I do not, however, agree that Alceste is figuratively the "elegant and informed mistress of Chaucer's wit" or art. McCall, *Chaucer among the Gods*, 119, rightly sees Alceste as a good woman, although he goes too far in seeing her through the daisy as the epitome "of all naturally trusting, pledged, and faithful women from antiquity." She is the model of wifely "fyn lovynge," however, and the calendar of goodness and bounty. She has a family relationship with the legends, but she stands apart, as myth does to history.

14 Both Fyler, *Chaucer and Ovid*, and Kiser, *Telling Classical Tales*, show Chaucer using source material selectively, altering likely sources to suit his purpose. This may well involve a humorous attitude toward his task, but it can also involve an effort at platonizing.

15 Lindahl, "The Festive Form of the *Canterbury Tales*," has convincingly worked out the carnival-like character of the Host's plan and the pilgrims' enactments. Kendrick, *Chaucerian Plan*, 126–27, sees this in an expressly Bakhtinian, carnivalesque sense: The "structure of the *Canterbury Tales* involves a contest between gentles and churls engaged on the playing ground of fiction, with the churls' fabliaux and beast fables repeatedly overturning with blatantly infantile desire the repressive authority embodied in the gentles' fictions, and with the gentles ever reasserting the powers of censorship and sublimation through their romances, saints' lives, tragic exempla, and sermons"—a contest that Chaucer directs for socially therapeutic ends, aiming at an image of restored social stability. This idealized view of both carnival and psychology does service to no tale, but it touches Chaucer's holiday structuring of the tale tellings. Moreover, Kendrick's view unfortunately divides the pilgrim company Chaucer has set into a holiday social group—not gentle mixed with churl, but pilgrims and companions all, "ruled" quite loosely by the Host.

16 See especially Gaylord, "*Sentence* and *Solaas* in Fragment VII of the *Canterbury Tales*," PMLA 82 (1967): 226–35.

Chapter 4: The Canon's Yeoman's Tale *and the* Manciple's Tale

 1 The fullest exposition of this is in Rosenberg, "The Contrary Tales of The Second Nun and The Canon's Yeoman." Studies that invite us to see a spiritual alchemy behind the Yeoman's language aid the kind of reading Rosenberg produces. See Grennen, "The Canon's Yeoman and the Cosmic Furnace," and Grenberg, "*The Canon's Yeoman's Tale*." Various readers see contrasting relationships, if not a definitive movement from true to false. See Muscatine, *Chaucer and the French Tradition*, 215–17; Peck, "Sovereignty and the Two Worlds of the *Franklin's Tale*"; P. B. Taylor, "The Canon's Yeoman's Breath"; Whittock, *A Reading of the Canterbury Tales*, 255; Norman T. Harrington, "Experience, Art, and the Framing

of the *Canterbury Tales*"; and Olson, "Chaucer, Dante, and the Structure of Fragment VIII (G) of the *Canterbury Tales*." Some of the contrasts noted concern blindness and sight, mere reason and revelation, calm and flux, and converse purgatories. For readings that do not see especially intimate connections between the two tales, see David, *The Strumpet Muse*, 234, and Pearsall, *The Canterbury Tales*, 256.

2 The fullest version of this is Dean's, "Dismantling the Canterbury Book"; also see Howard, *The Idea of the Canterbury Tales*, 305–6, for a sense of an ending that is "almost a mock apocalypse."

3 Only Chaucer's instances are given as exceptions in the *Middle English Dictionary*, a status they have only if they indeed refer forward to the treatise on penance and the seven deadly sins.

4 See notes in Robinson's second edition and in Benson's *Riverside Chaucer*.

5 As noted by Owen, "The Transformation of a Frame Story," 125–46.

6 References to time and place convince Charles Owen that the tale belongs, finally, at the beginning of the return journey from Canterbury. Whether one accepts this or not, and it has a lineage going back to Ten Brink, nothing links the *Manciple's Tale* to the *Canon's Yeoman's Tale* or, aside from a name, securely to the *Parson's Prologue*. The latter is the more significant point: in the Hengwrt MS. Christ Church, the Yeoman is named. Moreover, as many editors note, if it is morning still when the the Manciple begins his tale, it can hardly be four in the afternoon when he ends. Is Chaucer revising in this instance? Probably. If so, he has not progressed far, and we have only the ordering of tales in most manuscripts to link Manciple to Parson. That may have been how Chaucer left the matter (and how scribal editors understood it), but to build a sense of an ending upon these fragments is surely to build on uncertain foundations on either side of the *Parson's Prologue*.

7 Reames, "The Cecilia Legend as Chaucer Inherited It and Retold It," observes that Valerian sees the Angel before believing. Reames shows Chaucer revising the legend to emphasize a life in which the human soul "is incapable of responding in knowledge and love to the divine initiative. Nor are human fruitfulness and continuity very real possibilities in a world where converts are seized directly by a higher power and set on the shortest road to martyrdom" (54). Perhaps choice in one's spiritual life is just as troubling and just as influenced by temperament as is any other choice for Chaucer. He may have found the Second Nun's spirituality personally distasteful, or scrupulously reserving judgment, at least a spirituality that did not speak to him, however much he might credit this tale of Cecile.

8 See Pearsall, *The Canterbury Tales*, 255, on Cecile's triumphant, even rampant virginity. Howard, *The Idea of the Canterbury Tales*, 288, sees the tale as the last of a group of "ideal" tales and one that depicts a higher kind of marriage.

9 Patch, *On Rereading Chaucer*, 174, senses a gentle, sympathetic irony, less grim by far than Cecilia's hold on her chastity.

10 Shepherd, "Religion and Philosophy in Chaucer," 269, finds that Chaucer, although aware of what was going on in fourteenth-century religious movements, does not disclose his own commitments or judge others. Compared to Langland, Chaucer attenuates rather than obsessively enacts the burning issues of his day.

This seems right, even though Chaucer has sober, moral concerns, and returns several times to the pathetic in religious feeling.

11 Howard, *The Idea of the Canterbury Tales*, 292.

12 Cf. *Boece*, bk. 5, prose 4, ll. 141–66.

13 The practice is common, and always at the Canon's Yeoman's expense, even if the Yeoman is seen as changing his life in the course of joining the pilgrimage. See, for example, Brown, "Is the 'Canon's Yeoman's Tale' Apochryphal?" Sklute, *Virtue of Necessity*, 125, notes that the order of reading for these tales "reveals the theme of business, profit and 'multiplicacioun,' unusually. . . . Only by the retrospective contrast of *CYT* . . . does the literal story of Saint Cecilia assume the metaphorical richness we understand it to carry."

14 Howard, *The Idea of the Canterbury Tales*, 295, sees the Yeoman as continuing to believe in alchemic experiments as a possibility. Thus his tale of con artistry "is criticizing not science but the abuse of science." Lawler, *The One and the Many*, 136–44, indicates how strongly alchemic practice attracted the Yeoman in the past and how it seems to attract him still, although in joining the pilgrimage and telling his tale (becoming an author), he is "returned to the gay freedom he once enjoyed."

15 Muscatine, *Chaucer and the French Tradition*, 1964, 220.

16 Evidence of that vulnerability appears in his tale of con artistry and in his closing remarks. For a perceptive observation on the inconclusiveness of those remarks, see Burlin, *Chaucerian Fiction*, 179. However, Burlin overreads the Yeoman's specific ego investment here by not paying sufficient attention to the functional effects of the Yeoman's prosecutorial handling of his tale.

17 Nevertheless he believes in this craft at some level, despite attempts to debunk alchemy. Contrary to Grenberg, *"The Canon's Yeoman's Tale,"* the Yeoman never quite expresses a Boethian wisdom, although he eventually distinguishes between dull sight and forewarned thought (ll. 1418–19). He remains confused and a little fearful, a situation Ryan, "The Canon's Yeoman's Desperate Confession," ably articulates. The Yeoman confesses, but he holds back; he would repent, but he betrays a lingering hope in the quest still (Ryan, 307).

18 Lawler, *The One and the Many*, 1980, 134.

19 Ibid., 135.

20 Ruggiers, *The Art of the Canterbury Tales*, 137, appropriately notes a shift in tone, although he overreacts, I think, in characterizing it as "aggressively sardonic" and as resulting from the Yeoman's poisoned, personal grievance against his former master, "disguised as a righteous warning to canons about the Judas in their midst." This is a sharp move away from an older view, such as Patch's sense that Chaucer actually likes the Canon's Yeoman, even in his belching out of lists (*On Rereading Chaucer*, 179). That view has been championed by David Harrington, "The Narrator of the *Canon's Yeoman's Tale*," who sees the Canon's Yeoman as sensible and obligingly informative. Cook, "The Canon's Yeoman and His Tale," sees the Yeoman's helter-skelter lists as a deliberate attempt to portray the hopeless complexity of alchemic practice. For Cook this ingenious Yeoman is morally attractive and, very likely, permanently reformed (Cook, 24, 30). Burlin, *Chaucerian Fiction*, 178–79, has in part anticipated my point about clarification through the

tale of con artistry: reading the trickster illustration as a way for the Yeoman to settle his own guilt and stupidity (projected onto the trickster), Burlin sees the Yeoman as freeing himself, publicly at least. His closing use of philosophers is seen mainly as a way to distance himself further in an ego-boosting show of learning. The tale of trickery is a way of projecting guilt and freeing himself of complicity before taking on the theoretical problem of alchemy. But Burlin overreads the case without really entering into the psychological dynamics of this tale telling (which would have to entertain a dynamics of revenge and restitution that encompasses the entire performance, from sweaty entry to closing advice).

21 Burlin, *Chaucerian Fiction*, 178, notes that the Yeoman lacks the analytical ability to penetrate his master's obscurities as well as his own responses to alchemy. This seems right, although the Yeoman's continuing, lingering belief in alchemy is not clearly like that of the confirmed gambler's psychology (knowing better, but . . .), as Burlin would have it. The issue is complicated by clear authority, divine and otherwise, for the possibility of transmutation.

22 Scattergood, "The Manciple's Manner of Speaking," convincingly opposes a line of criticism that sees the Manciple as successful and discreet. He also notes parallels between the Manciple and the crow. Ruggiers, *The Art of the Canterbury Tales*, 248, finds the prologue both coarse and cruel, but he does not go on to see strong links between prologue and tale. Pearsall, *The Canterbury Tales*, 243, sees a low-level dramatic link between prologue and tale but not one that requires an elaborate characterization of the Manciple. Rather, the prologue and aspects of the tale better reflect Chaucer's stylistic experiments.

23 Hazelton, "The Manciple's Tale," takes hints of parody here and elsewhere into account when presenting the tale itself as a parody of parodies. It mocks those who would overlook its comic art and struggle for the moral within this fable of immorality. This view commends itself on two grounds: the fable of the crow is not taken with moral seriousness; and the Manciple's telling of the tale does involve him in comical gestures and evasions. But Hazelton does not pay sufficient attention to just what the Manciple does in the course of telling the tale and reducing its dimensions.

24 Howard, *The Idea of the Canterbury Tales*, 305, rightly tells us that the Manciple's style "is unsavory like the man himself. His tale destroys everything and does it coldly. . . . We are left in a bleak, mean world where the guarded tongue is the best counsel"—wordily given though it is. This meanness then becomes something to wrestle with: Does it actually take Chaucer to an ending to the collection? Does it suggest something we could almost call a "mock apocalypse"? I am doubtful (see earlier in this chapter). But even if the *Manciple's Tale* were meant to precede the *Parson's Prologue*, we still would have no good reason to take the Manciple in Chaucer's place.

25 Robert Payne, "Making His Own Myth," 200.

26 Payne, "Making His Own Myth," 207–8. Beauty, whether that of an actual or a literary daisy, a poem, or spring morning, incites desire, and that, Payne suggests, is Chaucer's essentially Platonic way of knowing the mystery of beauty, art, and love. Beauty does awaken us, arousing desire and wonder. But understanding what books tell us—getting at truth intermingled with falsehood—requires desire leav-

ened with feeling, reverence, delight, and those accords of mind and reason that Chaucer invokes in the *Prologue to the Legend of Good Women*. One wonders how such wonder and then such felt belief could be awakened in the Manciple.

27 Mark Allen, "Penitential Sermons, the Manciple, and the End of the *Canterbury Tales*," 83, sees the Manciple's discussion of lady and "lemman" as vaguely nominalistic. It may well be, for the Manciple's point is that a lewd thing is a lewd thing no matter how one conceptualizes it. As Chaucer's mean-spirited nominalist, the Manciple may reflect Chaucer's view of a movement that saw relations between things as merely conceptual.

28 The Manciple's cynicism about words and deeds is a hoary trope that Chaucer and others use in various ways—Chaucer early in the work when in the *GP* he cites Plato as saying the words must be cousin to the deed (l. 742). He, Chaucer the Pilgrim, thus asks our indulgence for his reporting of whatever words the pilgrims spoke, although they spoke rudely and broadly, as Christ did also in holy writ. Jean de Meun uses a similar defense in a wry approach to bawdy truth telling, while also recognizing that truth and language, words and deeds may never line up exactly. We should at least try for a relationship, if only a once-removed one. Returning to the Manciple, however, we probably should not think that the link with Plato is other than ironic or perhaps even absurd. See Paul Taylor, "Chaucer's Cosyn to the Dede."

29 In thinking about the tellers, I try to hear inside the Pilgrim "voice" in the prologue whenever possible. The Second Nun barely allows such hearing, but the Canon's Yeoman does, in full, and so does the Manciple. To think of the Manciple in his prologue encounter with the Cook and the Host as mainly an effect of stylistic choices by which Chaucer would simply delineate a possible behavior—that of the rude and crude man—or simply effect a transition into the tale, requires a withdrawal from the drama of the moment to a consciousness of linguistic surface. This is the direction in which Pearsall, *The Canterbury Tales*; Benson, "The Canterbury Tales"; and Lawton, *Chaucer's Narrators*, would like to go. Moreover it is the way in which Knight, *Ryming Craftily*, and Jordan, *Chaucer's Poetics*, have emphatically gone. It is as though we were to witness a violent argument and then, drawing back, were to muse not about our sense of the individuals involved—speculative as that may be—but mainly about the verbal and gestural conventions by which they have expressed their anger, abuse, or sarcasm. Of course in such a case we could not expect a full character analysis; but we could undertake a beginning that later knowledge might fill out or qualify—which is what we do when we attend to the ways a given pilgrim tells his tale and to precisely what he says in response to moments in his tale. We also, in many cases, have a *GP* portrait as a formally encapsulated but impressionistic, and often mixed, foundation. When we listen carefully, inferring whatever we can and then attend to the way a character tells his tale, in effect we attend to complex, self-creating rhetorical acts. The character materializes as we watch, forming a complexity of voice no matter what stylistic register is involved and complexity of motive (and therefore psychology) no matter what nuclear sense we have of the character at any given moment. As characters with labels like Manciple and Canon's Yeoman say things, they in effect express emotions, attitudes, and dispositions of mind. They have objectives and they

address others. Chaucer had available to him a subtle and profound analysis of emotion in Latin translations of Aristotle's *Rhetoric* 2. To take that analysis and individualize the psychologies involved within a verisimilar drama of characters and action is to generate a complexity and liveliness that is antirhetorical if we look only to the uses of stock "character" as similes and devices of amplification in post-Ciceronian rhetoric—a difference that even Quintilian registers when he places Aristotle's discussion within the compass of the common understanding of mankind. He will not pursue that discussion, because it would involve infinite labor and would take him from the narrow issue of credibility in considering those things that different people would desire or do (Butler, *Institutio Oratoria*, 5, 211).

30 Askins, "The Historical Setting of *The Manciple's Tale*," 104, n. 55, speculates that "ape-wine" is counterfeit wine, probably a mixture of French wine, cheap Spanish wine, pitch, and other unwholesome things. The Manciple's characterization of his own wine as of a ripe grape is thus a further insult, a further disparagement of the Cook's drink.

31 "Bourde" is used by the third, and worst, "riotour" in the *Pardoner's Tale* (l. 778) and by the duck in the *Parliament of Fowls* (l. 589)—who characterizes the turtledove's profession of constancy as a stupid joke (who can find reason or wit in loving causelessly?).

32 Contrary, then, to Scattergood, "The Manciple's Manner of Speaking," 136, who argues that the Manciple demonstrates "how, given a cynical disregard for truth and acute verbal dexterity, one can escape the implications of practically anything that one says."

33 Knight, *Ryming Craftily*, 1976, 174.

34 In effect, what the Manciple does is reduce natural inclinations to vileness, to whorishness. Nature becomes a bawd. The quotation is from Robbins, *The Romance of the Rose*, 158.

35 Knight, *Ryming Craftily*, 175, fails to see or hear the Manciple in any of this, especially not in this "complicated apology." Instead he hears a self-aware and rather subtle narrator, someone who is learned and generous with his learning. However, I think we have seen how the Manciple misapplies his sources, how he would lead his tale and control it, and how he stops himself; in that sense he is self-aware.

36 For recent commentary, in addition to Harwood, "Language and the Real," and Scattergood, "The Manciple's Manner of Speaking," see Grubar, "The Manciple's Tale"; Westervelt, "The Medieval Notion of Janglery and Chaucer's *Manciple's Tale*"; and Mark Allen, "Penitential Sermons, the Manciple, and the End of *The Canterbury Tales*." The range is from views of language in the tale as self-contained world to language as sin and language as penance. Implicitly, the "limits" of poetic language are also adduced, a theme partially invoked by Dean, "Dismantling the Canterbury Book," and Howard, "Chaucer's Idea of an Idea" as well.

37 Jordan, *Chaucer's Poetics*, 161–62, would see it otherwise. Indeed, all of the digressions effect for him a "decisive orientation toward the compositional surface," toward a foregrounding of textuality that makes the Manciple little more than "a loosely defined instrumentality" by which Chaucer calls attention to a wide range of the rhetorical (from bombast to irony). In setting out that range, Chaucer does not use the Manciple as a character, but merely as a rhetorical means to a loosely

exploratory end—the artful display of relations between speaker and what is spoken. Jordan has his eye and his ear on strands, on verbal registers that in fact are in the tale, are of the text that is the Manciple telling his tale. In this respect the digressions do indeed invite us to notice the teller. They intrude upon the tale. But how do we move the teller out of the way, reducing him to a loose "instrumentality"? This is done by properly debunking a circular realism within which everything the Manciple says somehow correlates with an a priori vision of his character and by pointing out that various opposites in the tale are "realistically incompatible—the classical and the vulgar, the shrewd and the ingenuous." There are no more powerful points of logical attack than these (noting the circular and the contradictory). But is this an adequate view, even granting that any character in any kind of fiction is foregroundable as a construct? Constructs can be powerfully imitative and exploratory, even deeply referential. What the Manciple says in his tale telling is consistent with what we have seen of him in the *Prologue* and coheres. We form a sense of his character from the whole, which includes what he means by not being textual (quoting bookish examples from memory).

38 See McCall, *Chaucer Among the Gods*, 152.

Chapter 5: The Squire's Tale *and the* Franklin's Tale

1 Howard, *The Idea of the Canterbury Tales*, 267, sees the tale as reflecting a decadent, aristocratic love for "courtly cliches and rhetorical posturings, bromides about love-longing, courtesy, honor, gentilesse, nothing but hearsay tales of distant princes." Kahrl, "Chaucer's *Squire's Tale* and the Decline of Chivalry," thinks mainly of the Squire as callow and of his tale as reflecting a late medieval decadence; Haller, "Chaucer's *Squire's Tale* and the Uses of Rhetoric," thinks of the tale as rhetorically jejune, showing lapses of taste; McCall, "The Squire in Wonderland," and Pearsall, "The Squire as Story-Teller," see the tale as rambling, as too given to incongruity (but see Pearsall, *The Canterbury Tales*). The Squire himself is thought of, mainly, as young and rhetorically inexperienced, although he has been flayed for presumed sins of spirit and flesh. See Fleming, "Chaucer's Squire, the *Roman de la Rose*, and the Romaunt"; Peterson, "The Finished Fragment"; and Wood, "The Significance of Jousting and Dancing as Attributes of Chaucer's Squire's Tale." Berger, "The F-Fragment of the *Canterbury Tales*," blames both callowness and social class for the Squire's confusions.

2 Jennifer Goodman, "Chaucer's Squire's Tale and the Rise of Chivalry," 135, thinks of the tale as a composite romance left unfinished by design. She thinks that a full-length version would have rivaled the entire collection of tales in size.

3 Pearsall, *The Canterbury Tales*, 141. In "The *Canterbury Tales* I: Romance," 115, J. A. Burrow points out that the admiration of Spenser and Milton is not negligible evidence for the tale's quality and that in fact the tale contains some rich passages of poetic narrative.

4 Lawton, *Chaucer's Narrators*, 106–29.

5 Lawton, *Chaucer's Narrators*, 119–29. He suggests the possibility that Hoccleve wrote the headlink. Kean, *Chaucer and the Art of Narrative*, has also suggested a likeness between the tale and a Renaissance poem—Spenser's *Faerie Queene*, which is certainly a composite romance.

6 Douglas Kelly, *Medieval Imagination*, 3.

7 See Wood, "The Significance of Jousting and Dancing as Attributes of Chaucer's *Squire's Tale*," 98–99.

8 Pearsall, "The Squire as Story-Teller," 89.

9 A point Lawton, *Chaucer's Narrators*, 115, makes convincingly. He also speculates that perhaps the ascription of the *Squire's Tale* to the Squire is not Chaucer's own but scribal—a case not made, but one that has some merit (126).

10 See Pearcy, "Chaucer's Franklin and the Literary Vavasour," Specht, *Chaucer's Franklin the Canterbury Tales*, and Carruthers, "The Gentilesse of Chaucer's Franklin," who together present a convincing case for the Franklin's status as gentleman, as worthy freeman.

11 I take "utopian" here in the sense admirably developed by Aers, *Chaucer, Langland and the Creative Imagination*, 160–61: The paradox of married lovers "comprises a utopian transcendence of conventional relationships based on an economic exchange and rampant male egotism." Aers places the Franklin as teller in a precarious position—neither as object of satire nor as master of this utopian view. Fair enough. The Franklin's confusions do "stem from the narrator's perpetuation of received categories and the attitudes they bear while wishing to transcend them" (164). But why the Franklin's error should come of a refusal to criticize established power and traditional attitudes is not as clear, for the Franklin can hardly refuse what he cannot think to do. Other readers, such as David, *The Strumpet Muse*, and Burlin, *Chaucerian Fiction*, are sympathetic toward the Franklin, but see him mainly as offering us views that are somewhat fantastical or foolish, if not entirely pretentious. One of the few readings to emphasize feeling in the tale is Robinson's, *Chaucer and the English Tradition*, although he focuses mainly on Dorigen's complaint and Arveragus's tears, while maintaining a strained analogy between the tale and D. H. Lawrence's *Women in Love*.

12 For example, see Pearsall, *The Canterbury Tales*, 152: After nicely thinking of the tale's representation of experience as somewhat enigmatic, he adds that we share the Franklin's pleasure in the marriage between Dorigen and Arveragus, because that relationship, particularly in its patience and mutual forbearance, is close "to what we recognise as the realities of such a relationship."

13 See Wenzel, *Summa Virtutum De Remediis Anime*, 152–216.

14 Carruthers, "The Gentilesse of Chaucer's Franklin," 296, thinks of patience as a form of generosity, "the ability to forgive human weakness and to . . . see beneath the appearances of temper and mood to the underlying integrity and goodness of another." This is an attractive idea, but I do not see it at work in the Franklin's gloss on freedom in marriage.

15 See Aers, *Chaucer, Langland and the Creative Imagination*, 164; Knight, *Geoffrey Chaucer*, 118–124, who emphasizes the tale's containment of threats to patriarchal aristocracy; Pearsall, *The Canterbury Tales*, 158, who agrees that line 793—servant in love, lord in marriage—is a little too neat (although it's not the Franklin's problem); Burlin, *Chaucerian Fiction*, 204, who sees the Franklin's ideals as both self-serving and quixotic; and David, *The Strumpet Muse*, 187, who sees the Franklin's ideal as essentially a contract, of a piece with keeping one's word and one's agreements.

16 See, for example, Mehl, *Geoffrey Chaucer*, 167, who sees Aurelius as in "plain,

sexual gratification." Gaylord's, "Sentence and Solaas in Fragment VII of the Canterbury Tales," is still the seminal essay on Dorigen's apparent promise.

17 Some readers, however, think that Dorigen's complaint is a rhetorical mistake and that the Franklin's efforts at characterization in these passages of complaint yield mixed, even humorous, results (with Chaucer looking over the Franklin's shoulder). See especially Burlin, *Chaucerian Fiction*, 199–202, where Dorigen is read as willful and somewhat silly. But see Baker, "A Crux in Chaucer's Franklin's Tale: Dorigen's Complaint," and Ruggiers, *The Art of the Canterbury Tales*, for more appreciative comments.

18 Aristotle, *Rhetoric 2* , notes that it is a necessary incentive to fear that there should remain some hope of being saved, a sign of which is that fear makes men deliberate, "whereas no one deliberates about things that are hopeless" (Freese, *Aristotle*, 207).

19 Mehl, *Geoffrey Chaucer*, 36, points out that "a certeyn thing" occurs also in Boece, where it refers to a fixed point "in the midst of a constantly changing reality." Mehl suggests that in the *Parliament* the phrase might mean some truly reliable, authoritative piece of information. See *Boece*, bk. 1, pr. 6, l. 12, where the notion is one of a governor or ruler of all things.

Chapter 6: The Shipman and the Prioress

1 Robinson notes a spurious link in sixteen manuscripts. The Host asks how we like the Pardoner's telling and tale, a tale that touches on "mysgouernaunce." This Host then turns to the Shipman and asks for a good tale.

2 Allen and Moritz, *A Distinction of Stories*, have used marriage as an organizing category for the tales.

3 The tale is humorous enough for most readers, although some find it especially amiable (Ruggiers, *The Art of the Canterbury Tales*), while others find something dark and vicious in it (Richardson, *Blameth Nat Me*). Howard, *The Idea of the Canterbury Tales*, 276, emphasizes the tale's unsavory quality, while Copland, "The Shipman's Tale," and Pearsall, *The Canterbury Tales*, 216–17, find its humor somehow impudent and exhilarating. Pearsall especially sees the tale as concerning the accommodating of the world and the circumstances thrown up to one. Other criticism has focused on the tale's presentation of a mercantile ethos and its penchant for puns—topics that have occupied readers for some time. See Jones, "Chaucer's 'Taillynge Ynough'"; Silverman, "Sex and Money in Chaucer's *Shipman's Tale*"; Donaldson, *Chaucer's Poetry*, 931–32, and Ruggiers, *The Art of the Canterbury Tales*, 81–86. See also, Scattergood, "The Originality of the *Shipman's Tale*"; Schneider, "'Taillynge Ynough'; and Keiser, "Language and Meaning in Chaucer's *Shipman's Tale*."

4 Knight, *Geoffrey Chaucer*, 133–35. He thinks of the tale as reflecting a world of fetishized commodities, taking a Marxist view of its relationships.

5 Hanning, "From *Eva* and *Ave* to Eglantyne and Alisoun," suggests that one way to synthesize the Prioress's "cheere of court" and "conscience" is to see her as needing the approval of others—something she cultivates in her carefully mannered way—with her good humor soliciting that approval and taking pleasure in it.

But her sympathy for little animals and children, for helpless things "trapped and punished in a world ruled by men" suggests something in herself that feels "imprisoned and vulnerable," menaced—a feeling of helplessness that could project cruelty and hatefulness, leading in turn to the attractiveness for her of the tale of the little child killed by Jews (588–89). This is an intriguing suggestion for the psychology of tale and teller, taking us farther than other readers go when they note the intense and special relation between pathos and cruelty that inexorably drives the tale. See especially Muscatine, *Poetry and Crisis in the Age of Chaucer,* 139–41, and Robinson, *Chaucer and the English Tradition,* 151–52.

6 Among the exceptions are Sister Madeleva, "Chaucer's Nuns," and Kean, *Chaucer,* 209.

7 See David, *The Strumpet Muse,* 212; Muscatine, *Poetry and Crisis,* 140; and Payne, *The Key of Remembrance,* 167–69.

8 Cf. Jacobs, "Further Biblical Allusions for Chaucer's Prioress," where we are told that *amor vincit omnia* "suited Chaucer well as an ironical inversion echoing a part of Paul's famous discussion of *caritas* in 1 Corinthians 13: 1–13."

9 Walters, *The Fire of Love,* 77.

10 Walters, *The Fire,* 90. Spiers, *Chaucer the Maker,* 179, thinks of this religious exaltation as something Chaucer fashions especially for the Prioress, producing an ecstatic note that rises above "the exaggerated horror of a folk-rumor of a child murdered in an alley." This rightly notes the ecstatic vein but allows it to transcend the tale. The folk-rumor of a child murdered, which embraces belief in the facticity of Hugh of Lincoln's murder by Jews, is part of the tale's complex tiding—the truth of evil butchery and Marian miracle that the Prioress credits and reveres.

11 The tale invites psychological speculation on several grounds: its link between anti-Semitism, anality (the privy), and castration (the child's slit throat, the drawn and quartered Jews); the sense of group hatred (Christians against Jews in competing communities of "reverence"); and the sadistic fantasy of beating the child (l. 542). One could explore all of this by way of analyzing the psychology of the tale—and the teller, if the tale is thought of as her dream. See Rudat, "The Canterbury Tales." But that assumes too much connectedness between tale and teller, obscuring the actual connections Chaucer makes in elaborating the prologue voice and having the Prioress respond directly to aspects of her tale. The point at the moment about the suckling infant's praise is that psychologically the mother's removal of the breast is experienced as a loss that could become traumatic, a trauma endured and then both transformed and transcended through praise of the exalted Mother. That loss could prefigure other feelings of loss focused anally and genitally in castration feelings (wherein the girl might feel aggrieved) at having suffered some loss or harm—a grievance that distances the girl from desire for the father and enhances a regressive focus on the Mother. Hanning's reading, "From *Eva* and *Ave,*" of a socially careful and accomplished, institutionally successful Prioress, who nevertheless feels powerless in a world of violent men, might be further elaborated in these terms, especially if the extreme character of that helplessness is emphasized. Why can't she stop men who would beat her dogs? Why can't she release injured mice and tend to them or search for traps and destroy them? She reacts to injury as to death: Who can revive the dead pet?

12 See Freud, *Group Psychology and the Analysis of the Ego*, 50–51.

13 Kean, *Chaucer*, 196, compares Chaucer's French source with the "ABC" and with this passage, arguing for organic unity of almost independently emphasized parts, noting that Chaucer avoids any interpretation of the images.

14 The glorified, mother Maid in effect here replaces the Father as active progenitor, suggesting the Prioress's substitution of the all-succoring Mother for the powerful Father, from whom, in greatly diminished, split, and earthly terms, one can expect pain, punishment, perhaps even murder in one direction and narrow justice (Provost) in another, with complete abasement for the Christian Father when confronted with Mary's miracle (recall the Abbot, who lies as still as though he had been bound). It makes sense to think of the Provost as non-Christian—see Edward Kelly, "By Mouth of Innocentz," although in itself this does not settle the issues of mercy raised by his summary punishment of the guilty Jews. Archer, "The Structure of Anti-Semitism in the *Prioress's Tale*," reads the Provost's law as neutral, open to conformity to the Old Law or to being informed by the New Law.

15 Various editors (Skeat, Robinson, Baugh, Donaldson) give "cheered"' or "illuminated" for "lighte."

16 See Murphy, *Three Medieval Rhetorical Arts*, 29–31.

17 If the preoedipal child feels competitive toward the mother for the father's sexual and progenitive attention, some such ravishment might be demanded, fantasized. A compensating gesture would be to exalt the mother and have her displace the father (see note 14).

18 Freud, *Collected Papers*, discusses fantasies of "a child is being beaten," drawing mainly upon cases of female children. To identify with the fantasy is to adopt a regressive masochism in the face of sexual competitiveness for the father's favor. To move, whether regressively or otherwise, to an observer's position—which seems the case in the Prioress's lack of response to this fear in the tale—is to renounce the early demands of the erotic life (187–96). But her pity for trapped mice or beaten dogs suggests an identification with the child beaten by a man (the father)—an identification expressed only by the emotion of her apostrophes against the cursed Jews (those who would murder the "sely" innocent).

19 See especially Pearsall, *The Canterbury Tales*, 249.

20 Schoeck, "Chaucer's Prioress," in the course of setting the Prioress and her tale within an implied criticism possible in medieval terms (given generous attitudes toward Jews and conceptions of charity and mercy), argues that the Prioress, bland and unmoved, tells with murderous satisfaction of the torturing of the Jews (Schoeck, "Mercy," 254). She covers this issue in six lines, the tones of which are open to interpretation but which seem more measured than not.

21 See Southern, *The Making of the Middle Ages*, and Frank, "Miracles of the Virgin, Medieval Anti-Semitism, and the 'Prioress's Tale,'" 177–88.

22 David, *The Strumpet Muse*, 211–13, takes this tack, but then he would, by noting the allusion to Rachel, follow Schoeck in seeing irony at the expense of the Prioress—she in whom the law of charity is not sufficiently alive.

23 Burnley, *Chaucer's Language and the Philosopher's Tradition*, 126–29. He quotes Gower: "Bot Pite, how so that it wende, / Makth the god merciable, / If ther be cause resonable / Why that a king shal be pitous. / Bot elles, if he be doubt-ous. / To slen in cuae of rihtwisnesse, / It mai be said no Pitousnesse, / Bot it is

Pusillamite, / Which every Prince sholde flee. / For if Pite mesure excede, / Kinghode may nought wel procede / To do justice upon the riht" (*Confessio Amantis*, 7, 3520–31).

24 With his entire intent set on Mary, the boy is much more like a mystic than is the Prioress. His being is love for the Virgin, a center of mysterious joy that the Prioress does not register in her confined hatred of his murderers.

25 Howard, *The Idea of the Canterbury Tales*, was one of the first to see that the tales of Fragment 7 were paired. For prudence as a public and private virtue, see Burnley, *Chaucer's Language*, 53.

Chapter 7: Sir Thopas *and* Melibee

1 For a contrary view, see Huppé, *A Reading of the Canterbury Tales*, 235–37. Olson, "A Reading of the Thopas-Melibee Link," has convincingly refuted that point of view. Dolores Palomo "What Chaucer Really Did to Le Livre de Melibee," following Hartung, "A Study of the Textual Affiliations of Chaucer's Melibeus," suggests that by "this tretys lyte" Chaucer means an earlier version of what comes to be "this murye tale" of Melibee.

2 Quintilian (Butler, *Institutio Oratoria*, 298–99). Quintilian writes approvingly of Cicero's style, noting only that the present age might add its taste for brilliant reflections (bk. 12, x, 46). Even the *Rhetorica Ad Herennium* (Caplan) advises restraint in the use of ornaments (bk. 4, 32), but Aristotle thinks of maxims as either the premises or conclusions of enthymemes, as concerning general things in relation to the objects of human action, and as especially useful when one's audience is vulgar or uneducated (*Rhetoric*, 279–87).

3 Howard, *The Idea of the Canterbury Tales*, 316, reads the tale as an address to a courtly audience, upholding an ideal of secular conduct, an ideal surpassed in turn only by the *Second Nun's Tale* and the *Parson's Tale*. For Ruggiers, *The Art of the Canterbury Tales*, 21, the tale is as close as we get to the counsel of reason in the *Canterbury Tales*.

4 Melibeus says that all her words "been sothe and therto profitable," but his heart is so grievously troubled that he does not know what to do (l. 1001). Kittay and Godzich, *The Emergence of Prose*, 152, suggest that medieval writers by the mid-fourteenth century were beginning to see prose as closer to truth than poetry. They cite Jean Le Bel as claiming to correct a minstrel's account of events Jean says he witnessed—a correction that will take the form of prose *pourtant que en ces hystoires rimees treuve on grand plente de bourdes* (because in these poetical stories one finds a great many tricksterish lies); whereas prose will allow him to get *au plus prez de la verite que [lui]! pourray, selonc la memoire que Dieu [lui] a preste* (much closer to the truth, as best [he] may, given the memory that God has bestowed upon [him]!). Memory and prose will get the "I" as the voice that writes as close to the truth as possible.

5 But see Hoffman, "Chaucer's Melibee and Tales of Sondry Folk," who urges the identification of Sophie's wounds with Christ (given wounds in the hands and feet especially). Askins, in an unpublished paper, urges an identification with the five parts of the body anointed in the fourteenth-century office for the dead.

6 Rhetoric 2, xxi, 2 (Freese, *Aristotle*, 279).

7 See especially Lawler, *The One and the Many*, 103–4. He applies the term to her advice in the choosing of counselors, this within a reading that sees Prudence as changing from an early reliance on proverbs to a later openness to experience (moving also from a prudential to a providential point of view). Melibeus goes through a similar though opposite movement, from his emotional understanding early to "a new appreciation of authority, a new understanding of his relation to general ideas" (103). These are interesting readings in that they are responses to actual movement in the tale, although they overdramatize that movement and misrepresent Prudence's early strategy. She is unsure of how to begin, not where to go.

8 Howard, *The Idea of the Canterbury Tales*, 312.

9 Patterson, "'What Man Artow?'" takes a darker view, suggesting that Prudence's teaching has been useless, largely because folded into a movement that subvert's the tale's program. He sees *Melibee* as counseling self-reflection but in fact enacting "a pedagogical program that forecloses true understanding" (160). Of course the tale reaches neither a Platonic nor a Boethian heaven, but it does move toward and reach a prosaic level of understanding, an embrace of prudence.

Chapter 8: *The* Monk's Tale *and the* Nun's Priest's Tale

1 For connections between the tales, see Hemingway, "Chaucer's Monk and Nun's Priest," and Watson, "The Relation of the *Monk's Tale* to the *Nun's Priest's Tale*."

2 Bk. 2, pr. 2, l. 70: "Tragedye is to seyn a dite of a prosperite for a tyme, that endeth in wrecchidnesse." In this section, Lady Philosophy impersonates Fortune and complains that Boethius has no right to dismay himself over the experience of misfortune. As ventriloquist, Lady Philosophy has Fortune say that she does no wrong in turning her wheel: Boethius is only experiencing the mutability of life in "the comune realme of alle." Of course, this presupposes a view of things that rises above misfortune, above this mutable realm. For various accounts of the Monk's inadequacy in his view of fortune, see Kaske, "The Knight's Interpretation of the Monk's Tale"; Mahoney, "Chaucerian Tragedy and the Christian Tradition"; and Pearsall, *The Canterbury Tales*, 283.

3 Olsson, "Grammar, Manhood, and Tears," suggests that in his learning, the Monk would wrap a cloak of language around himself, hiding his thoughts although remaining inspired by mere *curiositas*.

4 Howard, *The Idea of the Canterbury Tales*, 281, notes the three tragedies due to women but continues with a reading of the Monk's putative sense of powerlessness. For a social reading of the Monk's frankness, see Beichner, "Daun Piers, Monk and Business Administrator," who argues that the Monk has made his official duties as business administrator his way of life.

5 Too many personal emphases, even in the depictions of Fortune, work against seeing fortune increasingly personified as in itself a unifying factor. See Socola, "Chaucer's Development of Fortune in the *Monk's Tale*," for the opposite view.

6 Burlin, *Chaucerian Fiction*, 184, notes that for most of the pagan figures, aside from Nero, "the Monk's admiration waxes warmly enthusiastic, finding worldly

power and governance on an imperial level more impressive than virtue. The death of Alexander elicits his most extravagant rhetoric, filling an entire stanza with a bathetic revelation of the direction of the teller's true feelings." This perceptive remark, although mistaking the Monk's effusions, nevertheless complements Howard's notion that the Monk is obsessed with power and dignity, even though he himself can now never be a nobleman (*The Idea of the Canterbury Tales*, 280–82). I think the Monk greatly admires power and dignity but that his obsession is with wantonness and cruelty—both in men and in the "game" Lady Fortune plays.

7 Lenaghan, "The Nun's Priest's Fable," is one of the first to tie rhetorical play (and play at the expense of rhetorical handbooks) to a compound view of fable in the tale. But Shallers, "The 'Nun's Priest's Tale': An Ironic Exemplum," has more precisely investigated the tale's combination of beast fable and moral exemplum, although he sees the worldly beast fable dynamic as finally unsettling all resolutions of the tale into a secure moral. See also Mann, "The *Speculum Stultorum* (277, 282) for remarks on the fable analogues of the *Nun's Priest's Tale*, analogues that keep their morals separate from the tales (unlike Chaucer), applying them in exemplum fashion. Mann sees the comedy of the tale as operating in a Bakhtinian, carnivalesque fashion: at the expense of serious subjects without denying the power of those subjects (or views of the world). In Chaucer's hands, and in the work of Nigel of Longchamps to which Chaucer alludes, the beast story "stands for . . . the basic intractability of human nature and human experience, its resistance to organisation in terms of intellectual and moral analysis, and its awful tendency to suggest a common sense moral . . . just as often as a more elevated one" (277).

8 Donaldson, *Speaking of Chaucer*, 149, notes a number of inaccuracies and inconvenient details when discussing Donovan's "Moralite of the Nun's Priest's Sermon." Donovan's patristic reading of the tale marks an adversarial point on the way to Donaldson's own view that "the enormous rhetorical elaboration of the telling" suggests the tale's point: "Rhetoric here is regarded as the inadequate defence that mankind erects against an inscrutable reality. . . . Chauntecleer is not an alert Christian; he is mankind trying to adjust the universe to his own specifications and failing—though not, I am happy to say, fatally." For a reading similar to Donovan's, see Huppé, *A Reading of the Canterbury Tales*, 176–82. Dahlberg, "Chaucer's Cock and Fox," is in the same school but in a more specialized class. For him, the cock figures the parish priest and the fox is a figure of the friar, the priest's natural enemy. Judson Allen, "The Ironic Fruyt," admits that details in the tale support a priestlike view of the preacherly Chauntecleer but that the figuration achieved is disparate and ironic. All nonexegetical readings attempt to plot that disparateness and penetrate that irony in some rhetorical or strategic way. Myers (1973) even suggests, plausibly, that the tale has a tagmemic character, involving overlapping areas controlled by three centers of focus: the cock and fox story, the narrator's rhetorical elaborations, and the whole tale within the context of Canterbury tales.

9 Myers, "Focus and 'Moralite' in the *Nun's Priest's Tale*," 212–14.

10 Knight, *Ryming Craftily*, 214. Owen, *Pilgrimage and Storytelling*, 135, a sugges-

tion advanced much earlier in Owen, "The Crucial Passages in Five of the Canterbury Tales."

11 Jordan, *Chaucer' Poetics*, 136–41, sees Chauntecleer's massive response to Pertelote's advice as "the kind of rhetorical overkill, flamboyantly digressive, that we
have seen in numerous instances in the dream visions. This is Chaucer in color-
atura form." In this and other passages Jordan thinks of Chaucer as still "puzzling
over the place and validity of language in human experience"—producing satire in
this case on domestic relations, male pomposity, and the "flatulence and banality"
that interpretation can reach. All of this is perceptive reading, grounded as it is in
the shifts of narrative style we can trace in Chauntecleer's reply to Pertelote, but I
do not see Chaucer as especially puzzled over the place and validity of language.
That Chauntecleer is not a self-consistent, literary voice, or a realistic personality
hardly makes a case for Chaucer's puzzlement. Indeed, the shifts involved in this
passage are not confusing, nor is the comedy frustrating. Voices do not "collide"—
a cataclysmic image that Jordan relies on too much—nor is Chauntecleer's performance a whimsical mélange of vocal registers. Chauntecleer's voice is identifi-
able, beginning with "Madame . . . graunt mercy of youre loore" (l. 2970) and
breaking off with a recitation at line 2985. We then have a neutral, tale-telling
voice, which includes speaking parts for characters. Chauntecleer's voice points the
moral, then we move into another recitation, a tale told without intrusions, following which Chauntecleer's voice appears again, his earlier expostulations (such as
"By God" and "so moot I thee") now giving way to more energy, examples, and
stentorian conviction. This is consistent voicing, if not character deveopment. Then
we can consider the end of the tale's plot, at which point Chauntecleer's speech is
inspired and entirely efficacious. Why not take that as a cue for Chaucer's view of
language and its uses? Bloomfield, "The Widsom of the Nun's Priest Tale," has
done just that.

12 Jordan, *Chaucer's Poetics*, 143, thinks of the Nun's Priest as an illusion, a speaking
voice that breaks up "into kaleidoscopic fragments," rather than as a voice belong-
ing or giving us access to an internally consistent, reified speaker. The speaking
that goes on here in the ostensible person of the Nun's Priest is really just "spasmodic discourse" attributable only to the unreified poet. These observations are led
by an insistent foregrounding of textuality or rhetoricity and enforced by the dra-
conian insistence that no realistic characterization of an internally consistent personality appears here. This idea of imitated consciousness is beside the point. What
Chaucer's narrators say indicates something about their states of mind and their
preoccupations. Very few readers go away reeling, as though they had just listened
to the babble of fractured personalities and lunatic minds. To ask Jordan's question—"Can this be the voice of a priest, a voice that moves from tragedy to a reference ot Lancelot?"—is to ask facetiously and impotently if no imitation of human
nature is allowed here. The discourse seems spasmodic to Jordan and other readers,
because the Nun's Priest *is* in the habit of breaking away from the tale, given some
idea that has suggested something weighty to him. Then he returns to the tale
unself-consciously, not having been trained in recitation or in consistent, textual
commentary.

13 Animal fables in sermon literature enjoyed considerable popularity in the thir-

teenth and fourteenth centuries. Owst, *Literature and Pulpit in Medieval England*, 204–9, mentions Odo of Cheriton and Nicole Bozon as prominent preacher-fabulists in the thirteenth and fourteenth centuries, respectively. But Wycliff and others loosely associated with his type of purism inveighed against the use of fables.

14 See Gallacher, "Food, Laxatives, and the Catharsis in Chaucer's Nun's Priest's Tale," 63.

15 Pearsall, *The Canterbury Tales*, 232, sees the Nun's Priest as naive in his expansions, having no idea how funny he is to be applying serious thought to this tale. This is close to the mark, I think, if we insist that the Nun's Priest *does not* apply his serious material to the tale; he takes a "time out" given the appearance of a topic that merits expansion. Then he returns to the tale.

16 David, *The Strumpet Muse*, 229, 225, offers the attractive suggestion that satire in this tale focuses on "the tendency to look for a moral everywhere, to peck up the kernels of *sentence* and 'and ete hem yn.'" But the tale does have morals, clearly stated by two of the characters and rounded out by the Nun's Priest—morals that are not ridiculous. David also suggests that what he thinks of as the puffery of learned digressions and allusions becomes, "among other things, a satire on the medieval art of composition as it is taught in the rhetoric books, and particularly on the use of 'auctorite' to add weight and significance to a story." These suggestions are intelligent responses to the Nun's Priest's tale telling, but one can easily demur. The Nun's Priest is conscious, first of all, of his lack of rhetorical expertise; second, he becomes the target insofar as he thinks he should comment sententiously on topics encountered in the tale (and, as a priest, shouldn't he?). But to make the medieval art of composition or the use of 'auctorite' major targets is then to see much in Chaucer as similar satire. *The Tale of Melibee* becomes a much-enforced joke, for example, and a host of prologues and tales would follow suit. For views of rhetorical inflation similar to David's, see Manning, "The Nun's Priest's Morality and the Medieval Attitude toward Fables"; Donaldson, *Speaking of Chaucer*; Elbow, *Oppositions in Chaucer*, 110–11; and Burlin, *Chaucerian Fiction*, 230–33, which emphasize abuse of language; and F. Anne Payne, *Chaucer and Menippean Satire*, 201–6, who sees the satirical target as "men's habit . . . of idiotically believing in inane categories and outmoded theories."

17 Muscatine, *Chaucer and the French Tradition*, 242, has read this tale carefully, although his discussion is more summary than demonstrative. Still, he notes that scarcely a Chaucerian topic or style is excluded from the tale's purview or criticism. The assemblage of styles does not produce a negative or excluding effect; rather it seems to celebrate "the normality of differences," such that in the succession of topics we never rest long enough "to serve a single view or a single doctrine or an unalterable judgment." The parodic in the tale never quite demolishes its target. Elbow, *Oppositions in Chaucer*, 113, puts this assertively: the tale's brilliant debunking of rhetorical flights is itself a virtuoso performance that celebrates "imaginative creation and extravagant flights of inference." Chaucer has cast lowly animal fable as mock-heroic triumph and given such a tale, such a bearer of truth and feeling, to the Nun's Priest, who does not appreciate its rhetoric, but who takes the clear moral of its plot, its action—what he calls the tale.

18 See Allen and Moritz, *A Distinction of Stories*, 225.

19 Cf. F. Anne Payne, *Chaucer and Menippean Satire*, 205.

20 See Kendrick, *Chaucerian Play*, 102–15, for an extended account of the Host's exposing play.

21 For a fascinating, anthropological study of the body as an image differently expressive in differently organized societies, see Douglas, *Natural Symbols*.

22 Although I very much like Strohm's *Social Chaucer*, especially 172–78, his closing emphasis on unresolved polyphony and on the literary world as a safe exploration of social tensions does not, I think, sufficiently countenance the role of prudence in the building of community. Moreover, tellers do confront each other in this "game" of tales and tale telling; but their conflicts can be put aside, if not altogether resolved. The social Chaucer I see is one who profoundly embraces the community-building powers of prudence, mercy, and empathetic feeling.

23 The terms "grid" and "group" as either opposed or intersecting pairs for classifying social arrangements come from Mary Douglas's work. Societies can reflect strong or weak influences from group organization as well as from some overall grid of rules and expectations. A society might have little or no organization by group but a strong organization by grid, or strong group and weak grid, or both group and grid strong—as would be the case in an ideal, high-medieval England; or very weak group and no grid.

Chapter 9: Ending a "Feeste"

1 See David, *The Strumpet Muse*, 131–32, for a discussion of the two passages.

2 For these and other distinctions, see Douglas, *Natural Symbols*, ix–xii. The Miller's insistence is an instance of governance by veto and threat (the threat to leave, to diminish the company and dilute its fellowship). The Canon's Yeoman's appearance ratifies the group's boundary, both as a merry company and as a company further defined and gladdened by tale tellings, with a "merry" tale itself being one that forms or concerns or enhances community.

3 David, *The Strumpet Muse*, 132.

4 See Ebin, "Chaucer, Lydgate, and the 'Myrie Tale,'" for a survey of "merry" as it qualifies the notion of tale.

5 By emphasizing the Parson's talk about "the way," Lawler, *The One and the Many*, 162, overlooks the import of these negotiations. Lawler then seductively discusses the *Parson's Tale* as an organic closure to the tales of Canterbury, rather than as a radical departure from the play of tales, leaving the play behind. True, something of the one way does now replace the many ways of idiosyncratic pilgrims, and a community of souls now replaces a company of errant mortals. Moreover, transformation through contrition and confession of course replaces any other transformation on this earth, and finally an authorization does indeed replace opinion and qualification. But this is, as Lawler intuitively realizes, despite his arguments for an aesthetic of closure—a marked, sudden, and even drastic departure from the Canterbury project.

6 For an intriguing account in these terms of classical tragedy and comedy, see Trimpi, *Muses of One Mind*, 301–2. Also, note Redfield's claim, *Nature and Cul-*

ture in the Illiad, 59, that one can define a Homeric fiction as "the outcome of a hypothetical inquiry into the intermediate causes of action."

7 For a recent account of belief as cogitation rather than as an item of true belief (a proposition, perhaps arrived at inferentially) or as a disposition—an attitude toward such an item or group of items—see Bogdan, *Belief: Form, Context, Function,* 165–67, where he defines belief as a performance: Given a particular, cognitive issue, the cogitator "must *delineate* (or *retrace*) a theme, *activate, select,* and *retrieve* relevant portions from the memory knowledge as given information, *identify* the area where new information is needed," then consider competing possibilities for this new information, evaluate them, choose a particular possibility, and integrate this new information into the already given. The general notion of belief here is that its content is "a function of several parameters (of incrementation) whose joint valuation specifies an entire configuration of representational states. Belief remains a relation to a configuration of representations" such that the configuration both specifies informational content and is an occurrent reading of the relevant representations. This is belief as a purposive process without certainty or faith. Clearly, it is not the mere retrieval of items of belief from memory or from old books. One undertakes a reading, an evaluative process.

8 Konolige, *Belief and Incompleteness,* sketches out a conception of incomplete deduction for belief systems—incomplete because the believer does not have sufficient resources to deduce all that follows from his true beliefs. But such incomplete systems can reach closure given particular lines of sound inference within restrictions as to the depth and scope of inferential structures.

9 For definitions of consequentiality and derivability in a logical context, focused on systems of believer introspection about what one will also believe if one believes some statement "p," see Konolige, *Belief and Incompleteness,* 15–21.

❦ WORKS CITED

Aers, David. *Chaucer, Langland and the Creative Imagination*. London: Routledge & Kegan Paul, 1980.

Allen, Judson Boyce. "The Ironic Fruyt: Chauntecleer as Figura." *Studies in Philology* 6 (1969): 23–25.

Allen, Judson Boyce, and Moritz, Theresa Anne. *A Distinction of Stories: The Medieval Unity of Chaucer's Fair Chain of Narratives for Canterbury*. Columbus: Ohio State University Press, 1981.

Allen, Mark. "Penitential Sermons, the Manciple, and the End of *The Canterbury Tales*." *Studies in the Age of Chaucer* 9 (1987): 77–96.

Archer, John. "The Structure of Anti-Semitism in the *Prioress's Tale*." *Chaucer Review* 19 (1984): 46–54.

Armstrong, Edward A. *The Folklore of Birds*. 2d ed. New York: Dover Publications, 1970.

Askins, William. "The Historical Setting of *The Manciple's Tale*." *Studies in the Age of Chaucer* 7 (1985): 87–106.

——————. "Figures in Wax: Notes toward a Reading of the *Melibee*." Paper presented at NEH Summer Seminar for College Teachers, "Late Medieval Fictions," San Francisco, 1981.

Baker, Donald C. "A Crux in Chaucer's Franklin's Tale: Dorigen's Complaint." *Journal of English and Germanic Philology* 60 (1961): 56–64.

Bakhtin, M. M. *The Dialogic Imagination*. Trans. Caryl Emerson and Michael Holquist. Austin: University of Texas Press, 1981.

Baldwin, Ralph. *The Unity of the Canterbury Tales*. Anglistica 5. Copenhagen: Rosenkilde and Bagger, 1955.

Beichner, Paul E. "Daun Piers, Monk and Business Administrator." *Speculum* 34 (1959): 611–21. Reprinted in *Chaucer Criticism: The Canterbury Tales*. Vol. 1, ed. Richard Schoeck and Jerome Taylor. Notre Dame, Ind.: Notre Dame University Press, 1960.

Bennett, J. A. W. *Chaucer's Book of Fame: An Exposition of "The House of Fame."* Oxford: Clarendon Press, 1968.

Benson, C. David. "The *Canterbury Tales*: Personal Drama or Experiments in Poetic Variety." In *The Cambridge Chaucer Companion*, ed. Piero Boitani and Jill Mann, 93–108. Cambridge: Cambridge University Press, 1986.

Benson, Larry D., ed. *The Riverside Chaucer*. 3d ed. New York: Houghton Mifflin, 1987. Based on *The Works of Geoffrey Chaucer*, ed. F. N. Robinson.

Benson, Larry D., and Wenzel, Siegfried, eds. *The Wisdom of Poetry*. Kalamazoo, Mich.: Medieval Institute Publications, 1982.

Berger, Harry J. "The F-Fragment of the Canterbury Tales: Part One." *Chaucer Review* 1 (1966): 88–102.

Bloom, Allan, trans. *The Republic of Plato*. New York: Basic Books, 1968.

Bloomfield, Morton W. "The Wisdom of the Nun's Priest's Tale." In *Chaucerian Problems and Perspectives*, ed. Edward Vasta and Zacharias P. Thundy, 72–82. Notre Dame, Ind.: Notre Dame University Press, 1979.

Bogdan, Radu J. "The Manufacture of Belief." In *Belief: Form, Context, Function*, ed. Radu J. Bogdan, 149–84. Oxford: Oxford University Press, 1986.

Boitani, Piero. *English Medieval Narrative in the Thirteenth and Fourteenth Centuries*. Trans. Joan Krakover Hall. Cambridge: Cambridge University Press, 1982, 1986.

Boitani, Piero, and Mann, Jill, eds. *The Cambridge Chaucer Companion*. Cambridge: Cambridge University Press, 1986.

Brewer, Derek. "Gothic Chaucer." In *Geoffrey Chaucer*, ed. Derek Brewer, 1–32. Ann Arbor: Ohio University Press, 1974.

Brown, Peter. "Is the 'Canon's Yeoman's Tale' Apochryphal?" *English Studies* 64 (1983): 481–90.

Burlin, Robert B. *Chaucerian Fiction*. Princeton, N.J.: Princeton University Press, 1977.

Burnley, J. D. *Chaucer's Language and the Philosopher's Tradition*. Cambridge: D. S. Brewer, 1979.

Burrow, John A. "The *Canterbury Tales* I: Romance." In *The Cambridge Companion*, ed. P. Boitani and J. Mann, 109–24. Cambridge: Cambridge University Press, 1986.

Burrow, John. *Ricardian Poetry: Chaucer, Gower, Langland, and the Gawain Poet*. New Haven: Yale University Press, 1971.

Butler, H. E., trans. *The Institutio Oratoria of Quintilian*. 4 vols. London: Heineman, 1966.

Caplan, Harry, trans. *Rhetorica Ad Herennium*. Cambridge: Harvard University Press, 1981.

Carruthers, Mary J. "The Gentilesse of Chaucer's Franklin." *Criticism* 23 (1981): 283–300.

Cherniss, Harold F. *Aristotle's Criticism of Plato and the Academy*. New York: Russell & Russell, 1962.

Coleman, Janet. *Medieval Readers and Writers: 1350–1400*. London: Hutchinson, 1981.

Colish, Marcia L. *The Mirror of Language: A Study in the Medieval Theory of Knowledge*. New Haven: Yale University Press, 1968.

Cooper, Helen. *The Structure of the Canterbury Tales*. London: Duckworth, 1983.

Cook, Robert. "The Canon's Yeoman and His Tale." *Chaucer Review* 22 (1987): 28–40.

Copland, Murray. "*The Shipman's Tale*: Chaucer and Boccaccio." *Medium Aevum* 35 (1966): 11–28.

Culler, Jonathan. *The Pursuit of Signs: Semiotics, Literature, Deconstruction*. London: Routledge & Kegan Paul, 1981.

——————. *Structural Poetics: Structuralism, Linguistics, and the Study of Literature*. Ithaca, N.Y.: Cornell University Press, 1975.

Cunningham, J. V. "The Literary Form of the Prologue to the *Canterbury Tales*." *Modern Philology* 49 (1951/52): 172–81.

Dahlberg, Charles. "Chaucer's Cock and Fox." *Journal of English and Germanic Philology* 53 (1954): 277–90.

David, Alfred. *The Strumpet Muse: Art and Morals in Chaucer's Poetry*. Bloomington: Indiana University Press, 1976.

Dean, James. "Dismantling the Canterbury Book." *Papers on Language and Literature* 100 (1984): 746–62.

Delany, Sheila. *Chaucer's House of Fame: The Poetics of Skeptical Fideism*. Chicago: University of Chicago Press, 1972.

Donaldson, Talbot E. *Chaucer's Poetry*. New York: Ronald Press, 1958.

——————. *Speaking of Chaucer*. New York: W. W. Norton, 1970.

Donovan, Mortimer J. "The Moralite of the Nun's Priest's Sermon." *Journal of English and Germanic Philology* 52 (1953): 498–508.

Douglas, Mary. *Natural Symbols: Explorations in Cosmology*. New York: Pantheon Books, 1982.

Ebin, Lois. "Chaucer, Lydgate, and the 'Myrie Tale.'" *Chaucer Review* 13 (1979): 316–36.

Eco, Umberto. *Art and Beauty in the Middle Ages*. Trans. Hugh Bredin. New Haven: Yale University Press, 1986.

Economou, George D., ed. *Geoffrey Chaucer*. New York: McGraw Hill, 1975.

Elbow, Peter. *Oppositions in Chaucer*. Middletown, Conn.: Wesleyan University Press, 1973.

Eldridge, Laurence. "Chaucer's *House of Fame* and the *Via Moderna*." *Neuphilologische Mitteilungen* 71 (1970): 105–19.

——————. "Poetry and Philosophy in the *Parliament of Fowls*." *Revue de l'Université d'Ottawa* 40 (1970): 441–59.

Ferster, Judith. *Chaucer on Interpretation*. Cambridge: Cambridge University Press, 1985.

Fish, Stanley E. *Self-Consuming Artifacts*. Berkeley: University of California Press, 1972.

Fleming, John V. "Chaucer's Squire, the *Roman de la Rose*, and the Romaunt." *Notes and Queries* 14 (1967): 48–49.

Frank, Robert Worth, Jr. *Chaucer and the Legend of Good Women*. Cambridge: Harvard University Press, 1972.

——————. "Miracles of the Virgin, Medieval Anti-Semitism, and the 'Prioress's Tale.'" In *The Wisdom of Poetry*, ed. Larry D. Benson and Siegfried Wenzel, 177–88. Kalamazoo, Mich.: Medieval Institute Publications, 1982.

Freese, J. H., trans. *Aristotle: The Art of Rhetoric*. London: Heinemann, 1926; Harvard University Press, 1975.

Freud, Sigmund. *Collected Papers*. Vol. 2. Trans. Joan Riviere. London: Hogarth Press, 1949.

——————. *Group Psychology and the Analysis of the Ego*. Trans. James Strachey. London: International Psycho-Analytic Press, 1922.

Freund, Elizabeth. *The Return of the Reader: Reader-Response Criticism*. London: Methuen, 1987.

Fyler, John M. *Chaucer and Ovid*. New Haven: Yale University Press, 1979.

Gallacher, Patrick. "Food, Laxatives, and the Catharsis in Chaucer's Nun's Priest's Tale." *Speculum* 51 (1976): 49–68.

Gaylord, Alan T. "*Sentence* and *Solaas* in Fragment VII of the *Canterbury Tales.*" *Publications of the Modern Language Association of America* 82 (1967): 226–35.

Gendlin, Eugene. *Experiencing and the Creation of Meaning*. New York: Macmillan, 1962.

Gilby, Thomas, O.P., ed. *Thomas Aquinas Summa Theologiae*. Vols. 1 and 2. Garden City, N.J.: Image Books, Doubleday, 1969.

Goodman, Jennifer R. "Chaucer's *Squire's Tale* and the Rise of Chivalry." *Studies in the Age of Chaucer* 5 (1983): 127–36.

Goodman, Nelson. *Problems and Projects*. Indianapolis, Ill.: Bobbs-Merrill, 1972.

——————. *Ways of Worldmaking*. Hassocks, Sussex, U.K.: Harvester Press, 1978.

Grenberg, Bruce L. "*The Canon's Yeoman's Tale*: Boethian Wisdom and the Alchemists." *Chaucer Review* 1 (1966): 37–54.

Grennen, Joseph E. "The Canon's Yeoman and the Cosmic Furnace: Language and Meaning in the *Canon's Yeoman's Tale.*" *Criticism* 4 (1962): 225–40.

Grimaldi, William M. A., S.J. *Aristotle, Rhetoric I: A Commentary*. New York: Fordham University Press, 1980.

Grubar, Loren C. "The *Manciple's Tale*: One Key to Chaucer's Language." In *New Views on Chaucer*, ed. William C. Johnson and Loren C. Grubar, 43–50. Denver: Society for New Language Study, 1973.

Haller, Robert S. "Chaucer's *Squire's Tale* and the Uses of Rhetoric." *Modern Philology* 62 (1965): 285–95.

Hanning, Robert W. "From *Eva* and *Ave* to Eglantyne and Alisoun: Chaucer's Insight into the Roles Women Play." *Signs* 2 (1977): 580–99.

Harrington, David. "The Narrator of the *Canon's Yeoman's Tale.*" *Annuale Mediaevale* 9 (1968): 85–97.

Harrington, Norman T. "Experience, Art, and the Framing of the *Canterbury Tales.*" *Chaucer Review* 10 (1975–76): 187–200.

Hartung, Albert. "A Study of the Textual Affiliations of Chaucer's Melibeus considered in Its relation to the French Source." Ph.D dissertation, Lehigh University, 1957.

Harwood, Britton, Jr. "Language and the Real: Chaucer's Manciple." *Chaucer Review* 6 (1971–72): 257–73.

Hazelton, Richard. "The *Manciple's Tale*: Parody and Critique." *Journal of English and Germanic Philology* 62 (1963): 1–31.

Heintz, John. "Reference and Inference in Fiction." *Poetics* 8 (1979): 85–99.

Hemingway, Samuel B. "Chaucer's Monk and Nun's Priest." *Modern Language Notes* 31 (1916): 479–83.

Hill, John M. "The *Book of the Duchess*, Melancholy, and that Eight-Year Sickness." *Chaucer Review* 9 (1974): 35–50.

Hirshberg, Jeffrey Alan. "'Cosyn to the Dede': The 'Canterbury Tales' and the Platonic Tradition in Medieval Rhetoric." Ph.D. dissertation, University of Wisconsin, 1977.

Hoffman, Richard L. "Chaucer's *Melibee* and Tales of Sondry Folk." *Classica et Mediaevalia* 30 (1969): 552–77.

Holland, Norman N. *Five Readers Reading*. New Haven: Yale University Press, 1975.

Howard, Donald R. "Chaucer's Idea of an Idea." *Essays & Studies*, n.s. 29 (1976): 39–55.

——————. *The Idea of the Canterbury Tales*. Berkeley: University of California Press, 1976.

Huppé, Bernard F. *A Reading of the Canterbury Tales*. Albany: State University of New York Press, 1967.

Hyman, Arthur, and Walsh, James J., eds. *Philosophy in the Middle Ages*. 2d ed. Indianapolis, Ill.: Hackett Publishing, 1973.

Iser, Wolfgang. *The Act of Reading: A Theory of Aesthetic Response*. Baltimore: Johns Hopkins University Press, 1980.

Jacobs, Craney. "Further Biblical Allusions for Chaucer's Prioress." *Chaucer Review* 15 (1980): 151–54.

Jones, Claude. "Chaucer's 'Taillynge Ynough.'" *Modern Language Notes* 52 (1937): 570.

Jordan, Robert M. *Chaucer and the Shape of Creation*. Cambridge: Harvard University Press, 1967.

——————. *Chaucer's Poetics and the Modern Reader*. Berkeley: University of California Press, 1987.

Kahrl, Stanley J. "Chaucer's *Squire's Tale* and the Decline of Chivalry." *Chaucer Review* 7 (1972–73): 194–208.

Kaske, R. E. "The Knight's Interpretation of the Monk's Tale." *English Literary History* 25 (1957): 249–68.

Kean, P. M. *Chaucer and the Making of English Poetry*. Vol. 2, *Chaucer and the Art of Narrative*. London: Routledge & Kegan Paul, 1972.

Keiser, George R. "Language and Meaning in Chaucer's *Shipman's Tale*." *Chaucer Review* 12 (1977): 147–61.

Kelly, Douglas. *Medieval Imagination*. Madison: University of Wisconsin Press, 1978.

Kelly, Edward H. "By Mouth of Innocentz: The Prioress Vindicated." *Publications of the Modern Language Association of America* 5 (1969): 362–74.

Kendrick, Laura. *Chaucerian Play: Comedy and Control in the Canterbury Tales*. Berkeley: University of California Press, 1988.

Kiser, Lisa J. *Telling Classical Tales: Chaucer and the Legend of Good Women*. Ithaca, N.Y.: Cornell University Press, 1983.

Kittredge, George Lyman. *Chaucer and His Poetry*. Cambridge: Harvard University Press, 1967.

Kittay, Jeffrey, and Godzich, Wlad. *The Emergence of Prose: An Essay in Prosaics*. Minneapolis: University of Minnesota Press, 1987.

Knight, Stephen. *Geoffrey Chaucer*. Oxford: Basil Blackwell, 1986.

——————. *Ryming Craftily: Meaning in Chaucer's Poetry*. Atlantic Highlands, N.J.: Humanities Press, 1976.

Kolve, V. A. *Chaucer and the Imagery of Narrative: The First Five Canterbury Tales*. Stanford, Calif.: Stanford University Press, 1984.

Konolige, Kurt. *Belief and Incompleteness*. Report CSLI-84–4. Stanford, Calif.: Center for the Study of Language and Information, 1984.

Lawler, Traugott. *The One and the Many in the Canterbury Tales*. Hamden, Conn.: Archon Books, 1980.

Lawton, David. *Chaucer's Narrators*. Cambridge: Boydell & Brewer, 1985.

Leff, Gordon. *The Dissolution of the Medieval Outlook*. New York: New York University Press, 1976.

Leicester, H. Marshall. "The Art of Impersonation: A General Prologue to the *Canterbury Tales*." *Publications of the Modern Language Association of America* 95 (1980): 213–24.

Lenaghan, R. T. "The Nun's Priest's Fable." *Publications of the Modern Language Association of America* 78 (1963): 300–307.

Leyerle, John. "Chaucer's Windy Eagle." *University of Toronto Quarterly*, 40 (1971): 247–65.

Lindahl, Carl. "The Festive Form of the *Canterbury Tales*." *English Literary History* 52 (1985): 531–74.

Lumiansky, Robert M. *Of Sondry Folk: The Dramatic Principle in the Canterbury Tales*. Austin: University of Texas Press, 1955.

McCall, John P. *Chaucer among the Gods: The Poetics of Classical Myth*. University Park: Pennsylvania State University Press, 1979.

—————. "The Squire in Wonderland." *Chaucer Review* 1 (1966–67): 103–9.

Madeleva, Sister Mary. "Chaucer's Nuns." In *A Lost Language and Other Essays on Chaucer*. New York: Appleton, 1951.

Mahoney, John F. "Chaucerian Tragedy and the Christian Tradition." *Annuale Medieavale* 3 (1962): 81–99.

Mann, Jill. *Chaucer and Medieval Estates Satire*. Cambridge: Cambridge University Press, 1973.

—————. "The *Speculum Stultorum* and the *Nun's Priest's Tale*." *Chaucer Review* 9 (1974–75): 262–82.

Manning, Stephen. "The Nun's Priest's Morality and the Medieval Attitude toward Fables." *Journal of English and Germanic Philology* 59 (1960): 403–16.

Martin, Graham Dunstan. *Language Truth and Poetry*. Edinburgh: Edinburgh University Press, 1975.

Mehl, Dieter. *Geoffrey Chaucer: An Introduction to His Narrative Poetry*. Cambridge: Cambridge University Press, 1986.

Merleau-Ponty, M. *Phenomenology of Perception*. Trans. by Colin Smith. New York: Humanities Press, 1962.

Murphy, James J. *Three Medieval Rhetorical Arts*. Berkeley: University of California Press, 1971.

Muscatine, Charles. *Chaucer and the French Tradition*. Berkeley: University of California Press, 1964.

—————. *Poetry and Crisis in the Age of Chaucer*. Notre Dame, Ind.: University of Notre Dame Press, 1972.

Myers, D. E. "Focus and 'Moralite' in the *Nun's Priest's Tale*." *Chaucer Review* 7 (1973): 210–20.

Nuchelmans, Gabriel. *Theories of the Propositon: Ancient and Medieval Conceptions of the Bearers of Truth and Falsity*. Amsterdam: North Holland Press, 1973.

Ogden, C. K., and Richards, I. A. *The Meaning of Meaning*. New York: Harcourt, Brace, 1948.

Olson, Glending. "A Reading of the *Thopas-Melibee* Link." *Chaucer Review* 10 (1975–76): 147–53.

——————. "Chaucer, Dante, and the Structure of Fragment VIII (G) of the *Canterbury Tales.*" *Chaucer Review* 16 (1982): 222–36.

——————. *Literature as Recreation in the Later Middle Ages.* Ithaca, N.Y.: Cornell University Press, 1982.

Olsson, Kurt. "Grammar, Manhood, and Tears: The Curiosity of Chaucer's Monk." *Modern Philology* 76 (1978): 1–17.

Owen, Charles A. "The Crucial Passages in Five of the Canterbury Tales: A Study in Irony and Symbol." *Journal of English and Germanic Philology* 52 (1953): 294–311.

——————. *Pilgrimage and Storytelling in the Canterbury Tales.* Norman: University of Oklahoma Press, 1977.

——————. "The Transformation of a Frame Story: The Dynamics of Fiction." In *Chaucer at Albany,* ed. Rossell Hope Robbins, 125–46. New York: Franklin, 1976.

Owens, Joseph. *The Doctrine of Being in the Aristotelian Metaphysics.* 2d ed. Toronto: Pontifical Institute of Medieval Studies, 1963.

Owst, G. R. *Literature and Pulpit in Medieval England.* Cambridge: Cambridge University Press, 1933.

Palomo, Dolores. "What Chaucer Really Did to *Le Livre de Melibee.*" *Philological Quarterly* 53 (1974): 304–20.

Patch, Howard Rollin. *On Rereading Chaucer.* Cambridge: Harvard University Press, 1948.

Patterson, Lee W. "The 'Parson's Tale' and the Quitting of the 'Canterbury Tales.'" *Traditio* 34 (1978): 331–80.

Patterson, Lee W. "'What Man Artow?': Authorial Self-Definition in *The Tale of Sir Thopas* and *The Tale of Melibee.*" *Studies in the Age of Chaucer* 11 (1989): 117–75.

Payne, F. Anne. *Chaucer and Menippean Satire.* Madison: University of Wisconsin Press, 1981.

Payne, Robert O. "Making His Own Myth: The Prologue to Chaucer's *Legend of Good Women.*" *Chaucer Review* 9 (1975): 197–211.

——————. *The Key of Remembrance.* New Haven: Yale University Press, 1963.

Pearcy, Roy J. "Chaucer's Franklin and the Literary Vavasour." *Chaucer Review* 8 (1973–74): 33–59.

Pearsall, Derek. *The Canterbury Tales.* London: George Allen & Unwin, 1985.

——————. "The Squire as Story-Teller." *University of Toronto Quarterly* 34 (1964): 82–92.

Peck, Russell A. "Chaucer and the Nominalist Questions." *Speculum* 53 (1978): 745–60.

——————. "Sovereignty and the Two Worlds of the *Franklin's Tale.*" *Chaucer Review* 1 (1966–67): 253–71.

Pegis, Anton C., ed. *Introduction to St. Thomas Aquinas.* New York: Modern Library, Random House, 1948.

Peirce, Charles. *Writings of Charles S. Peirce: A Chronological Edition* 1. Ed. Max H. Fisch. Bloomington: Indiana University Press, 1982.

Pepper, Stephen C. *Concept and Quality: A World Hypothesis*. LaSalle, Ill.: Open Court Publishing, 1966.

Peterson, Joyce E. "The Finished Fragment: A Reassessment of the *Squire's Tale*." *Chaucer Review* 10 (1975–76): 62–74.

Reames, Sherry L. "The Cecilia Legend as Chaucer Inherited It and Retold It." *Speculum* 55 (1980): 38–57.

Redfield, James J. *Nature and Culture in the Iliad: The Tragedy of Hector*. Chicago: University of Chicago Press, 1975.

Richards, I. A. See Ogden, C. K.

Richardson, Janette. *Blameth Nat Me: A Study of Imagery in Chaucer's Fabliaux*. The Hague: Mouton, 1970.

Robbins, Harry W., trans. *The Romance of the Rose*. New York: E. P. Dutton, 1962.

Robertson, D. W. *A Preface to Chaucer*. Princeton, N.J.: Princeton University Press, 1962.

Robinson, Ian. *Chaucer and the English Tradition*. London: Cambridge University Press, 1975.

Rodway, Allan. *The Truths of Fiction*. New York: Schocken Books, 1971.

Rosenberg, Bruce A. "The Contrary Tales of the Second Nun and the Canon's Yeoman." *Chaucer Review* 2 (1968): 278–91.

Rudat, Wolfgang. "The *Canterbury Tales*: Anxiety, Release and Wish Fulfillment." *American Imago* 35 (1978): 407–18.

Ruggiers, Paul G. *The Art of the Canterbury Tales*. Madison: University of Wisconsin Press, 1965.

Ryan, Lawrence V. "The Canon's Yeoman's Desperate Confession." *Chaucer Review* 8 (1974): 297–310.

Scattergood, V. J. "The Manciple's Manner of Speaking." *Essays in Criticism* 24 (1974): 124–46.

————. "The Originality of the *Shipman's Tale*." *Chaucer Review* 11 (1976–77): 210–31.

Schneider, Paul Stephen. "'Taillynge Ynough': The Function of Money in the *Shipman's Tale*." *Chaucer Review* 11 (1977): 201–9.

Schoeck, Richard. "Chaucer's Prioress: Mercy and Tender Heart." In *Chaucer Criticism: The Canterbury Tales*, ed. Richard Schoeck and Jerome Taylor, 245–58. Notre Dame, Ind.: University of Notre Dame Press, 1960.

Schoeck, Richard, and Taylor, Jerome, eds. *Chaucer Criticism: The Canterbury Tales*. Vol. 1. Notre Dame, Ind.: University of Notre Dame Press, 1960.

Shallers, A. Paul. "The 'Nun's Priest's Tale': An Ironic Exemplum." *English Literary History* 42 (1975): 319–37.

Shepherd, Geoffrey. "Religion and Philosophy in Chaucer." In *Writers and Their Background: Geoffrey Chaucer*, ed. Derek Brewer, 268–89. Athens: Ohio University Press, 1975.

Silverman, Albert H. "Sex and Money in Chaucer's *Shipman's Tale*." *Philological Quarterly* 32 (1953): 329–36.

Sklute, Larry. *Virtue of Necessity: Inconclusiveness and Narrative Form in Chaucer's Poetry*. Columbus: Ohio State University Press, 1984.

Socola, Edward M. "Chaucer's Development of Fortune in the Monk's Tale." *Journal of English and Germanic Philology* 49 (1950): 159–71.

Southern, R. W. *The Making of the Middle Ages*. New Haven: Yale University Press, 1953.

Spearing, A. C. *Medieval Dream-Poetry*. Cambridge: Cambridge University Press, 1976.

Specht, Henrik. *Chaucer's Franklin in the Canterbury Tales: The Social and Literary Background of a Chaucerian Character*. Department of English, University of Copenhagen 10. Copenhagen: Akademisc Forlag, 1981.

Spiers, John. *Chaucer the Maker*. London: Faber and Faber, 1964.

Strohm, Paul. *Social Chaucer*. Cambridge: Harvard University Press, 1989.

Taylor, Karla. *Chaucer Reads 'The Divine Comedy'*. Stanford, Calif.: Stanford University Press, 1989.

Taylor, Paul B. "Chaucer's *Cosyn to the Dede*." *Speculum*. 57 (1982): 315–27.

—————. "The Canon's Yeoman's Breath: Emanations of a Metaphor." *English Studies* 60 (1979): 380–88.

Thundy, Zacharias. "Chaucer's Quest for Wisdom in the *Canterbury Tales*." *Neuphilologische Mitteilungen* 77 (1976): 582–98.

Travis, Peter W. "Affective Criticism and Medieval English Literature." In *Medieval Texts and Contemporary Readers*, ed. Laurie A. Finke and Martin Shichtman, 201–15. Ithaca, N.Y.: Cornell University Press, 1987.

Trevisa, John. *On the Properties of Things*. 2 vols. Oxford: Clarendon, 1975.

Trimpi, Wesley. *Muses of One Mind: The Literary Analysis of Experience and Its Continuity*. Princeton, N.J.: Princeton University Press, 1983.

—————. "The Ancient Hypothesis of Fiction: An Essay on the Origins of Literary Theory." *Traditio* 27 (1971): 1–78.

—————. "The Quality of Fiction: The Rhetorical Transmission of Literary Theory." *Traditio* 30 (1974): 1–118.

Vasta, Edward, and Thundy, Zacharias P., eds. *Chaucerian Problems and Perspectives*. Notre Dame, Ind.: Notre Dame University Press, 1979.

Walters, Clifton, ed. *The Fire of Love*. Harmondsworth, U.K.: Penguin, 1972.

Watson, Charles. "The Relation of the Monk's Tale to the Nun's Priest's Tale." *Studies in Short Fiction* 1 (1964): 277–88.

Wenzel, Siegfried, ed. *Summa Virtutum De Remediis Anime*. Athens: University of Georgia Press, 1984.

Westervelt, L. A. "The Medieval Notion of Janglery and Chaucer's *Manciple's Tale*." *Southern Review* 14 (1981): 107–15.

Wetherbee, Winthrop. "Some Intellectual Themes in Chaucer's Poetry." In *Geoffrey Chaucer*, ed. George D. Economou, 75–91. New York, 1975.

Whittock, Trevor. *A Reading of the Canterbury Tales*. Cambridge: Cambridge University Press, 1968.

Wood, Chauncey. "The Significance of Jousting and Dancing as Attributes of Chaucer's Squire's Tale." *English Studies* 52 (1971): 116–18.

❦ INDEX